Janey Lee Grace

imperfectly
naturalwoman

getting life right the natural way

Crown House Publishing Limited
www.crownhouse.co.uk
www.chpus.com

First published by
Crown House Publishing Ltd
Crown Buildings, Bancyfelin, Carmarthen, Wales, SA33 5ND, UK
www.crownhouse.co.uk
and
Crown House Publishing Company LLC
6 Trowbridge Drive, Suite 5, Bethel, CT 06801-2858, USA
www.CHPUS.com

First published 2006. Reprinted 2006 (twice), 2007.

British Library of Cataloguing-in-Publication Data
A catalogue entry for this book is available from the British Library.

10 digit ISBN 1904424899
13 digit ISBN 978-190442489-5

LCCN 2005931364

Edited by Fiona Spencer Thomas
Designed and typeset by Thomas Fitton
Printed and bound in the UK by Cambridge University Press, Cambridge

This book is dedicated to my family
and friends and everyone who has a
vision for a healthier world.

I was gonna take over the world but I got distracted by something shiny

Acknowledgements

Hard to know where to start but huge thanks to Caroline Lenton and all at Crown House Publishing for giving me this opportunity to share my top tips with you!! Thanks to Steve Wright and Tim Smith for giving me the airtime to argue the 'alternative/holistic' viewpoint, and thanks to the many Radio 2 listeners who wrote in to say please write a book so we can find out where to buy and how to use this stuff.

Going way back in time I must acknowledge Ron and Linda Grace who introduced me to the whole concept of naturopathy and natural living. In more recent years thanks to Grace Hall for keeping my health on track and Gowri Motha for helping me through four pregnancies and natural births.

Much of my info has come from a very special bunch of ladies, my virtual support group – Imperfectly Natural Parents, you are such inspirational, knowledgable mums. Special mentions must go to Hatty, June, Julie, Claudia, Helen, Mink, Nikki and of course the founder of it all – Sue.

Thanks also to the Imperfectly Natural People dotted throughout the book, some fantastic tips in there for us all.

Thanks to all the companies who have given us the info to promote their work and loan us a few items to photograph (for a full list see page 241). Thanks to Richard and Mary at the Dutch Nursery Garden Centre Hatfield for the lushious plants.

Thanks to Geoff Crawford for great 'reportage style' photos, Tina Bolton for the use of the photograph on pages 92–3 and Rosi Flood for helping to style the shots and remind Geoff to shoot my good side when possible!!

Thanks to my excellent editor Fiona Spencer Thomas and finally to my wonderful husband Simon – I couldn't have done any of it without you.

Contents

Introduction

If the closest you've ever come to natural living is choosing the 'light' version of mayonnaise - this book is for you. If the only recycling you've ever done is chucking your wine bottles into the car park's bottle bin just to rejoice in the crashing sound - it's still for you.

The title is all-important you see. It's 'Imperfectly Natural Woman'. After all, if you're one hundred per cent 'natural' that wouldn't be 'natural'. We've all got imperfections and we're all at a different stage in our life journey.

What you won't find in this book is padding. You won't find pages and pages of diagrams or photographs of people exercising. Be honest, when did you last get up in the morning, decide to do a workout, pick up a book and follow the diagrams? It just doesn't happen. A video or CD maybe, but a book? Never. Also, I haven't bulked it out with pages of recipes. Sure, I may have sneaked in one or two but, mostly, I'll try to point you in the direction of a healthy attitude to eating. Once you know which ingredients you need, you'll find that there are millions of books and websites dedicated to the recipes you'll need.

There is also not too much in-depth technical information or analysis of the products or treatments I've recommended. I am not a medical expert, nor am I a nutritionist, and there are even those who think my little bit of learning is a dangerous thing!

As H H Munro said in the last century, 'A little inaccuracy sometimes saves a ton of explanation.'

I know what I'm passionate about. I figure that, like me, you're busy and most of the time you'll settle for whether or not something works and forego much of the in-depth knowledge as to how it works. In case you want to check out something in detail, I'll also list references and web addresses.

What I really want to offer is recommendations you can trust - stuff that is safe, ethical and has really worked for me.

You know what it's like when your girlfriend bounces in looking ten years younger with shiny hair and bright eyes? You just want to know what she's on and where can you get it. All you ask at that point is, will it do me any harm, what does it cost, how soon can I buy it? Sometimes it's hard to prise it out of them because, after all, they don't need you looking ten years younger too! Girlfriend - I'll fast-track you to all those secrets

The other really exciting sections of the book are the Imperfectly Natural People. With the best will in the world I can't 'guinea-pig' everything and, for example, I don't have pets, so I can't make any recommendations there. Alas, because of my imperfections, especially when it comes to recycling, I need a steep learning curve too, so I asked some colleagues and friends whom I respect for their lifestyle and they've given you their best tips too. I've already stolen several of their ideas so the whole thing is escalating wildly!

As I said, you'll already know some of these products and treatments. You may disagree vehemently with some of my suggestions and be convinced that the one you use has the edge, in which case, please take the time to write or email and we can spread the word. All these little ripples of holistic living will some day add up to a sea of health.

By the way, if looking at any part of this book just makes you feel guilty, just move on and find another section that appeals to you. I really believe we all need to make these changes at our own pace. You may not be ready for some of these suggestions yet, while other ideals you'll have been practising for years. But one thing is for sure: once someone is informed, if it's meant to be, their conscience will nag away till they give it a go.

So, thanks for buying this book and I hope you'll find it incredibly useful and inspiring. Hopefully, if you take up some of the ideas, you'll be living a little more simply and saving a good few quid into the bargain. You'll be healthier and, in a sense, wealthier and, in the currency of doing your bit for the environment, you'll be richer indeed!

naturalyou

Now I lay me down to sleep, I pray the Lord my shape to keep.
Please no wrinkles, please no bags,
And please lift my butt, before it sags.
Please no age spots, please no grey,
And as for my belly, please take it away.
Please keep me healthy, please keep me young,
And thank you Dear Lord for all that you've done.

ANON

Save Your Skin

You know, gals, like me, you probably pick up the Saturday or Sunday supplements along with various women's mags and avidly read the beauty pages, reviews of new products, best buys and celebrities' tips. Then you'll be told by someone who looks gorgeous, and whose photo has probably been airbrushed, what new moisturiser or under-eye or anti-wrinkle cream we absolutely must have, but have you ever actually been out and bought any of these astronomically expensive items on their recommendation? A few, probably, and, if so, are you still using them years on? The truth is that most of us hit upon some kind of skincare regime when we're in our late teens or early twenties. We throw money at it and then, give or take 'two for one' offers from Clarins or Clinique, we just stick with the same brands. Also, if you're anything like me, you feel a bit miffed that these beauty journalists just sit there in their flash offices being sent freebies of all the latest products for publicity purposes and all they're really telling me is what the big companies want to sell me, rather than whether they're really any good or going to work for me. I'm far more inclined to buy a new beauty item or makeup if a girlfriend recommends it. I can see it works for her so it's got to be worth a try.

Most of us know that washing our faces with soap and water is a very bad idea – not the water bit, that's just fine, but most conventional soaps have had the naturally moisturising glycerine removed and many contain harsh chemicals. There are, thankfully, bees-wax soaps and natural soaps made of essential oils if you are a soap-and-water fan.

When it comes to our favourite skincare products, without wishing to be too scaremongering, I feel I must tell you a little of what's in them. There are incredibly sophisticated anti-ageing formulas on the market now and they all claim to have unique ingredients. An article in the *Ecologist* claimed in 2004 that there is little difference between them, and many contain ingredients that can actually accelerate skin damage and could even have more serious health implications over the long-term.

Most contain skin irritants such as strong perfumes and colours. The *Ecologist* found at least one well-known brand that contained carcinogenic acrylamide and triethanolam (an additive in shampoo), which can form cancer-causing oily compounds called nitrosamines, and also Teflon (yes, that of the pans), which has been dubbed by scientists as the new DDT. Sunscreens in moisturisers and anti-wrinkle creams have now become de rigeur and many contain a range of ultraviolet filters, enough to have a powerful additive effect on the process of skin damage.

In case you are technically minded, the *Ecologist* listed the common ingredients in many skincare products including: dimethicone, ethylhexyl salicylate, disodium EDTA, ethylparaben, methylparaben, propylparaben preservatives and *parfum*.

All the above can cause skin irritation; some have hormone-disrupting potential, alter skin structure and allow chemicals to penetrate the bloodstream and, in the case of the preservatives, have been known to mimic oestrogen and been linked to breast cancer.

I could go on with a list of the scary chemicals found in sunscreens and shampoos. An excellent book is *Living Dangerously: are everyday toxins making you sick?* by Pat Thomas (Newleaf). But, for now, let's just say – Save Your Skin.

Now, you think I'm going to tell you about my favourite, really expensive French or Swiss skincare range that, remarkably, doesn't contain harmful chemicals, don't you? Wrong, I'm going to let you into a couple of incredibly well-kept secrets (and they're very cheap!).

Soften up

Let's start with your face. As we get older most of us find our skin gets drier; but, if you load on the moisturiser, it becomes greasy. In my case my skin is so sensitive that usually I also erupt in spots from an allergic reaction to the chemicals used in the product (have you ever actually tried to read the ingredients on a tube of face cream?).

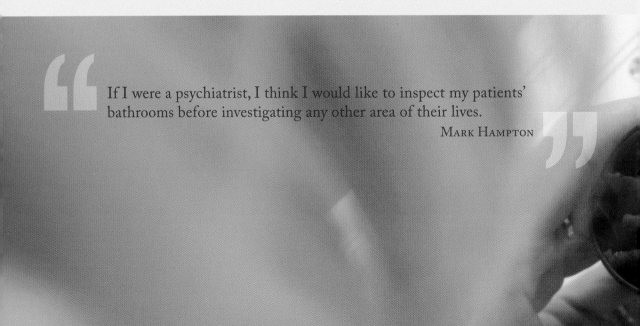

If I were a psychiatrist, I think I would like to inspect my patients' bathrooms before investigating any other area of their lives.

MARK HAMPTON

I've tried most of the brands over the years; I went to department stores, had free facials and got talked into buying the whole expensive range of a certain 'flash' product. I tried mail order for an allegedly natural product and I got conned into buying a frighteningly expensive one that was on offer at a beauty salon. I can honestly say none of them made any difference and some made my skin worse.

About twelve years ago, I had my first ever aromatherapy massage. It seems incredible to wait until your late twenties, I know, but I just thought that kind of pampering was only for rich women. I found Janice, an incredible beauty therapist local to me, and she really made me feel as if I'd died and gone to heaven for an hour. The blend of oils she used smelled amazing and the cold that had been threatening with a sore throat and headache miraculously disappeared. I was intrigued that the full body massage also included a treatment of the face and said, 'Surely, using oils on my face will make my already greasy skin really greasy.' She said, 'Not at all - you'll be amazed.'

Well I was: my skin was the best it had ever been and I've never looked back. Janice made up for me my own special blend of face oil and I used it night and morning. When I'd used it all she made me up another, slightly different blend, depending on what she felt I needed. She liked to see if she could determine by my aura, how stressed I was, whether I was tired, pregnant and any other factors that would help her choose the right oils. I've continued to this day to use nothing but essential oils to nourish and moisturise my face.

This tip is twofold. First, if you haven't tried an aromatherapy massage, have one. They're wonderfully therapeutic on so many levels (see the chapter on 'Touch Therapies'). Second, if you know a good aromatherapist, ask them to recommend some oils for you and, if possible, 'tailor-make' you a face oil. A good basic oil, which should be varied each time, might be made up of a base of cold pressed grapeseed oil, plus carrot oil and, occasionally, add a vitamin E capsule or evening primrose oil. To a 30ml bottle of this you could add:

eucalyptus 5–10 drops
clary sage 5 drops
thyme linalol 5 drops
lavender 15 drops
geranium 5 drops
bergamot 5 drops

Occasionally, you can substitute neroli, fennel, rose or myrrh.

Your aromatherapist may take offence if you give her a recipe but there's no reason why you couldn't actually make this kind of oil up yourself, as long as you source good quality essential oils (not blends) and, of course, you'll need a little dark glass bottle with a dropper.

I reckon that, like me, you'll never buy another 'commercial' skin product. Try to get good quality, pure essential oils. They're widely available now and, if you do want to buy a blend, you'll find that Neal's Yard Remedies sell some wonderfully relaxing oils along with a fabulous range of bath products and herbs. (See www.nealsyardremedies.com.) You can get excellent face oils from www.greenpeople.co.uk and www.spieziaorganics.com.

By the way, when it comes to making up your own simple concoctions, when I've felt I needed a skin toner, I use a simple solution of rose water and witch hazel. You can buy both from any good chemist or ask them to make up a bottle for you by mixing two parts rose water to one part witch hazel. It's cheaper and better than any chemical toner you'll find on the market.

So that's the face. What about the body? Well again, like me, you probably started with talcum powder as a child (what is that stuff?), moved on to body lotion as a teenager and then tried a variety of creams, lotions and butters in order to find the one that really did seem to care for your skin. Again it must have been around fifteen years ago when one of my best girlfriends, Rosi, put me on to this absolute wonder of a body moisturiser. She gave me a jar of what looked like lard and had a price tag of £1.80. (It's gone up slightly since then, but not a lot.) She said, 'Slap this on after you shower or bath and tell me how your skin feels.' I couldn't believe it. It felt amazing. What was it?

Coconut oil. Yes, that stuff that's usually sold in Indian food stores, good enough to eat (because that's what it is, a cooking oil) and certainly good enough to put on your skin. It's odd to get used to at first because it solidifies if left in normal to cold temperatures, and you need to spoon it out of the jar, rub your hands together and then apply it, making sure you don't

lose too many of the drips on the bath-room carpet. When the weather is warm or if you heat it gently on a radiator, it turns to liquid and you just smear it over your body. Now you'd think it would be greasy or smell of coconuts, which, let's face it, is OK if you're on the beach, but not ideal all year. However, incredibly, it has only a faint smell and it's not greasy. You just need to give it a minute to soak in and you can be off.

Now I don't wish to brag, girls, but I'm a fairly old bird and I've had four children and I don't have stretch marks. (OK, maybe all my bits are going south but my skin's good! Maybe I'm like the late Barbara Cartland, who claimed that, at ninety, she had no wrinkles on her body and many people asked how her eyesight was!) Honestly, I put it all down to coconut oil. It's fantastic for pregnancy, so you can forget all those expensive pregnancy 'tummy oils'. This is all you'll need.

I really think that the most important thing is to find the purest oils you can for your skincare products, since they are safer to use in the long run and also, without a doubt, moisturise the skin much more efficiently than petrochemical-laden products.

It's worth remembering, too, that sweet almond oil, borage and even just extra virgin olive oil are all wonderful for skincare. In Europe and Asia, these have been the mainstay of women's skincare and beauty regimes for centuries.

Coconut oil can be tricky to get hold of. You'll find it in some health shops and food stores but the best places are those big food markets, often those that specialise in Indian or Caribbean foods. Try to buy a tub or a jar. Occasionally, it's sold in bottles, but if the bottle has a small neck you'll need to warm it up to get it out because it solidifies at around 65°F. If it's in a jar or tub, you can just spoon out what you need.

Also, something I've only recently realised is that I can use it as a hair conditioner. Some beauticians swear by it. It softens the hair and conditions the scalp. It's rich in various nice minerals such as calcium, potassium and iron and, if you have dry damaged hair, using the oil as a prewash conditioner can revitalise it and rid you of dandruff better than a medicated shampoo. My dear friend Rosi says, 'Whenever my hair feels dry I slap a load of it onto dry hair, wrap my head in a towel, sleep on it, then wash it all off in the morning and my hair's shiny again.' Rosi, I've always hated you for having such great hair!

It seems there are a lot of very sensible people using coconut oil, not just as an oil for cooking up a coconut-style curry but for everyday cooking and as a food supplement. In fact, it is a great health food. You can use it in cooking to replace butter or margarine, though you may want to source organic virgin coconut oils for the purpose. It is claimed that this type of oil is less refined in its extraction process. There is a fantastic website that can give you more information on the organic oils: www.coconut-oil-uk.com.

They say,

As a 'functional food', coconut oil is now being recognised by the medical community as a powerful tool against immune diseases. Several studies have been done on its effectiveness and much research is currently being done on the incredible nutritional value of pure coconut oil. Coconut oil is not stored in the body (liver) as fat, but is converted into pure clean-burn energy. It does not raise cholesterol levels. It's the only oil you should use in cooking.

Check it out for yourself: it's called Virgin Coconut Oil, 440ml, and it's £14.97 from www.coconut-oil-uk.com. My favourite is the ethically traded Coconoil, from Sri Lanka www.coconoil.com.

My 'cheapy' one, which is fabulous for your skin and hair at least, is KTC Coconut Oil. It's 100 per cent pure and made by KTC Edibles. You can usually buy it for around £2 for a 500ml jar.

Talking of virgin coconut, if you do want to smell wonderful rather than just being lubricated (in the skin sense), here's the best solution ever. A little tub of virgin coconut oil gently scented with gardenia - heavenly. It's made by the Sensitive Skincare Company (read on for more).

Enough on coconuts!

I instinctively knew it was not a good idea, or at all necessary, to use any soap when bathing my first baby. B4 for Baby did the lot in one. The Sensitive Skincare Company is run by Amanda Hughes from her own home in Monmouthshire. She started off with totally natural oils and body washes for those with sensitive skin and eczema, and for years I've used her B4 range (so-called because you smear on a little of the oil before you shower or take a bath.) It's fantastic stuff and brilliant for babies' bottoms, dry flaky patches and mild eczema.

Amanda has since done loads more research and refined her range. The Sensitive Skincare Company range of pure, gentle organic skincare products is made specifically for people with dry and sensitised skin. Natural botanical oils have been carefully blended to create the most effective natural moisturising film on the skin, while gently soothing, cleansing and restoring the skin's missing protective moisture function. Amanda believes it's this all-important moisture protection that is usually lacking when skin has become sensitised, irritable and dry and it needs restoring immediately.

The range also consists of natural essential plant oils that have been chosen for their anti-inflammatory and antibacterial properties to help soothe and heal irritated skin. If you use this stuff, your skin really does feel moisturised, smoother, softer and less prone to irritation. All the products in the range contain the purest blends of natural botanical ingredients.

They contain no petroleum or chemical preservatives, all the ingredients are sustainable and almost all are organic.

There's a deep nourishing moisturiser, a protective lip balm (until then I hadn't found a regular one that didn't make sore lips worse), a soapless body wash, gentle shampoo and luscious hair conditioner. There's also a range for babies including an all natural pre-bath and shower oil and a gentle wash.

Not everyone wants to be scented, or they may have ultra-sensitive skin, so all the products are offered without the essential oils added, and you can order the scentless ones if you prefer.

I've never been a fan of scent in body products, but (going back to that virgin coconut oil with the amazing smell) the Sensitive Skincare Company has taken my favourite product and added the most sensational scent ever – gardenia. It has to be smelled to be believed. I wish I could include a scratch-and-sniff page to demonstrate what I mean! I take a big sniff of it and then smear it all over before having a bath or shower and I can detect a very subtle but luscious smell coming off my skin all day. (See www.sensitiveskincareco.com.)

Spiezia Organics

I had the absolute joy of being able to meet the founders of the UK's only complete range of 100 per cent organic skin and body care products that is Soil Association – accredited (and that really does mean something). I arrived at their farm in Cornwall, had an organic salad in the farm shop and then walked across the yard to the reception area, where a heavenly aroma of flowers hit me. This is one wonderful little 'factory'. I met Dr Mariano Spiezia and his wife Loredana, and they told me a bit about their family-run business.

Mariano began his healing career in 1981 as a graduate in medicine and surgery in Italy, where he worked for eight years in city medical emergency departments. He had a strong desire to find a gentler way to treat disease and a passionate belief in the extraordinary power of nature, and that led him to combine this with his wealth of orthodox medical experience. His studies convinced him that by using the whole plant, whether flower or herb, and carefully combining it with carrier oils, essential oils or seeds, he could create products to help maintain and improve our bodies and wellbeing. He still works as a holistic doctor in a practice in Truro, but his main passion is for his fabulous products.

Everything is handmade using herbs, flowers, oils and nothing else. They don't even use water in their creams and you need apply only a small amount to obtain the best results. A little seems to go a very long way.

Mariano took me on a little tour of their workshops. He explained that 99 per cent of their ingredients are of high edible food grade and they're 100 per cent organic. Their products are made from combinations mostly of camomile, propolis, calendula, rosemary, comfrey, jojoba oil, almond oil, apricot kernel oil, extra virgin olive oil, wheatgerm oil, carrot oil and sesame oil. First, he showed me the little greenhouse where the process starts. There were around fifty huge jars of herbs, flowers and petals infusing in olive oil. He leaves them in a warm environment exposed to the sun and the moon. As we closed the door he winked and said goodnight to his 'babies', leaving them to sleep peacefully. When they are ready, they are pressed and this oil becomes the main ingredient for their excellent range, which includes a wonderful daytime moisturiser made with jojoba oil, wheatgerm oil, rose petals and vanilla pods. They also produce a fantastic floral skin toner with lavender, camomile and sage flower water, and their essential oils.

They also do night cream, hand cream, body balm, a fabulous face oil and many more skincare products, too many to list here. They have products for guys, too, and a fabulous revitalising room spray (see the section on air fresheners under 'Get Your House in Order').

The products are not cheap, as you may expect, but it's possibly the purest and best complete range anywhere in the world. You can get them in some large department stores or from their website, www.spieziaorganics.com.

Other companies who offer totally natural skincare products include Living Nature, whose range has a lovely mix of ingredients, including manuka honey (www.livingnature.com) and Green People, who do a nice non-greasy makeup remover and 'body butter', a good alternative to the coconut oil (www.greenpeople.co.uk).

You'll also find excellent skincare products from www.avea.co.uk, www.naturallyTejas.com, www.purelyforyou.com, www.akamuti.co.uk, www.lavera.com and www.thenaturalskincarecompany.co.uk.

Always go for the most natural beauty and skincare products you can find. If you've got problem skin or scarring, remember that harsh chemicals will only make it worse. I read this from one of the Yahoo! discussion groups I'm a member of:

> I have a scar on my cheek, resulting from a badly stitched bite when I was four. Anyway, last time I was at the dentist he told me that if we had applied Vitamin E Cream (or the oil straight from the capsules) as soon as possible after the injury had occurred, the scarring would have been much less. Even then, twenty odd years later, I started using vitamin E and now you would hardly notice there is a scar unless you were looking for it.

I've never tried it myself but it makes sense.

As Simon, who runs Making Waves Vegan Guesthouse in St Ives, says (see 'Imperfectly Natural People'), 'Never put anything on your skin that you can't eat.' That really is food for thought. After all, if your skin is supposed to 'drink' moisturisers and creams, why feed it chemicals?

Mariano

Mariano Spiezia, 50, medical doctor and herbalist. Moved to Cornwall in 1998 with wife Loredana and children Marco, Maria Chiara and Francesco to start a new adventure and live closer to nature.

In 2001 founded with Loredana (we have always worked hand in hand) Spiezia Organic Care, producing the first 100 per cent organic skin care and ointments certified by the Soil Association. Still very enthusiastic about the work we are doing, maybe missing a bit of sunshine during the English winters! (See www.spieziaorganics.com.)

Bright and early
I wake up very early and I like listening to nature talking in the silence.

Typical brekkie
Some raisins and nuts.

Lunch
A bowl of soup or hummus with some veggie.

Dinner
A huge mixed salad with seeds, wheatgerm and yeast flakes dressed with extra virgin olive oil.

Drinks – water – bottled or tap?
Rarely, a glass of a good organic red wine or a little shot of our handmade herbal liqueur. Definitely no tap water.

Favourite superfoods I couldn't live without
Spirulina tablets, pasta with tomato sauce, black olives and capers but made by Loredana!

Vitamins and minerals
Vitamin C.

Favourite treatments
Acupuncture and zero balancing – aiming to bring your energy and physical body into balance.

For exercise
Walking and squash.

For relaxation
Reading and yoga.

Save my skin
My wonderful products.

Sunscreen
None.

Recycling and composting tips
After pressing the herbs we use for making our products I use the leftovers in the compost. The result is magic.

Pets
Veggie dogs! I love my beloved 'bilingual' vegetarian Max (pointer crossed with lurcher).

For the kids
Vitamin C and bee pollen grains.

Top parenting tips
Always ask them 'whys'. Always wait for their answers before telling them what you think. One hundred per cent TLC no matter their age.

I'd also like to recommend...
... to be vegetarian and eat a big bowl of salad before meals.

To achieve balance in my life...
I try to see beauty in everything and everyone (Sanskrit: Om Namaha Shivaya).

To revitalise my soul I go to...
... immerse myself in nature. Meditate.

The one thing I couldn't live without
Joy and compassion.

Guilty secrets and imperfections
I find hard saying 'no'.

If I had a magic wand, I would...
I would pay all the Third World debts and help them use their resources. I would make all the sad children in the entire world happy.

Bathtime bliss

Just a word here about bathtime – my favourite time of the day (that is my bathtime, not the kids'!). If you're a take-a-quick-shower kind of person you may not identify with my wallowing in the bath with a candle and a glass of wine, but similar principles apply. Before you step into the cubicle or lower yourself into the bath, try to get into the habit of dry skin brushing. Yes you've read about it in every detox diet you've ever seen but it really is invigorating and it only takes a few minutes. You need to use a natural-bristle brush and work upwards from your feet, not forgetting the soles of your feet and the backs of your knees. Firm long strokes work best and you should work towards your heart. You'll find it might even tingle at first but you'll soon notice the benefits. For starters, all those dead skin cells will be sloughed away and with them all the nasty toxins. Second, it will help with lymphatic drainage (very important for your immune system, too) and boost your blood flow. You'll feel all tingly and warm because your circulation has been stimulated.

To further eliminate toxins, Epsom salts are wonderful. I try to get a big bag of commercial Epsom salts from an independent pharmacy. It works out much cheaper than buying a small box designed to help you with digestion. Put a cupful into your bath and soak. Check out the chapter 'Natural Cures for Common Ailments' to see how the salts can help with colds and flu, but, in general, they will help relax the muscles and encourage elimination of toxins. You can of course also use sea salt, which is sold in many forms. Dead Sea salt is popular but more expensive than my good old-fashioned Epsom.

For a deluxe treatment, though, it's worth investing in a bag of Himalaya salt. This is lovely and soft and pale pink in colour. The website www.soothingsouls.net makes some impressive claims about its benefits both in the bath and as an aid to health (it can be taken internally). It's claimed that unrefined Himalaya salt is better than table salt because the regular stuff has been stripped of its 'companion elements' and can contain additives such as aluminium silicate to keep it powdery. Himalaya salt is also said to contain 84 mineral elements that the body needs.

It's claimed Himalaya salt can prevent osteoporosis, is a strong natural antihistamine, can benefit the extraction of excess acidity from the cells in the body, in particular the brain cells, can be beneficial for balancing the blood sugar levels particularly for diabetics – and the list goes on.

I've never taken it internally, I must confess, though it is suggested that you make a 'sole' (salt with water) and drink it daily for the most beneficial effects. I do use it in the bath from time to time when I'm feeling rich (it's quite expensive). See www.saltshack.co.uk. Also treat yourself to salt lamps, which give a beautiful orange glow.

You can buy himalayan salt and salt lamps from www.kudosrocksalt.co.uk.

It goes without saying that I'd never go near a bubble bath or foam, because they're usually loaded with skin irritants. A drop or two of essential oil is enough for me or, if one of the children has a rash or eczema, it's hard to beat the oatmeal bath. Just fill a muslin bag or an old stocking with oatmeal, tie it at the top and let the water soak through. It feels rather as if you were bathing in milk!

You can make your own bath bomb by mixing 3 tablespoons of bicarbonate of soda with 1½ tablespoons of citric acid and a few drops of essential oil. Drizzle a scant teaspoon of water over the ingredients and mix well. This can be used as it is or pressed into a mould and stored in a plastic bag.

"There must be quite a few things a hot bath won't cure but I don't know many of them.

SYLVIA PLATH "

Sunscreen

The sun has had such a bad press in recent years that most of us now avoid it totally. We plaster ourselves in sun factor 30, even under our moisturising creams during the winter months, and stay out of the sun. The problem is that, when we get one or two weeks' holiday, we go completely mad, forget all our beliefs about the dangers of burning and cook ourselves until we're fully roasted and basted with a nice chemical concoction. Then, because a tan makes us feel so great, we top up with sun beds on our return to make our tan last a little longer. It really is this sporadic exposure to sunlight that harms most skin types.

I am extremely fair-skinned and remember clearly being sunburned as a child. My dad was of the school of thought that if you cooked yourself for hours the red bits would 'go brown'. Not so with me. My poor red-raw skin just stayed puce, itched and then flaked off, which of course makes me a very high risk for the big killer cancer, malignant melanoma. But I still don't accept that smothering myself in chemical creams is the answer.

Over the years I've tried them all, I think, certainly most of the high-factor sun blocks, and none really worked on me, apart from one that actually smelled of hot rotting rubber (what on earth was that doing to my skin?). I don't trust the sun-factor ratings, either. They lure me into a false sense of protection. Most ratings measure only protection against UVB rays (that's ultraviolet, type B), whereas UVA rays (type A) are also part of the sun's ultraviolet energy and a factor in skin damage.

Some of the ingredients of sunscreen being absorbed into your skin that you might want to avoid include dioxybenzone, oxybenzone and PABA (p-aminobenzoic acid). At the same time, these chemicals actually inhibit the formation of vitamin D, the one

thing it's actually essential to get from the sun. It's thought that around fifteen to twenty minutes daily of being in the sun 'safely' will give us enough vitamin D for our needs. There's no doubt it makes us feel better, increases our oxygen levels and gives us a great sense of wellbeing. Remember feeling depressed on that grey winter day and the first sunshine in spring has us leaping for joy? (See also 'See the light!' under 'Get on the Right Wavelength'.)

Richard Hobday's book *The Healing Sun* claims that each year lack of sunlight probably kills more people than skin cancer. I remember talking to a very naturally minded woman who had her babies in the late 1950s. She was fairly out of synch with everyone else in that she refused vaccinations, formula milk and any processed foods for her children, feeding them instead a total wholefood diet, fresh vegetables from her organic garden (everyone's garden was organic then) and religiously

putting them outside in their prams for a sleep in the fresh air and sunlight every single day. The interesting thing we've probably all forgotten is that, many years ago, heliotherapy (exposure to sunlight) was an amazing medicinal tool before we had many of the drugs and invasive treatments that are available now.

So what do I do? Well, it's a balancing act. Get a little sunlight and, if you use the sun creams, make sure they're the more natural ones. Urtekram Sun Lotion factor 24 is a good one. It has to be kept in a cool place when not in use, since it is organic and preservative-free. The ingredients are water, organic apricot kernel oil, plant-based sunblock, coconut oil products, peanut butter, vegetable stearic acid and nothing else! Most of all, I cover up, especially during the hottest part of the day. Clothes are the best sunblock. I go for the film star image (in my dreams!) and wear a huge sunhat, big sunglasses and

pashminas. Silky sarongs and light throws look pretty cool too.

The Australians have a huge anti-sun-cancer campaign going. Their message is slip, slap, slop – slip on a T-shirt, slap on a hat and slop on some sunscreen, or something like that. Well the first two I absolutely endorse and you can get a great range of UV-protective all-in-one 'sun-suits' for the children. But, if you know you're going to be exposed to the sun and it's not practical to cover up – if you're on a boat, say, in and out of the swimming pool or on a walk – think carefully about your choice of sunscreen.

The surfers have got it right, I reckon, with their total blocks (we've all seen them with bright white noses). They usually protect themselves against wind and sun damage by reflecting UV light away from the surface of the skin. They're usually titanium oxide and zinc oxide creams, which are opaque and stay on your skin as a block.

Urtekram products are in health shops or at (www.urtekram.dk).

For other highly recommended natural sunscreens and lotions try: Green People (www.greenpeople.co.uk) and www.oliveorganic.co.uk and, for the kids, there's a brilliant range of cover-up clothing at www.suntogs.co.uk.

If you're concerned about your moles get a full body screening www.themoleclinic.co.uk.

Hands and nails

I guess I should include feet but here I am, as imperfect as they come, so I slap on coconut oil and hope for the best.

When it comes to my hands I must confess I'm not much better, but I do realise there are those who judge us by our hands and nails. They absolutely deserve to be well looked after and they give away our age without a doubt. I know I should wear rubber gloves for washing up but I just can't feel the dishes. I do try to wear protective gloves for gardening (ha, when's that, then?) and, in recent years, I've started to have regular manicures because, quite frankly, left to their own devices, my nails look as if I'd used them for digging potatoes without the gloves. The only thing that seems to clean them properly is a soaking in lemon juice.

When I first started taking care of my nails I noticed they had little white flecks all over them and I was advised that this is usually a sign of a zinc deficiency. I took 25mg of zinc daily and that seemed to sort them out. It can also be a sign that you need more B vitamins and calcium and, at the time, I upped my intake of calcium and magnesium.

Silica is also good for nails (and hair), and of course for healthy nails we need essential fatty acids (see 'Essential fatty acids and dietary supplements' in the chapter 'Let Food Be Your Medicine') and, since I've been taking regular amounts of

Omega 3, 6 and 9, I'm fairly sure my nails are stronger.

There are lots of natural treatments for hands and nails. I never use regular soap (far too drying) or conventional hand creams (full of chemicals) because, as with the feet, I just slap on the coconut oil. If I'm sleeping alone I soak my hands first, then lather on the oil and wear protective gloves in bed (surgical ones do the trick). You look a sight but wake up with very soft and silky hands – but I only do it when no one's looking.

To replace the oils in nails you won't go far wrong with extra virgin olive oil, but sweet almond oil works just as well and is not as heavy. If you need to exfoliate your hands, use a paste of almond oil or ground almonds and sunflower oil with rock salt, honey and lemon juice.

If you really prefer creams and lotions to oils, find a chemical-free one. Living Nature make a good one, as do Neal's Yard.

There are now some more 'natural' nail polishes, 'Suncoat nail polish' from www.avea.co.uk has less synthetic chemicals and is certainly less smelly. Of course 'buffing' is great and makes the nails shiny and healthy. Got to : www.greenhands.co.uk for a 'natural' salon manicure.

Always go for a high quality polish and at least make sure it's not tested on animals. And, when it comes to nail polish remover, use an acetone-free one to avoid further weakening and drying of the nails.

Perfumes

I can tell you exactly when I stopped wearing perfume. It was 1998. When I was pregnant for the first time, I suddenly found I hated the smell of just about any perfume. My friends did pretty well that Christmas, because I gave away all the expensive ones I'd been stocking up on at duty-free shops during trips abroad. Now that I'm more aware of the dangers, I'm glad my nose protected me. I even have a friend who is so allergic to any chemical 'parfum' that she reels if anyone goes near her wearing the stuff.

In her book *Drop Dead Gorgeous: Protecting Yourself from the Hidden Dangers of Cosmetics*, Kim Erickson says,

Most contemporary perfumes are complex mixtures of more than 4,000 chemicals, most of which have never been tested for safety. Yet the US National Academy of Sciences says that many of these ingredients are capable of causing cancer, birth defects, central nervous system disorders and allergic reactions.

I now just use essential oils if I want to smell nice. My friend Rosi puts a dab of pure rose oil on her wrist for a really sensuous whiff, but it's easy to blend your own scent or buy ready-made natural scents, usually based on essential oils. As with the face oils above, if you know a good aromatherapist, get her to create a scent especially for you. She should be very knowledgeable about the bass, middle and upper aromas needed for the perfect combination.

You can now buy natural perfumes and colognes, which are usually based on the principles of aromatherapy.

Aubrey Organic Colognes offer five fragrances that are 100 per cent natural and vegan. My favourite is Lemon Blossom. (See www.aubrey-organics.com.)

Neal's Yard Remedies do a fab little roll-on bottle of essential oil blends. (See www.nealsyardremedies.com.)

Cosmetics

Here's a factoid for you girls. I've read that the biggest cosmetic-related medical problem comes from women stabbing themselves in the eye while applying mascara in the car!

Well, I haven't done that (yet) but I have spent all this time talking about caring for your skin and, I must be honest and say I am not very au naturel when it comes to makeup. I have girlfriends who look fantastic without makeup – the real outdoor types who look fresh-faced and gorgeous without a scrap of slap. However, I am not blessed with those looks. My features are very undefined and I really believe I look like Winnie the Pooh (no offence to Winnie, of course).

I do wear makeup, though not as much as I used to and not every day, but I couldn't venture out to anything vaguely important without at least a bit of base colour, some highlighter, concealer, mascara and lipstick. If it's a night on the town, (haven't actually had one of those for as long as I can remember) I'll go for blusher, eye shadow, eyeliner and lip gloss too, but at what cost to my skin? Well, I've preferred, up until very recently, not even to think about what's in your average tube of makeup. For years, I stupidly thought that, if I washed it all off religiously before bed, it wouldn't actually affect me. What was I dreaming of?

Have you ever noticed how, when you're tired (I've no idea why that is) or the weather's warm, your makeup disappears and you need to reapply it? Where does it go? Maybe you're fortunate enough to have had your lippy kissed off but, if not, it goes anyway. It seeps into your skin and all those lovely chemicals are being ingested. Particularly so with lipstick, because, every time you eat, drink or lick your lips, a potentially harmful brew, including wax, is getting in. It can be argued that these are only tiny amounts but, according to Charlotte Vohtz, a pharmacologist and founder of the organic Green People Company, most women absorb around 2kg of chemicals through cosmetic products every year.

Reports have shown that some cosmetics may be loaded with a host of potential carcinogens, neurotoxins and other irritants that can be absorbed through your skin into the bloodstream and end up in your internal organs. Let's face it, absorption is what many creams and foundations are designed for. The 2005 scare with Sudan 1 food dye was a wake-up call for us all, yet Sudan 3 is still being used in some cosmetics as I write this. Although it's not in eye products or lipstick, you may find it in skin creams, sometimes labelled as C1 26100. It's legal, yes, and scientists say it is only loosely connected to Sudan 1; but, then, Sudan 2 and 4 were also legal until they were banned in 1976. Scientists do like to change their minds, don't they?

Legislation is in place that's designed, of course, to protect us from potential hazards, but legislators are historically slow to act. It was only after years of lobbying from pressure groups that the European Union finally banned the use of phthalates, substances, which had long been used in cosmetic production and known to cause hormone disruption. The case histories of hundreds of these substances are all in the public domain for your perusal, if you're that way inclined. What bothers me is the continuous, cumulative effect of the cocktail of worrisome chemicals that we are using on a daily basis - formaldehydes, coal tars, parabens, nitrosamines and others - many of which are linked with health problems from mild irritation to cancer and hormone disruption. The list of suspects is endless. A study by the US organisation Environmental Working Group (EWG) found that the average adult uses nine cosmetic products a day containing around 126 chemicals in total. I just don't buy into the attitude that if a government says it's legal it's therefore safe to be consumed by me and my family. Labelling is also a problem: it may as well be in Klingon as far as I'm concerned. The word 'parfum' on a label, for example, can be used to describe 200 different substances.

Apart from avoiding make-up completely, there are alternatives. There are more and more companies coming onto the market now offering complete ranges of natural cosmetics. Living Nature is one of the most natural ranges around – they use no synthetic parabens, grain alcohol or sulphates and its GM free. Their foundation is one of the nicest I've tried. And I haven't had the pleasure of trying one yet but they offer facials in their therapy rooms with natural spa products from the Living Nature Professional range. See www.livingnature.com. There is also an Australian company Miessence who claim they are the world's first certified organic cosmetics outlet (Australian certification indicates a very high standard). Check them out, they offer translucent foundation and powder, concealer, bronze dust, shimmer crème, and jaffa lip balm, all in a range of colours. (See www.sheerorganics. com. and www.totallyorganics.co.uk).

Lipsticks in particular are often seen as the worst culprits. Living Nature have Luscious Lips, coloured with nontoxic minerals and oxides that are intended to form a natural sunscreen. There are no petroleum-based chemicals and all the lipsticks are cased in recycled plastic. (See www.livingnature. com.)

'Good for you gloss' with a built-in mirror is my favourite from Eccobella from www. lemonburst.co.uk.

Stilla Cosmetics are available in Selfridges and Dr Hauschka has some fab lipsticks and lip liners made with rose petals, almond extract, jojoba oil and plant water. (See www.drhauschka.co.uk.)

For complete makeup ranges, the one known as The Skincare Makeup is by Jane Iredale. There's a whole host of products all claiming to be nonallergic, composed of inert minerals, all environmentally friendly and not tested on animals. (See www.janeiredale.com.) Possibly the best-known kind-to-animals range is Beauty Without Cruelty. I've been using their makeup for years and find it stays on well but washes off easily. (See www.bwcv.com.)

Also take a look at the excellent Sante range of make-up from Germany available from www.avea.co.uk.

I never keep makeup for more than a few months. Like anything else, it can go off. Throw stuff away if it changes colour, or starts to smell different, because it could indicate that bacteria are building up. Remember that, apart from being absorbed by your skin, this stuff is going near your eyes and is even eaten! Never use saliva to moisten anything that's a bit dried up, since it could create even more bacteria. Be even more vigilant with the non-preservative kind. Yes, you avoid the chemicals but the shelf life is shorter (I think of it as more of a 'fresh' product).

You may want to go for the beach girl look and lose the cosmetics altogether, but, because I'm imperfect, the reality is that I will continue to use some cosmetics regularly. Natural product tipsters or cosmetic companies, if you could find me a totally chemical-free product to rival YSL Touch Eclat, the light-reflecting concealer that helps (slightly) to get rid of the bags and dark circles under my eyes after my 3 a.m. Saturday show, I'd pay good money for it.

For further information, contact: Women's Environmental Network (www.wen. org.uk); Environmental Working Group (www.ewg.org); Cosmetic, Toiletry and Perfumery Association (www.ctpa.org.uk).

"I don't believe makeup and the right hairstyle alone can make a woman beautiful. The most radiant woman in the room is the one full of life and experience.

SHARON STONE

Easy for her to say! JANEY LEE GRACE "

Crystal deodorants

Have you ever worried about what's actually in all those spray and roll-on deodorants that you use, or thought about what the inhibition of one of the body's most natural and important processes, namely sweating, is actually doing to your health? Enter crystal deodorant stones!

If you've heard *Steve Wright in the Afternoon* on Radio 2 you'll know that I often bang on about these little gems. As soon as the conversation comes around to body odour (delightful), the boys discuss their favourite brands of aerosol deodorants and antiperspirants. The trouble is, they mix up the smells and often they don't work. Add that to the fact that they're terrible for the environment and clog up your pores, and there is a school of thought that says they can lead to serious disease. What's more, they also often cause allergic reactions, as they usually contain petroleum, emulsifiers, alcohol, aluminium chloride, propellants and, of course, perfume.

I have never really found a satisfactory deodorant. When I did dance classes in the 1980s, I was constantly asking my girlfriends what they used. Some would pull a roll-on out of their leg warmer when they needed a top up, even during the class; others would stink out the changing rooms with a heavily fragranced aerosol. It was a revelation to me when I finally chanced upon crystal deodorants.

Crystal deodorants are thought to be 300 times more effective than conventional deodorants and 100 per cent eco-friendly and not tested on animals. They have been used in Thailand for hundreds of years as a traditional control for body and foot odour. They contain natural mineral salts, which inhibit the growth of odour producing bacteria on the skin.

What we often don't realise is that it's not our sweat that smells: it's when bacteria forms that we get whiffy. The whole concept of antiperspirant is a weird one to me. It's hopeless trying to block the pores so that your body can't perspire. That's asking for trouble. The bacteria won't be destroyed and the odour will only temporarily be masked with a perfume.

A natural deodorant doesn't stop perspiration and therefore doesn't clog the pores; also, it doesn't cover up odours with a perfume. What it does is attack the cause of the problem: the bacteria that cause the odours. When applied, it leaves a tiny layer of mineral salts on the skin that can't be felt or seen. The combination of these salts has the unique ability to prevent bacteria growing and, because of the large molecular structure of the crystals, nothing is absorbed into the skin to leave toxic residue or by-products, and there's no smell! It's a revelation for me. Another wonder of nature.

There's another good rule of thumb here. Anything that seems to be what I call 'overly advertised', such as insurance, double glazing and cars, usually means that it's good for the manufacturers but not for you. Ignore all those thousands of TV ads for deodorants, buy yourself some crystal deodorants. They come in the form of 'stick' like a roll-on, stones or even sprays.

You use them like this. After a bath or shower, while your skin is still wet, simply apply the deodorant to the areas that need protection. If the body is dry then wet the deodorant with water and use as you would a roll-on, making sure the entire area is covered.

Don't leave the deodorant in water, because it will dissolve, and if it's a stone and you drop it on a hard surface it will probably break. Rinse the stone before and after each application, especially if more than one person is using it. You'll find it is neither sticky nor greasy and will not stain clothes, and each deodorant if used by one person, should last at least six months and probably as long as a year.

This is my top tip, which you probably won't read anywhere else. These crystal deodorants also work great on minor skin complaints and spots! If you get a huge zit

on your chin (incredible that it happens even when we've outgrown our teenage angst, isn't it?) just rub the slightly dampened stick gently on the area. It'll go – trust me. And boys, it's great when you've slashed yourself during the morning shave, so there's no need for the patch of loo paper!

Favourite brands

There are lots of crystal deodorants around now. Personally, I've found the ones in health stores or independent shops to be better than the big name, packaged ones found in chemists' shops. They vary in price from around £3 to £8. A good one is the 'Crystal Travel Stick' from www.lemonburst.co.uk. All types are available from www.crystaldeodorant.com.

If you want a natural deodorant but like the idea of a roll-on, try Weleda and Green People, See 'Imperfectly Natural People' for individual recommendations and www.weleda.co.uk for anthroposophic, homoeopathic medicines and skincare products.

Amanda

Amanda Hughes, 46, businesswoman, married to Garry Hughes, 47.

Bright and early
We rise later than most people, because we can. We are both self-employed and live in a lovely old town called Monmouth situated in an absolutely stunning area of Wales, the Wye Valley.

Because we work from home, I prefer to go to the gym and work out for an hour and a half each morning. Then I take care of two businesses for the rest of the day. One business is a skincare company called the Sensitive Skincare Company, which was set up to provide pure products designed to help adults and children with very, very sensitive eczema-prone skin, because one in ten people suffers from itchy, dry skin at some point in their lives (see www.sensitiveskincareco.com).

The other business is a music-related company called Parallel Universe. Garry is a record producer and I look after all the paperwork for his company.

Typical brekkie
Muesli and Oatli, an oat drink instead of milk. Two cups of tea.

Lunch
Usually some leftover dinner and salad. Herbal teas.

Dinner
Veggie four times a week at least, usually Indian, and the other days only organic meat and fish. We use organic vegetables as much as possible bought from our wonderful local greengrocer Phil.

Drinks – water – bottled or tap?
Mostly tap water but purified first. We installed a purification system that takes out all the chlorine from our household water. A water softener adds in salt to soften hard water for the shower and washing. Then we have another filter especially for drinking water that removes everything but the minerals down to viral level for all our drinking and cooking water.

Favourite superfoods I couldn't live without
Almost all vegetables, fruits and salads, nuts, coconuts and all types of spices.

Wild horses wouldn't get me to eat…
… lamb's liver.

Vitamins and minerals
Oils, Omega 3 and 6, which are great for skin and hair. They also help to regulate hormones.

When I'm under the weather
I like clear, thin miso soups, with just a little spice.

Favourite treatments
Pedicures are great. They revitalise tired feet, and get rid of those hard-skin areas. Feet are very overlooked.

For exercise
I have started walking over 10,000 steps per day and doing yoga every second day.

For relaxation
I listen to music and read.

Save my skin
For skincare I use – well, I have to say I use my own products. I have very sensitive skin and they really work; plus, I know exactly what is in them!

Sunscreen
Hats, long-sleeved shirts and sit in the shade.

Favourite beauty products
A water filter that takes out the chlorine from the bath and shower, water and pure, cold pressed, organic plant oils. There is truly nothing better for your skin!

Haircare
The Sensitive Skincare Co. has a range of gentle haircare products that are beautiful, derived from plants, and they smell divine; plus, they make hair so shiny and there is absolutely no dandruff or irritated scalps.

Cleaning and laundry products

I use microfibre cloths without any additional products to clean stainless steel surfaces. In the bathrooms I use soda crystals and sometimes I use Ecover bleach in the toilet. I sell, as part of my skincare products, washing balls. I add some essential oils so that the wash smells lovely, and washing balls are great for people with sensitive skins.

Recycling and composting tips

We use a compost bin, then recycle bottles, cardboard and paper. I try really hard not to accept plastic bags when out shopping. Instead, I take a basket. Plastic bags really are an enviromental hazard.

Gardening naturally

I get horse manure and chicken manure to use on the garden and I use my own compost. I don't use pesticides at all and we have a family of hedgehogs that eat the snails. I encourage birds by putting seed out for them.

Babycare

Use pure, natural, cold pressed plant oil (preferably sweet almond), without scent, on babies first to clean them a few days after they are born. Later, use very mild soapy cleanser to make them smell nice and use oil on them around the nappy area so they don't get rashes. Massage babies – they love it and you will, too, because it chills them out.

To achieve balance in my life...

Garry and I try to take breaks of a month or more to gain perspective on our lives. Taking time out really does let us see where we are going and lets us think; plus, we discuss how we would like to live out our lives. We really don't like being told how to live our lives by others. As far as I can see, for most people life today is increasingly hectic. There are so many expectations of people worldwide to be perfect parents, perfect partners and also have well paid, demanding work lives.

There are also increasingly unchecked pressures on the environment, wildlife, etc. We humans have to consider the implications of our actions deeply. Do we want future generations to curse us for our insatiable greed and for leaving this precious planet of ours in a huge enviromental mess?

The one thing I couldn't live without

Love!

Guilty secrets and imperfections

I have recently become a nonsmoker yet again. It's a totally crazy habit and we all know of the negative health implications for smokers and for those around them. I also like my wine very much and have limited myself to only drinking at weekends. I must say I feel better for that adjustment. Sugar and refined foods are another thing I've cut down on. I love white pasta and white bread, but it doesn't like me. The sugar thing is because I love chocolate – I totally binge at Easter and Christmas.

If I had a magic wand, I would...

Mmm, so many things! From studying much harder when I was younger, doing art instead of the subjects I was told to take, to not falling off a motorbike and breaking my bones. We all make mistakes, so trying to learn by them and live with them, without beating ourselves up, is the key.

Feminine Care

Girls' monthlies

Guys, you know you're very welcome to read this and, trust me, I like a guy who knows his clitoris from his vulva (if you see what I mean!), but really this chapter is just for the girls. It's not that we don't want you to know this stuff just that its not for the faint-hearted and I think, if truth be told, most of you are about as fascinated by our menstrual cramps as we are with the intricacies of your electric razor. So women only – this chapter is for you and, whatever you do, don't skip it, as it's incredibly important.

I remember when I was in junior school and first learned about periods. My mum had made some half-hearted attempt at giving me a book to read, which seemed terribly confusing. I thought I understood the bit about periods and was horrified. I remember asking, 'So, once you "start", you can never go swimming again?' I had no concept that the menstrual blood lasted for a period of only a few days. A very kindly teacher gave us sex-education classes in her lunch hour and of course we were highly competitive as to who would be first to begin this adventure. At the time, I was mortified that, at eleven, I'd still seen not so much as a drop of blood to prove my 'grown-up-ness'. Of course it came before too long and I was issued with the regulation huge sanitary towel with elastic ties that worked their way up outside the top of your skirt if you weren't careful and the incinerator in the girls' loos smelled as you'd imagine a scene from a scratch-and-sniff horror movie would smell.

Thankfully, we've moved on since then and most women use tampons or very light-weight and discreet disposable sanitary pads. All OK, then? Certainly not. You will have read over the years scaremongering stories about women who've had toxic shock syndrome (TSS), a serious form of blood poisoning, and other serious infections from wearing tampons and, like me, you've dismissed it as too small a risk to care about.

But what about the other factors? There are the environmental considerations of course. Landfill sites are full of the horrors, not to mention the cost of calling out Dyno-Rod to unblock your drains if a well-meaning (not) girlfriend disgustingly flushes one down your loo.

I was absolutely horrified to read not so long ago about the chemicals used in the production of some sanitary products: bleaching agents, chlorine and even, allegedly, a 'chemical' that encourages more bleeding. There are fears that many tampons contain dioxins and there is evidence that even low levels of dioxin may be linked to cancer, as well as adversely affecting the immune system. There are even worries about the rayon used in the materials during manufacture and its contribution to the onset of TSS. Now if that's not alarming I don't know what is, but it certainly made me think again before inserting the little gems.

So what's the alternative? Well just as there are cloth nappies there are cloth menstrual pads that are totally reliable and washable. However, for those who simply can't function with padding around their private parts, there's the menstrual cup. The best known is the Mooncup and, boy, is it an amazing little invention! It's basically a tiny 'cup' that is inserted high into the vagina to catch the flow of blood and, when it's full (you get to know how often you need to check), you simply flush the blood away and rinse out the cup. During the course of your period you lose on average about 30 to 40ml of blood (6 to 8 tablespoons), so it's not as much as it may seem, but I know what you're thinking: 'There's no way I'm going ferreting up there getting blood on my hands to insert a plastic flying saucer five times a day.'

I do sympathise. When I first tried a contraceptive cap many years ago, I faffed around for what seemed like hours in a bizarre half-seated, half-lying position, legs in the air, only for it to flick out again the moment I sat up. I never could get on with the cap but, trust me, this is easier. For a start, the cup is very small and mouldable and, once you've got the knack of sort of 'clicking it' into position, it doesn't drift and really is no more hassle than a tampon. The really big advantage with the menstrual cup is that it seems to help with erratic, heavy periods and menstrual cramps. To be honest, I don't think there's any scientific research to prove this as yet, but several women I know have reported that their periods have become regular after years of irregularity. The blood flow has seemed considerably less - unless they just weren't really able to monitor it on an absorbent tampon; but, best of all, they suffered less bloating and menstrual cramping. The theory for this could be that tampons, because of their absorbency and chemical toxins, actually dehydrate the vaginal area and it is the dehydration during blood loss that can cause pain and discomfort. Obviously, if a tampon, or even a sanitary towel to a lesser extent, has a high absorbency, then it soaks up all the natural fluids as well as the menstrual flow. As for making periods more regular, well, I can only guess that it's more natural, so allows your body to regulate itself.

As well as the Mooncup, there's also the Keeper, and both are incredibly good value at around £20-30. They should last up to 10 years if you look after them and, if you compare that with what you spend on tampons and panty liners, even in a year you're up on the deal. Also, you've really nothing to lose because the Mooncup

comes with a guarantee: you can try it for three menstrual cycles and, if you're not satisfied, they'll refund your money. Can't say fairer than that.

If it's just not your thing or you want to use tampons when you're out and about because you can't face rinsing out the cup in public loos, then make sure you only ever use organic sanitary protection. NatraCare are one firm who make an excellent range of tampons and disposable sanitary pads and they are 100 per cent organic, GMO-free cotton, so much less potentially toxic. It's interesting that, even if you get the 'super' ones, they don't have anything like the absorbency of the conventional makes. That's actually a good thing, because it makes you change the tampons more frequently. It scares me to think what really is in the others when you compare it to the idea of a commercially bought slice loaf, which lasts nearly a week, whereas the one that just popped out of my breadmaker lasts two days – if I'm lucky. Interesting, isn't it? Those preservatives and chemicals are leaching into you, literally. (If any guys have defied me and are reading this, don't even *think* about the gag that follows that statement!) (See www.natracare.com and check out www.mooncup.co.uk.) NatraCare tampons and towels are available in most health-food shops. They are slightly more expensive than regular brands but well worth it. For cloth menstrual pads see www.familyfrench.co.uk. You can also buy many eco-menstrual products and get loads more info from www.treehugger-mums.co.uk.

Heavy periods and pain

While we're on this subject, I've been fairly lucky over the years, though I have noticed that what I eat and drink has a definite effect on me just before and during menstruation. Try to cut down on wheat, sugar, caffeine and alcohol, the usual suspects, and drink copious amounts of water.

I've also recently tried a great little product called the Ladycare Magnet. This clips onto your knickers and really does seem to help relieve pain. The theory is that the magnet improves blood circulation to the pelvic area, which reduces the pain caused by a build-up of lactic acid in the uterine muscles.

If you can afford one, try a Rare Earth Magnet. It is meant to be the birds' and the bees' knees, but it's expensive. My cheaper one does seem to work. The Ladycare Magnet is available at most Lloyds Pharmacies and from www.magnopulse.com at around £15.

For those who want to try homoeopathic remedies, agnus castus is meant to be very effective for heavy periods. It's renowned for its hormone-balancing properties and it can significantly increase the progesterone levels in women, thereby helping with PMS and menopausal symptoms.

Magnesium can help with reducing bloating and cramps, and can reduce irritability. If you can't eat copious amounts of green, leafy vegetables, take a magnesium supplement for a few days before your period is due. Many women also swear by evening primrose oil capsules but GLA (gamma linolenic acid) is an essential fatty acid that plays a key role in easing premenstrual syndrome. Biocare make Mega GLA complex capsules that contain four times more GLA than 500g of evening primrose oil capsules. (See www.bio care.co.uk.) Lots of Omega products too at www.revital.co.uk.

The bitterest pill

While we're talking menstruation and monthly cycles, let's get onto contraception. This was probably the catalyst for my becoming interested in holistic health. I had the usual run of heavy troublesome periods as a teenager and went to see the GP. He put me on the contraceptive pill to 'regulate' my periods. Now quite what periods they're meant to regulate I'm not really sure, because, as you're aware, when you're on the pill, you do not have 'proper' periods. The bleeding, which can be as heavy as during a normal period, is merely a withdrawal bleed triggered by the seven day pill break.

Most women go for this option just so they can continue to feel 'normal' by having monthly periods, but actually you can ask for four consecutive packs and have a 'bleed' only every five weeks. So it's not in fact helping to 'regulate' anything, just artificially creating hormonal change.

I wasn't even having sex at the time, choosing instead to 'save myself' for Mr Right, but knowing that I could have un-

protected sex of course made me consider the possibility and, indeed, go for it once I was in a stable relationship. Now I'm not blowing my own trumpet but I was not a girl who put it about: I was practically celibate and, for two of the three years I was on the pill during my time at university, my long-term boyfriend was working abroad. Why then did I continue to take this beastly little pill? I guess because just about every other girl I knew was doing the same and rumours spread about the particular brand, saying that it seemed to make you skinny or lessen your appetite – oh, and allegedly helped clear up acne.

I duly attended the GP's surgery or the family-planning clinic (excuse me, but what family planning? – they never asked me!) every six months and the doctor would ask, 'Do you smoke? Are you very overweight? Do you get severe headaches?' No to all of the above. 'OK, then, here's another prescription for a little horror that will totally mess up [I'd like to use a stronger word] your hormones and interfere with the natural rhythms of your incredible female reproductive system.'

But of course they didn't say that. It takes us a while before we realise that we're women, we're meant to have our cycles and they're a natural process that we should embrace. It never crossed my mind to question why I continued to take the contraceptive pill when I wasn't even having regular sex. I think I was afraid to see what would happen if I stopped taking it.

Years later, I lived with a very special partner for a decade. Now, I'll be honest: after the initial excitement of the first year or so, like most 'married' couples, we didn't have sex very often. Sometimes weeks would go by and, with professional commitments and because we were both downright knackered, sex was the last thing on our minds. Well, it may have been on our minds, but the body was just too weak. In any case, I continued to take that stupid pill. Every three years, I had my routine cervical smear and one day a letter plopped onto the mat telling me to contact my GP. Abnormal cells had been found and may need treatment. Well my heart missed a beat. The 'C' word sprang to mind. I had never been ill other than with a cold or tummy bug and I was terrified. A colposcopy revealed I had 'CIN3', which apparently meant pre-cancerous cells were developing rapidly and, if left untreated, could develop into cervical cancer.

I've always had a bit of an enquiring mind and I just couldn't accept I'd got this problem. I wanted to know the reasons why. I went to see a colleague who is a doctor but, with one foot firmly in the world of alternative medicine, she said this is fairly common in women who have had many sexual partners (not me), who had sex at an early age (not me) and who have had continuous use of the pill for several years (me). She asked why I'd been on it for so long. Was I very sexually active? She asked very nicely. I suddenly saw, in the cold light of day, what I'd been doing to my poor body. I'd been putting chemicals into

it that changed my hormonal patterns on a daily basis.

Even now we're told that the pill is largely very safe, even offering protection in some cases against breast cancer, but recent reports show it lowers women's libido (won't be needing it, then!) and can increase the risk of osteoporosis.

In 2004, a study found that women aged 18 to 25 who had been using the pill for several years had significantly reduced bone density in their bodies. The theory could be that, in your twenties, bone is still developing and the hormones in the contraceptive pill may interfere with that process. How scary!

I think that it was all those years ago, when I realised the implications of messing with my hormones, that I became interested in holistic health. I went to see a nutritionist, threw away the pill and started to learn about the whole picture.

The biggest revelation was this simple little question and it's not one you will hear many doctors asking you. Why do you need to take the pill? I really believe I was using a sledgehammer to crack a nut. I was having sex (if I was lucky) once every couple of weeks, yet altering my body clock on a daily basis for years on end. I can't say this emphatically enough but, unless you are at it like rabbits, you do not need the contraceptive pill. In fact, even if you are a bright-eyed lucky little bunny, I'd still say there are other ways to ensure you don't have an unwanted pregnancy. It seems so obvious to me now. We should not mess with our God-given monthlies. Go with the flow – literally. Get in tune with your own body and its rhythms and you'll be far better equipped, both physically and emotionally, to decide what family planning really means.

All forms of contraception are a pain but you'll find something else that works for you. Condoms are very effective now, and perfectly fine once you're used to them, and also there's no longer any need for messy spermicidal creams. I told you the diaphragm was not for me but I have several friends who get on fine with it and some who use the more natural version, the Honey Cap. Apparently, honey works as a spermicide (sticky old mess if you ask me but each to her own). I know you're probably shouting, 'Yes, but the pill is the only sure-fire way of not getting pregnant!' Think again, sister. My treasured part-time mother's help has just handed in her notice (sob) because she's discovered that she is unexpectedly pregnant at the age of 45 with her fourth child, and she has been on the pill for years. She is convinced she did not miss one and has had no illness that would interfere with its effectiveness, but there's a baby whose middle name should be 'meant to be'.

More and more of my girlfriends are using natural family-planning techniques. The rhythm method, as it's known, takes a bit of getting used to, as you have to monitor your own menstrual chart with a basal thermometer and graph, but I know women for whom it's been successful both in preventing pregnancy and for knowing the best time to conceive. Get a copy of the old-fashioned way – *The Billings Method* (www.billings-centre.ab.ca).

You can also of course get a kit now to help determine whether you are ovulating. The Persona is the best known make but, to be certain, I'd use it in conjunction with your own temperature chart and vaginal mucus check. (Guys, I told you this wasn't for you!) You can get detailed information at www.fertilityuk.org.

Menopause

Before we move off matters concerning periods and related subjects, I thought I'd add just a word about the menopause. I'm not there yet but, rest assured, I'll have plenty to say on it when I am.

My much-quoted friend Rosi feels sure she is perimenopausal. It's a buzz word just now, and basically means she is gearing herself up for the big stuff.

Mary Taylor, her homoeopath and astrological counsellor believes that the journey through the menopause should not be a traumatic experience of hot flushes and sleepless nights. Mary tries to find a match between the homoeopathic picture and the astro-logical picture for each woman she tries to help down this route. With Rosi, she's used the homoeopathic remedies, pulsatilla (made of the flower of the same name), sepia (made of cuttlefish ink) and lachesis (venom from the highly poisonous snake of the same name) which she feels are 'indicated' and they are remedies that work both on the emotional and physical symptoms.

My feeling right now is that I would not touch hormone-replacement therapy (HRT) with a bargepole, largely for the same reasons as I believe the contraceptive pill to be un-necessary, overused and a contributory factor to illness. There are many natural ways of helping to alleviate the very real symptoms of the menopause, not least embracing the 'change of life'. You can see it as your transformation into the next wonderful phase of being a woman and, just think, no more monthlies! Bliss.

I should shut up now because, if you're having a hot flush on a crowded subway as you read this, you'll be shouting aloud, 'How do you know, you condescending cow, you haven't experienced it.' You're right. This book is only recommending things I've expe-rienced personally and, if you have some tips to share on this one, please do send them on. It's easy for me to say what I think I'll do when I'm not yet in that situation. Much more helpful is to read a personal account and there are plenty of books out there that go into the phase in more detail. You could try *Dynamic Menopause* by Beth MacEoin or *Your Change, Your Choice* by Michael Dooley and Sarah Stacey.

My friend Janice has had a tough old time of it. Here's her story:

My menopause and I are not quite good friends. At 32, I had a very early partial hysterectomy, leaving both ovaries, because of benign problems which caused constant bleeding. Luckily, the procedure left me symptom-free and carefree for many years. Perimenopause started at the usual sort of time, around 45, and a new, at that time, progesterone cream (only on prescription in the UK and over the counter in the USA) kept mild hot flashes at bay for some time. Gradually sleepless, sweaty nights added to menopausal tiredness and gratefully I started using HRT patches, keep-ing the dose as low as possible and playing with the dose till I got it right. Before and during the HRT treatment, I experimented with every sug-gested herb and potion. Some helped a little but it seemed that, as soon as my body readjusted, the problems were back. Increasing HRT slowly over time added too much hormone and, consequently, breast tenderness became a real problem. That plus the adverse publicity made me decide to give nature another chance, so I stopped the HRT. Eighteen months later after suffering real misery, sleepless nights, nightmares and panic attacks, incredible tiredness and lethargy, plus high blood pressure, made me feel one hundred years old and I have returned to patches of oestrogen, with great relief. Within two weeks, I had some energy back, the panic attacks disappeared and, although a little 'rounder', I look ten years younger again. At the same time I have continued to maintain an increase in soya products, including soya milk (organic and GM-free), which does seem to help and is good for your bones too.

The only real help I find when either on or off hormone treatment is that strenuous exercise, walking uphill on a treadmill for example, or spin classes, and now regular swimming and skipping, seems to help all the signs and symptoms. It really does seem that if 'you don't use it, you lose it'. Finding time for yourself and your mental as well as physical needs seems important too. When discussing male menopause it is usually about the direction the man's life is taking at this midlife time and, combined with the physical symptoms, I feel women can find it difficult to adjust to their changing roles in middle age. The physical changes can mask the mental and emotional adjustments that need to be accommodated.

So, every 'body' is different. The best advice is to find a GP you can relate to, who is willing to give you time and really listen to your needs, get regular check-ups, mammograms, cholesterol, blood pressure and bone density scans and a colonoscopy too, if indicated. Ask for them, because they aren't always offered. Listen to your body and don't be afraid to obtain whatever help is available.

There are masses of good books on the various herbs available. Checking out your bone density is very important. It is underreported and easily addressed. Bone density scanning is available on the NHS and can prevent bone loss with early treatment, either by HRT or other medication, and a yoghurt a day (whatever type you like) is often enough to help prevent it. I take calcium supplements now and wish I'd started it earlier.

JANICE ESTERMAN, 2005

If you're wondering whether you're perimenopausal and gearing up for how you'll react when it all happens, get a copy of *Before the Change: Taking Charge of Your Perimenopause* by Ann Louise Gittleman. She's a nutritionist who recommends some dietary changes even before the full symptoms appear. Also, take a look at www.marilynglenville.com for some helpful suggestions. See also the sections 'Homoeopathy' and 'Herbs' in 'Natural Cures for Common Ailments'.

Wonderful at any time is the Hormone Replacement Therapy Cake - yes, a cake that's hormone-balancing (www.anniebakes.com/favorites.htm#hrt). Here's the recipe:

Grease and line two 1lb loaf tins.

Preheat oven to 190°C.

Put all the following dry ingredients into a large bowl and mix thoroughly:

4oz soya flour

4oz wholewheat flour

4oz porridge oats

4oz linseeds

2oz sesame seeds

2oz flaked almonds

2 pieces stem ginger, finely chopped

7oz raisins

½ a teaspoon each of nutmeg, cinnamon and ground ginger

Add 1pt 7fl.oz soya milk and 1 tablespoon malt extract.

Mix well and leave to stand for 30 minutes.

Spoon into tin and bake for about 1 hour 15 minutes until cooked through.

Test with skewer.

Turn out on to rack to cool.

Serve sliced and spread with soya spread or butter. Divine!

Breast care

I don't need to tell you the frightening statistics regarding breast cancer. I'd take a guess that every woman reading this has either had a scare or knows someone who has.

All I'd like to do here is remind you of what you probably already know. It's a great idea to be aware of your own body and check your breasts regularly. Many people think that just means feeling to see if a lump has developed. Not so. It can be anything irregular. My girlfriend Sue was diagnosed with breast cancer and her lump was less than pea-sized. She hadn't even noticed it but, what she had noticed was a kind of puckering on her nipple. She had a mastectomy and reconstructive surgery and now, seven years on, she's a picture of health, but she often wonders whether it might have been a different story had she not gone and got that little irregularity checked out. But what is irregular? Well, only you know your own breasts and (there may be some guys volunteering for this job too) you should check them every month. In the shower is best because it's soapy.

We interviewed Olivia Newton-John last year on Steve Wright's Radio 2 show. It's well documented that she had breast cancer and, again, it was thirteen years on and she looks incredible. She is endorsing an excellent little product called Liv - The Revolutionary Breast Self-Exam Kit. It's basically a reusable, one-size 'glove' made of soft, latex-free polyurethane, filled with a nontoxic lubricant that enables you to feel your breasts, and it kind of magnifies any changes. It's hard to describe but well worth getting hold of. It comes with a little user guide on what to look for and also a journal in which you can chart month by month any changes you find. In that way you can start to see a pattern of what is normal for you. They cost around £15-20 from www.natural-woman.com or www.goodforhealth.com.

By the way, it's worth noting Olivia's personal story. She found a lump and saw her doctor, who was fairly sure it was benign but sent her for a test anyway. She had a mammogram and a needle biopsy. The results came back as a benign cyst, but instinctively she was sure something was wrong. She got another appointment and asked for a surgical biopsy and this time it showed she had breast cancer, so she went on to have treatment. Don't be alarmed by this because many lumps and changes are benign and obviously our breasts do change through menstruation, pregnancy, breastfeeding and the menopause - but do always trust your own instincts.

Talking of breastfeeding - which is heartily recommended and covered in detail in *Imperfectly Natural Baby and Toddler*. I'd like to give you just a couple of points to bear in mind. During pregnancy 'toughen' up your boobs as much as you can by exposing them to sunlight. Give the neighbours a treat in the garden! Seriously, the nipples will get some stick once the baby's born and sunlight and fresh air really help them prepare for the arrival. Once your milk 'comes in' three or four days after the baby is born, if you find your breasts are engorged or if they're sore, keep a couple of cabbage leaves chilling in the fridge and apply them often. They're wonderfully cooling. One more suggestion for if your nipples do get sore: it's difficult, I know, but try to continue to feed the baby from that breast – they are wonderfully self-correcting if you can persevere. Absolutely the best thing to apply to sore nipples is breast milk. I tried every type of cream and potion and nothing helped, but breast milk worked a treat.

If you are having difficulties breastfeeding, it's often due to poor positioning, so don't suffer in silence. There's lots of help available from telephone support by trained counsellors, even local people who will come and sit with you while you feed to make sure the baby is latching on and feeding in the right position.

Contact the Association of Breastfeeding Mothers (www.abm.me.uk), the Breastfeeding Network (www.breastfeeding network.org.uk) and La Leche League (www.lalecheleague.org).

For every woman, a very important factor in breast health is 'lymphatic drainage'. If you can get even one session with a Bowen therapist (see 'Touch Therapies') get them to show you a simple little movement that you can do for yourself. It helps to drain the breasts and helps with any fluidy lumps or mastitis if you're breastfeeding. If you can get a full session of lymphatic drainage, too, you'll find that's a wonderful treatment.

When it comes to bras, I bet you know what I'm going to say! Leave them off when you can. Now I speak as a very small-boobed person, so it's easy for me to say, and I appreciate that, if you're well endowed or pregnant, you need a good support bra; but go for the minimum 'scaffolding' you can manage. Whatever you do, avoid underwired bras like the plague. They are very, very bad news. They press on the lymphatics and prevent general drainage.

Not exactly bras, but, while we're on the subject of underwear, don't forget thongs are also bad news. Bizarre, I know, but get into those Bridget Jones–style big knickers. It was explained to me by my Bowen therapist that thongs irritate the coccyx, that very important bit at the bottom of your back and top of your bum. Remember when you were kids how there was always some smart Alec who thought it funny to pull a chair out from under you just as you sat down? It was a frighteningly dangerous prank. Bowen therapists believe the coccyx is a very important part of the body, which, if it gets irritated or hurt as in a bad fall, can have serious implications on the mouth and the jaw. Interestingly, studies show that it can also lead to depression, so treat it with care. During pregnancy, Bowen therapists never work on the coccyx area, as this can induce labour.

Recent advice also says leave off the thongs (or cheese wires, as I've heard them called!), since they can cause infection and skin problems if worn too tight in that sensitive area. They also, in my humble opinion, look terrible poking out the top of the trousers, but that's not the only reason I'd also say, even if you're gorgeous and slim, cover up your midriff.

The UK's foremost writer on Chinese medicine, Giovanni Maciocia, whose books are now studied by all acupuncture students in this country and abroad, says this in his massively heavy tome, *Obstetrics and Gynaecology in Chinese Medicine* (Churchill Livingstone):

> Invasion of Cold is a very common cause of infertility in young women. Indeed, it is probably the most common cause of primary infertility in young women in Britain. If a girl undergoing puberty is exposed to cold and dampness (especially during her period) when exercising or playing sports, Cold invades the Uterus, turns into internal Cold and obstructs the Uterus and the Directing and Penetrating Vessels (2 of the meridians), preventing fertilization.... When Cold invades the Uterus and settles there... it frequently leads to stasis of blood causing infertility, a delayed cycle or painful periods characterized by red blood with small dark clots... External cold invades the lower burner (lower abdomen area) more easily (especially when a girl plays sports in shorts in winter) causing amenorrhoea or dysmenorrhoea (lack of periods or painful periods).

An acupuncturist friend of Tiggy Walker's (see 'Imperfectly Natural People'), Sarah, is convinced that fashion-conscious young girls could be reducing their chances of fertility by exposing their midriffs, coming out of a nightclub in a vest top in winter and wandering around in jeans and a strappy top. She says, 'I can't believe the amount of girls I meet and treat now who were put on the pill almost from the start because of painful periods. And then everyone's wondering why they don't get pregnant 15-20 years later!' Of course, cold isn't the only culprit, but it is definitely one of the main ones.

Janice

Janice Esterman - well over 40!! Married to Mel, three grown-up children are twins James and Joanna and Lara. For years, I ran my own business as an aromatherapist/beauty therapist. We now live part of the year in Florida and part in Hertfordshire.

Bright and early
Fall out of bed, swim (here in Florida, in London I walk on the treadmill for half an hour), up by 8 a.m. usually, but I don't always sleep well.

Typical brekkie
Oats and soya milk, poached egg on tomato, or Kashi slim cereal.

Lunch
Fish/chicken and occasionally steak, vegetables steamed with nothing, yams roasted or done in microwave, salads.

Dinner
Same as lunch if main meal but soup and salad for lunch or dinner otherwise. Homemade minestrone or bean soup, rye bread with whole flours, Small amounts of cheese, or cold meats (only from places that meat is organic and has no additives etc.) Only olive oil, little soya if necessary, no sunflower or 'vegetable' oils (very strict about this now).

Drinks - water - bottled or tap?
Definitely a tap lady since I saw some info on what is in bottled water (although I buy it for travelling)

Favourite superfoods I couldn't live without
Almonds. Fig cake made with nuts from very expensive health store. Pears. Peanut butter is a recent addition as I don't eat fruit or carbs without some protein.

Wild horses wouldn't get me to eat...
Ham or bacon, or snails.

Vitamins and minerals
Are you ready for this?
- One a day Woman's vitamin
- Q10
- L Lysine (for my hair health)
- Calcium (since my bones are thinning)
- Omega 3 oil capsule (Deep sea fish, pharmaceutical quality all vitamins only USDA)
- 1 aspirin 85 mg enteric coated
- My blood pressure lowering pills (otherwise I'd have a stroke)
- Statin for high cholesterol

When I'm under the weather
A dram of scotch single malt whisky - neat or with hot water, honey and lemon if I have a cold.

Favourite treatments
Massage. Facials. Try and have one of each on alternate months, if not every month or six weeks.

In Florida, pedicures - they know how to do them here!

For exercise
Swim and exercises in the pool with dumbbells, skip one hundred skips a day, also treadmill and in Florida we cycle almost everywhere.

For relaxation
Sex, reading, studying,drawing, in no particular order, and sitting in the hot tub before bedtime.

Save my skin
For skincare I use Eve Lom skin cleanser daily Aromatherapy oils. If you are frightened to make your own mix, then use lavender oil neat on your skin on blemishes or dryness at night.

Don't spend a lot of money. If you are hard up the important thing is to wash with hot water and soap and rinse, rinse, rinse, first with hot , then cold, using a daily clean flannel, and use a cheap moisturizer. In the wind in England or at sea I use Vaseline.

Sunscreen
I like P20, it stops me burning, I'm very fair and I use it every day. It is a vitamin based UVA stopper, but you need to use a top-up cream if you sunbathe for UVB. I always wear

a visor to keep the sun off my face – but still have freckles and slight tan.

Haircare

Cheap and cheerful – your hair is dead. All you are adding is silicone to thicken the hair and a simple serum thickener does the trick. Only a sixpence size is enough for most heads. To treat flaky scalp and itching use Oilatum hair shampoo for sensitive scalps. L'Oreal Regenerist clears up redness around the cheek and nose area, often stubborn and difficult to treat, the serum is the one that works, but the cream is good too. Good for Roseaca.

Cleaning products

Hot water and if necessary for grease, washing up liquid, the milder the better. Bleach for toilets and down sinks and on cloths for work surfaces and floors. Newspaper to finish windows and glass surfaces. Beeswax preparations for wood furniture occasionally, no sprays allowed in my house. Use the new microfibre cloths, expensive but you can wash them in the machine or boil them.

Laundry products

No fabric conditioner, we have a salt water softener, best thing in the world, for skin and clothes and machines. Wash balls are good and work when I'm feeling like saving the planet occasionally.

Recycling and composting tips

Usual stuff recycled, they are better at it in USA, collect at the door twice a week. Keep saying I will compost but never start it.

Gardening naturally

No chemicals. Ground cover plants mean little weeding. Lawns are for sitting on not looking at.

I'd also like to recommend…

All women need woman friends to talk to and learn from. If you have lots of acquaintances you will find a gem or two for lifelong soulmates. You need opposites to bounce off ideas and good friends to tell you what you need to hear occasionally.

To achieve balance in my life…

Balance is pretty boring, trying to get balance is the fun of life, it never happens and, when it does you get bored.

To revitalise my soul I go to…

… the sea shore and watch the waves, paddle and find shells. If I'm not near the sea, I walk near water.

The one thing I couldn't live without

Right now – Melvyn and my kids – but life tends to teach you that you can live without anything except your health.

Guilty secrets and imperfections

Impatience, bad temper, little sympathy for fools, and the rest is private! Apart from the fact that chocolate eaten when no one can see you has no calories.

I do need some 'unnatural' help with menopausal symptoms. (See chapter on 'Feminine Care'.)

If I had a magic wand, I would…

There are no magic wands… understand that each day is a new one and you can make it new all over if you want to every morning. Attitude is everything. Like the song 'Live like you are dying'. Easy to say, hard to do, but good to remember when things are tough.

Organic Clothing and Fabrics

I'm afraid that, with this one, I'm still very imperfect. With my 'charity-shop chic' approach to fashion, I only recently started to take notice of eco-friendly clothing. As with so many things, I began to address it when I wanted to buy decent baby clothes. It seemed perfectly sensible to want to dress that perfect skin in gentle, unbleached cotton.

Growing conventional cotton involves many of the kinds of practices associated with other nonorganic crops, including the indiscriminate spraying, both on the ground and from the air, of chemical toxins to eliminate insects, control weeds and strip the plants of leaves for harvesting. Sometimes cotton is sprayed up to ten times a season with chemicals so poisonous that they can leave the land barren for long periods of time. There are the obvious environmental problems associated with such practices, such as when chemicals are washed away and absorbed into our ecosystem and, ultimately, the food chain. Much use is made of GM technology, too, the biggest funder in this area being the United States. According to the Council for Biotechnology, 68 per cent of the Chinese cotton crop is GM. Here I am doing my best to avoid GM products, but how bizarre it is that I might pop out and buy a cotton T-shirt made in China and actually end up wearing GM!

Organic cotton feels lovely. It has a sheen about it that I don't see on conventional cotton. In the case of white cotton it has a vibrant and 'alive' glow and, when it's dyed, the colours are so much richer. Conventional cotton can be blended in the style of some cheap wines, where high quality is spun with lower quality to create an easily marketable 'average'. Organic cotton can look and feel more uniformly 'high quality'. You even get the feeling the plants were happier.

Over the last two years, sales of organic and environmentally friendly textile products have increased by 20 per cent in the UK, so the word's on the street, and there are some great companies out there championing the cause.

Gossypium do a great range of casual wear, including T-shirts, vest-style tops and some good stretchy, roll-over-at-the-waist leggings. There are also some kaftan-style pyjamas that, quite frankly, are too good to be worn only in bed (see photo on page 82, and see also www.gossypium.co.uk).

For 100 per cent raw cotton, it's hard to beat the Earth Collection. They sell through shops around the world and there are ten or so in the UK. (See www.theearthcollection.com.) A great range too from www.peopletree.co.uk and www.howies.co.uk.

Also, look at the fairly traded organic cotton T-shirts from www.funkygandhi.com, and the latest designer range is Bono and Ali's label, Edun, in large department stores. It's a range of fair-trade organic cotton clothing, not cheap but certainly hip. www.edun.ie.

For babies and children, there is a wealth of companies that now offer organic cotton ranges, including www.tattybumpkin.com and www.greenfibres.com; and, if you want a really sensual bathtime, check out the Organic Towel Company. They sell really soft luxurious bath linens at reasonable prices. (See www.organictowel.co.uk.)

Natural Hair Care

It won't be news to you to hear that your hair will be healthy if you are healthy. It's our 'crowning glory' and for many of us a bad hair day means simply a bad day.

As we get older, our hair tends to get thinner, seems much drier as the oil glands have slowed down, and loses much of its colour intensity, even if we haven't actually gone grey. This is because the pigment fades and we produce less melanin. We'll talk more about colour in a while but, for now, I want to tell you what we can do to feed our hair, or rather ourselves, if we work on the basis that healthy shiny hair comes from within.

We need a diet rich in essential fatty acids and certain vitamins and minerals. In her excellent book *Ultrahealth*, Leslie Kenton suggests that there are 'magic foods' that protect hair from age-related changes. They include liver, a rich source of vitamin A, which is essential for the proper functioning of the scalp's sebaceous glands, and black molasses (the sun-sulphured variety), which can be added to a bowl of yoghurt or taken on its own every day. It contains 2 milligrams of iron, lots of calcium and magnesium and is also chock-full of many B vitamins, including pantothenic acid.

Sea vegetables and seaweed of all varieties are the single most potent strengthener of hair (and, incidentally, nails) you can find in nature. They are a veritable treasure house of essential minerals, including organic iodine, as well as the B vitamins and vitamins D, E and K.

You can buy many kinds of dried seaweed to use in vegetable dishes, soups, and curries or, as an alternative, take kelp tablets with every meal. (See 'Seaweed' under 'Let Food Be Your Medicine' for more on this food source.)

Here are some commonsense tips when it comes to hair care:

- don't wash your hair too often;
- avoid harsh shampoos and conditioners (more later);
- always make the final rinse in cold water to 'close pores' and make the cuticle lie flat;
- never rub or wring wet hair: just pat it dry and wrap it in a towel;
- use a natural bristle brush and keep your brushes and combs clean by removing hairs from them and washing them in water and a bit of bicarbonate of soda;

- leave hair to dry naturally whenever you can and avoid using hair straighteners, heated brushes and rollers too often; and

- look at your diet and ensure you are getting the essential nutrients you need if your hair is looking the worse for wear.

A few 'recipes' for treatments include…

Massaging fresh apple juice into the scalp and then rinsing with a few teaspoons of cider vinegar and water is excellent for dandruff and flaky scalps, and far less toxic than your average shop-bought medicated shampoo.

Coconut oil, which can be left on overnight if you wrap your hair in a towel, is also great. Wash thoroughly in the morning. (See the chapter 'Save Your Skin' for more on coconut oil.) This also works with olive oil and, indeed, extra virgin olive oil.

Use three parts jojoba to two parts wheatgerm oil to make a great base for a revitalising hair treatment. You can then add a few drops of essential oils – tea tree, lavender and geranium work well. Apply it to dampened hair and leave on for about half an hour.

Hair is clever stuff, even self-cleansing if you let it. I once had a friend who didn't wash his hair for two months and, instead of looking like a drowned rat, he sported the most luscious mop I've ever run my fingers through! Now you can't do that sort of thing living in the city, with fumes and grime all over the place, but it does prove that your hair does have a natural balance that you can easily destroy with sustained heavy duty chemical intervention. I can't go that route myself, since I can't stand the itching until it finds its equilibrium – but go easy, and go natural.

> " Life is an endless struggle full of frustrations and challenges, but eventually you find a hair stylist you like.
>
> AUTHOR UNKNOWN

Shampoos and conditioners

Well, you know what I'm going to say, now, don't you? If you've read the chapter on skincare above, you will know that I'm going to tell you that the average bottle of shampoo and conditioner contains a hair-damaging, certainly hair-raising number of chemicals and toxins. At the very least, if you wash your hair every day with these shampoos, you will be stripping your hair and skin of essential oils and creating a potential skin irritation on your hairline and face.

As a teenager, my nephew developed terrible acne and dry patches all around his face, but mostly around the forehead. Then he changed his diet, cut out sugar, started cleansing his face in really hot water and applying tea tree oil. The skin around his nose seemed to clear up well but he still had the same irritation around his forehead and ears. Eventually, he realised it was because he was washing his hair in the shower every day with a so-called gentle shampoo. Well, not gentle enough. He switched to a natural brand and cut down his hair washing to twice a week. His hair became less greasy and the dry skin and acne cleared up within a week. It's not easy to make shampoos without a load of chemicals. It's a detergent, after all ('It's all washing up liquid with scent,' my old granddad used to say), but there are some alternatives.

When it comes to shampoo there are now lots of companies offering natural ranges. One of the best I've found is the Sensitive Skincare Company (see 'Save Your Skin'). This is a lovely organic shampoo containing rosemary and lavender essential oils. It has no parabens or sodium laurel sulphate (or any other nasties found in most shampoos), yet it lathers fairly well and really washes your hair effectively. Similarly, the conditioner contains essential oils and leaves your hair silky smooth. They're really good value £8–£10 a bottle. (See www.sensitiveskincareco.com.)

You won't go far wrong with any of the shampoos from Jason at www.kinetic4health.co.uk or from www.aubrey-organics.com. Green People do a lovely organic shampoo for babies.

The other really fab way to wash your hair naturally and ethically is to use soapnuts. You can make an infusion by boiling six or seven shells in a saucepan and the amazing thing is that it makes a fantastic shampoo that leaves your hair really soft and silky and it protects against head lice. Soapnuts are 100 per cent natural, so great for anyone with allergies and totally environmentally friendly. They are also very economical at around £3 for 100g. See the chapter 'Those Washday Blues' for more information on soapnuts (yes, they wash your clothes too!).

Hair to dye for

Are you one of the few women who have never coloured their hair? Oh, how I bow to your good sense! That's the stuff we should be taught in school. If you've got even a *half*-decent natural hair colour, keep it, at least until there's too much grey to see the colour. I was lucky enough to have naturally blonde hair in great condition, that is until I started messing with it when I was around twenty. I could see all my friends going for punky haircuts and bleaching their hair and, while peroxide seemed a bridge too far, when the hairdresser suggested some highlights just to 'lift' it for the winter, I jumped at the chance. Of course, once you start down that slippery slope you'll be forever at the hairdresser's shelling out hard-earned cash to pile those chemicals into your hair to keep up what you've started. If only I had known back then how cool it would be to stand out for having natural hair in great condition – there would have been no messing.

As we get older our hair colour changes gradually, as does the texture and condition. All kinds of factors play a part from diet and stress to pregnancy and childbirth. My hair was luscious through pregnancy but fell out in handfuls while I was breastfeeding. My girlfriend Alison had slightly wavy hair, which grew noticeably darker and went really curly after her first child was born.

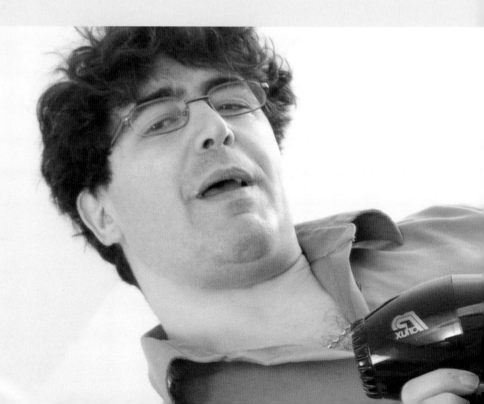

Apart from the cost and the hassle of having to go back to the hairdresser's every six weeks, there's the issue of the chemicals. Most people reading this will be aware of chemicals in food and skin products and will do their best to limit them or avoid them altogether. But, when it comes to hair, we just troll off to the salon to come back stinking of peroxide and a toxic blend of chemicals. Is there an alternative?

Being the inquisitive kind, I once again trawled the Internet and found some worrying information. When you dye your hair, most of the harm is done in the thirty minutes that the chemicals (some of them possibly carcinogenic) sit around on your head, being absorbed into the scalp.

Studies first appeared in the 1970s that linked hair dye with breast cancer, one test showing that 87 out of 100 breast-cancer patients used hair dye on a regular basis. Another test, in 1979, showed that women who started dying their hair at age twenty were twice as likely to develop cancer than those who started at forty.

Research has continued to this day. Japanese and Finnish studies made links between cancer and dyes in the 1990s. Another test gave a threefold increase in cancer risk if dye was used as a colour change rather than to eliminate greyness, black, brown and red dyes giving the greatest risk. Tests in 2001 also linked hair-dye use with bladder cancer. However, it would appear that there is conflicting

evidence over this whole issue and there are later research studies that can find no link between cancer and hair dyes. It may come down to who you choose to believe. In fairness, there are problems with studies into hair dye and cancer risk. Some involve small numbers of women working in the cosmetic industry. These women are exposed to the known carcinogens in hair dyes such as solvents, nitrosamines and formaldehyde-releasing preservatives (plus a host of others) in much greater concentrations than the rest of us will experience. Some of those chemicals have now been removed from hair products altogether but it is still worrying.

Once you start to enquire about all the various chemicals in these products you're practically into a new career. Phenylene-diamines, ammonia, naphthol, chlorides, propylene glycol, solvents, isopropyl alcohol – the list is endless. It's probably no coincidence that some manufacturers cover themselves by giving a warning on their product labels alerting people to the presence of some ingredients.

It's easier of course if your hair is in the red spectrum. Henna is a wonderful natural product that works brilliantly but, for us blondes, peroxide is the only answer – or so I thought. As soon as I became interested in all things holistic I started to notice how my hairline would itch when the hairdresser did a root tint on my hair. I could feel how dry my naturally greasy hair became and I could smell the chemicals for a couple of days after my hair had been treated. I started asking hairdressers if there was another alternative apart from henna and the answer was 'no'. I must have asked ten or fifteen hairdressers over the same number of years.

When I became pregnant for the second time, I decided that something had to be done. I contemplated letting my roots just grow out but I knew that would look terrible and depress me greatly. I started wearing scarves and headbands to cover up the roots while I sought an answer and, amazingly, it came from a makeup artist one day when I did a spot on GMTV. I explained to this lovely lady how awful my roots were but that I couldn't bear to put all this toxic stuff into my system while pregnant. She said, 'Go and see Daniel Field. He does organic and mineral hairdressing with plant-based colours.' She happened to have gorgeous beach-blonde hair that she'd just had lightened there.

Girls, aren't there just moments when you want to run to the top of a mountain and shout, 'Thank you, God'? And, boy, was it meant to be because, though not on my doorstep, Daniel Field's main hair salon in Barnet is only about thirty minutes' drive away! I know that, after what you read here, if you are dependent on colouring your hair, you'll make the trip.)

So why are Daniel Field and his team so good? Daniel is a top hairdresser and salon owner and a pioneer of organic and mineral hairdressing. He was the first professional hairdresser to ban animal-tested products from his salon. His products are animal-ingredient-free and ideal for vegans, and he cares for the environment. Daniel was one of the original founders of the Ark Environmental Foundation and, for a long time, its chair. He has also promoted the philosophy of sustainable consumption around the world, and, for us gals, Daniel has adopted a policy of best practice for the elimination of toxins in all his haircare, he uses hair colours that are recommended by oncologists as being safe enough to be used by chemotherapy patients.

His team colour and highlight using only high quality organic and mineral products. These contain safer and gentler alternatives to the usual chemical concoctions on offer. Daniel offers 'Water Colours' for covering grey hair described as 'the world's first non-peroxide, nonammonia, semi, demi or permanent hair colour' and Mineral Colours for darkening and enriching hair colour.

Seaweed highlights

The big one for me, though (needing to lighten my hair) is Seaweed Lightener. Bleach is a very effective lightener but, as we know, bleach and peroxide are very harmful to us, so how do they do it? (I know at least fifteen hairdressers who need to read this!) Daniel and his research team developed his Seaweed Lightener in 1981. It's a combination of Fruity Booster with a 'natural catalyst' system made from seaweed and mineral extracts. I couldn't believe it. When I went for my first consultation I was sceptical to say the least. 'I'm pregnant,' I told the stylist, not that she didn't know that by the fact I needed an elephant-size chair, 'so no chemicals. I realise you won't be able to make it as light as it is now but just do what you can.'

Oh, doubting Thomas! She applied a couple of colours and it smelled heavenly rather than that terrible bleach whiff I was used to. She then left it on for forty minutes and, shock horror, beautifully soft, natural-look blonde hair. It lasted for six to seven weeks, which, for me, was exactly the same as if I'd used conventional colour, and it was only slightly more expensive than my usual salon. For blonde hair, this lightening is offered only in the salons, so, sadly, you can't use it at home, but it really does lighten and condition the hair and really does achieve the same degree of lightness as peroxide. A miracle!

The really wonderful thing is that my hair feels in better condition than it has for years, even though I'm still colouring it and, thank goodness, I don't get that terrible itchiness and tingling around the hairline after it's been tinted.

The bottom line, then, if you intend to keep dyeing your hair, is to consider the safer options. If you want a 'salon job', Try Daniel Field or see www.herbuk.com.

If you go for home colouring, try to buy plant-based dyes and tints. Leave the maximum amount of time between applications and leave the colour on for the minimum time. There are companies now who offer herbal and plant-based hair colours, usually by mail order. One of the purest is by Logona from www.avea.co.uk. Be careful though if your hair is very porous, some of the plant based tints can 'stain' the hair and won't always cover grey effectively. Ask your own hairdresser if they'd be willing to colour your hair with the product you supply. Who knows, it could raise interest and result in more organic and mineral salons across the country.

Rosi

Rosi Flood, painter/fashion stylist (www.rosi flood.co.uk). I live in Herefordshire. Age depends on how I feel each day.

Bright and early
Glass of water. Let dogs and chickens out and feed. Fresh coffee.

Typical brekkie
Porridge with goat's milk, laced with fresh pear, maple syrup and organic cream. Glass of fresh orange juice, more coffee and water.

Lunch
Varied, soup, bread, fruit, leftovers from previous day or sometimes I forget, then it's Green & Black's chocolate and banana.

Dinner
Varied, always fresh. Veg, meat, fish, etc., no ready meals. As organic as possible.

Drinks – water – bottled or tap?
Water, carrot, ginger and celery juice (own concoction). More water.

Favourite superfoods I couldn't live without
Fruit.

Wild horses wouldn't get me to eat...
... plastic ready meals, sugary 'hypo' drinks and animal produce from intensive and non-ecological farming.

Vitamins and minerals
Vitamin C, oils (EFAs).

When I'm under the weather
Sleep. Gargle with two drops of tea tree in water for sore throat. Vitamin C. Peppermint tea.

Favourite treatments
Mary Taylor's miracle techniques. Face-shaping fingertip facelift, body–shaping massage and mind–shaping astroprofile (see www.marytaylor.co.uk). Alexander technique with Sally Tottle (www.bodysenseuk.com) – brilliant for posture and horse riding.

For exercise
Walking, tennis, chi kung, helping at stables.

For relaxation
Walking, painting, learning, gardening.

Save my skin
Sensitive Skin Care Company Face & Body Wash. Own mix of rosewater and witch hazel astringent. Wheatgerm, almond and avocado oil with a drop of tea tree, lavender, chamomile and manuka oil, shaken well. (See www.sensitiveskincareco.com.)

Sunscreen
Usually forget, remember when burning, have shower, plaster myself with coconut oil and lavender and stay out of the sun until it has all soaked in, otherwise in danger of frying.

Favourite beauty products
Sensitive Skin Care Company. Aromatherapy oils, coconut oil.

Haircare
Sensitive Skin Care Company. Olive and almond oil plastered on hair.

Cleaning and laundry products
All Ecover. Ecocloths and tea tree oil, lemon, bicarb for fridge and freezer. Washing: Ecover, tea tree.

Recycling and composting tips
As much as poss. Buy a shredder and use waste for pet beds (chickens, rabbits, stables, etc.). Carry shopping in boxes, not plastic bags. Compost heaps.

Gardening naturally
No chemicals, totally unnecessary. Use companion planting, comfrey liquid (stinks but very effective), dig in good rotted manure. Always work back from the native environment from which the plant came – that should give you clues as to how to give them the best position, compost, food etc.

Pets
Homoeopathy works really well with animals. Dogs like veg and fruit, add a few chopped carrots, blackberries, etc. to food plus cod

liver oil and wheatgerm (used sparingly). Tea tree and citronella oil on bedding is good for banishing fleas. If you only eat good, healthy food then your animals should too.

I'd also like to recommend...
... Tui Na with Nadia Smith de Nekludoff (nadiasmith@tiscali.co.uk). Buy from the farm gate if you can, shop locally and support farmers' markets. Half a lamb straight from the organic farm, in the freezer, is not only cheaper but far healthier and helps keep small producers in business, otherwise we're going to be taken over by intensive, multinational, pro-GM organisations who believe in profit before health. Field Fayre in Ross on Wye for local organic produce. Irma Fingal-Rock, Monmouth, the best wine merchant around who also sells organic wines (www.pinotnoir.co.uk).

To achieve balance in my life...
I paint and think a lot.

To revitalise my soul I go to...
... anywhere near water. Sunshine. Daydream.

The one thing I couldn't live without
One thing! Impossible to decide... the beauty of the natural world.

Guilty secrets and imperfections
I've only just given up smoking.

If I had a magic wand, I would...
I wouldn't do anything different because it's about continuing to learn, but I'd like the bigger picture to change towards a peaceful and more intelligently run world.

Look Out for Those Pearly Whites!

I was an old soul before I finally got around to caring for my teeth. When you're young you really do think the little gems will last for ever and you can eat sweets to your heart's delight. I had a nasty shock at age four and a half, when I 'needed' to have four teeth removed (allegedly – not sure if they'd have done that now). I can still remember the smell and feel of the gas anaesthetic. I'm afraid that, through my teenage years, I was addicted to mints and, looking back, never really brushed my teeth properly, so, by the age of about 21, I had a mouth full of fillings, two crowns and a bridge.

Many years later, I finally went to a frighteningly expensive but brilliant dentist who told me the four magic words: see a hygienist regularly.

Oh, and the other four: clean your teeth properly.

Seems like a simple tip but it's absolutely vital and not something most of us do. I'd heard of hygienists: my mum used to go for a six-monthly check-up and then her teeth would be cleaned and polished. I think I once had it done too many years ago, but this superficial 'cleaning' has nothing to do with the rigorous scraping and removal of the plaque that I now experience at a hygienist's appointment every four months. Without a doubt it's plaque remaining on the teeth that leads to decay.

The hygienist has, on several occasions when I've left it too long between visits, noticed problems that need to be referred to the dentist. These people are trained to spot potential problem areas that, if dealt with quickly, can result in less intervention.

As for cleaning your teeth properly, well, you're thinking 'What is this, a book for five-year-olds?' Well I wish someone had instilled it into me at five. Cleaning your teeth has nothing to do with flicking a soft worn-down brush with a load of fluoridated toothpaste on it across your pearly whites, and it's not even about an up-and-down rather than a side-to-side motion. It's about small circular movements around the gum for a good five minutes. This was such a revelation to me when the simple fact was pointed out that it's the gums that need attention, while the teeth can almost look after themselves. It's where they meet the gum that bits of food stick and the plaque forms.

Flossing

I remember geography lessons at school. I can tell you anything you need to know about irrigation in the Ganges Delta. And moraines. But what I wish they'd taught me, what I *really* wish they'd taught me, is how to floss my teeth. That's something that might have been actually useful to learn. (I feel a whole new book on education coming on here!) I didn't know anything about that simple little trick till I was over thirty.

Flossing is essential. It has an effect on your overall health and wellbeing. The bacteria that cause gum disease can even trigger an immune response that could result in an inflammation of the arteries. There was a study done in Sweden that confirms the link between gum disease and cardiovascular disease. Try a few different brands of floss till you find the thickness that suits the gap between your teeth, otherwise it really does feel as though you're crocheting in your mouth.

Toothbrushes

The important thing here is to change them often, whenever the bristles look splayed out or worn down. Electric toothbrushes are much more popular now and I'd highly recommend one, because the head is circular and helps brush in little circles around the gum, but you still need to change the head frequently.

There's also a fab new 'invention' that is a great alternative to the electric toothbrush.

It's the first solar-'powered', toothpaste free toothbrush: the Soladey. The idea is that the brush cleans your teeth without toothpaste. Apparently, the titanium rod in the brush creates negative ions when hit by light (artificial or natural). Those negative ions then attract the positively charged bits of food and plaque on your teeth, which is essentially the same way fluoride in toothpaste works. It leaves a slightly metallic taste in the mouth but I think these are really going to take off. At around £12.50, they can be ordered from www.hippyshopper.com.

A really neat replacement for toohbrush and paste when you're travelling is The natural toohbrush. It looks like a twig but works a treat to get around the gums particularly. www.thnaturaltoothbrush.com

Toothpaste

The jury's out on fluoride, but my inclination is to steer clear of it. Yes, it will help fight tooth decay, but at what cost? Fluoride is a toxin, a by-product of aluminium, which itself has been linked with Alzheimer's disease. It's one of those poisonous substances that are apparently OK for us all to consume because there are 'permitted levels'. Excuse me, it's either a poison or it isn't! Fluoride helps teeth fight decay by making bones denser but more brittle, so intake of it affects not just teeth, but, with prolonged use, all the bones in your body. Tests have been carried out that show that fluoride can adversely affect developing brain functions as well. As you might have guessed, I'm dead against it in water supplies. Most health-food shops stock a good range of natural toothpastes. My favourite is Kingfisher. They do a great fennel flavour, which the kids love, too. Weleda also do a good range of natural toothpastes and Green People do a good one for babies.

You can make your own toothpaste too, mix ¾ cup baking soda with ¼ cup of sea salt, add 2 teaspoons of glycerine and enough water to make a paste. After brushing, rinse well and gargle – cheap, effective and healthy.

The simplest mouthwash is a couple of drops of peppermint or sage tincture in a cup of water. If you've got mouth ulcers, a great mouthwash to use is essential oil of myrrh (yes, of Wise Men fame) in water.

Mercury

Here's another 'nice' poison that is allegedly OK for us to consume. I read of someone who had suffered from migraines for years. A holistic doctor suggested the removal of her mercury fillings. Now it seems obvious, doesn't it? One of the most poisonous substances known to man should not be in our mouths for the whole of our lives, leaching its nastiness into our systems. The effect of mercury on our bodies is just too horrible to mention, yet we gladly lie back and let our dentists do their work.

Is it that 'permitted levels' thing again? Some reports show that 'silver amalgam' fillings contain up to 50 per cent mercury by weight. Not everyone believes their removal is a good idea – 'don't mess with it' is the theory – but I know many others who have found that serious health problems have literally disappeared (and in one case a 47-year-old woman conceived naturally for the first time!) after the removal of a mouthful of mercury fillings. We should never underestimate the effects that exposure to mercury and, indeed, all dental problems, can have on our health. There have been several lifelong cases of migraine 'cured' by a visit to the dentist.

This message was posted anonymously on an alternative health site.

> For the last several months I have had difficulty walking and terrible stiffness on the right side. I was beginning to suspect old age until last week... I had a molar completely cleaned [which was] full of caries under a biocomposite filling from two years back. The next day, I ran down the stairs and stopped midway and howled for joy... Obviously stiffness and achy symptoms were due to an infection in my tooth... As I write I am still coping with pain in my jaw but I can run again!

To have your mercury fillings removed, though, is a big undertaking. Never consider it without seeking the advice of a dentist who specialises in the removal of amalgam fillings. Make sure the dentist uses a 'rubber dam' to ensure that you don't swallow any of the filling being removed. You will also need to follow a programme of detoxification and supplementation to counteract any ill effects of any mercury that has entered your system.

'Well, Janey (smart bottom), why haven't you got your silvery choppers sorted, then?' I hear you ask. Well, believe me, I intend to, but it's not advised during pregnancy or breastfeeding and I've been one or the other for the last seven years, in fact, ever since I became aware of the situation. Check out Dr Graeme Munro Hall's holistic dental practice (www.hallvtox.dircon.co.uk; 07050 611333), or contact the Holistic Dental Association on www.amalgam.org.

Tiggy

Tiggy Walker, 44. Commercials producer and currently developing a feature film that I've written. Married to Johnnie Walker. No kids of my own but about to become a step-granny.

Bright and early
Start every day with a mug of warm water and juice of half a lemon, a swig of noni juice or aloe vera and then if there's time I go for a power walk and stretches in the park.

Typical brekkie
The most important meal of the day to get right - it has to be healthy and nutritious. I usually have fruit with seeds and nuts. Because it's not good to mix fruit types I have a different one each day - berries (blueberries, raspberries, strawberries); citrus (orange and grapefruit); papaya (good for the gut); mango; apples and pears; or cooked fruits such as plums or rhubarb. On top I put lots of seeds - pumpkin, hemp, sesame, sunflower and linseed - and a few almonds, walnuts and Brazil nuts. A good addition to this mix is some raisins soaked overnight in water. Occasionally, I have homemade, wheat-free muesli with soya milk. I make this with buckwheat, oats, barley, rice flakes, seeds, nuts and dried cranberries or blueberries. If I plan ahead I soak it in soya milk overnight, as it makes it easier to digest.

Lunch
A healthy salad or a homemade vegetable soup. I'm into the 'superfoods' like seeds, mung beans, avocado, and chick peas on a bed of leaves. I make a great salsa to go on top of a salad, which was suggested to me by an Ayurvedic doctor: diced tomato, garlic, mint leaves, coriander leaves, desiccated coconut and olive oil. It gives a salad a real kick.

Dinner
I try not to eat too heavily in the evenings, as it can affect my sleep. I usually make a vegetarian or fish dish - stir fry veg, kedgeree or vegetable curry. Always use brown rice. Tilda's Brown Basmati is good. Only have meat once a week, which is generally a roast organic chicken (because he loves a roast spud and parsnip). I don't have puddings any more. I just cannot cope with the sugar. But I do like a square of Green & Black's dark chocolate to take away any sugar craving.

Drinks - water - bottled or tap?
Always bottled water. I always have a stack of half litre bottles of Evian or Volvic in the house. I sip throughout the day. Otherwise, I drink herbal teas, Eleven O'Clock rooibosch tea and Ayurvedic spicy teas. I have a selection of twenty different teas in a drawer. I never drink coffee and allow myself just one cup of Earl Grey tea a day.

Favourite superfoods I couldn't live without
Avocado, chickpeas, nuts and seeds.

Vitamins and minerals
I started taking supplements twelve years ago and they changed my life. I used to have annual 'MOTs' to see what I needed. My doctor passed away and so now I try to listen to my body's needs. Currently on CoQ10, vitamin C, magnesium, calcium, zinc, fish oils, chromium, spirulina, SucroGuard, noni juice or aloe vera juice.

When I'm under the weather
I go and have a treatment. It could be a facial or a massage or, if really low, I go to Dame Diana Mossop who does phytobiophysics. She measures your vibrational levels and then makes up homeopathic remedies. She works on a physical, emotional and spiritual level. No idea how it works, but it does. (See www.phytob.com.)

Favourite treatments
Cranio-sacral therapy - especially for back or hip aches; acupuncture - for energy flow; Reiki, reflexology, facials and massage.

For exercise
Goes in phases of gym, yoga and walking. The gym takes too much of my energy if I am not on top form. Right now I have been told to do yoga and walking, which suits me very well. It is so important to find stillness, which both of these provide, as well as toning and mild cardiovascular work.

For relaxation
A candlelit bath with Ren High Altitude Lavender Bath Oil before bed works.

Save my skin
Dermalogica Ultra Calming Cleanser, Daily Microfoliant, Multi Active Toner and Skin Smoothing Cream. There are no perfumes in it and many makeup artists recommend it. It's fantastic. Sisley is gorgeous too made with essential oils but is soooo expensive.

Sunscreen
None.

Favourite beauty products
Not very holistic but – Jo Malone Grapefruit Body Cream, Clarins Bust Firming Gel, Clarins Hand and Nail Cream, Crabtree & Evelyn Goats Milk Hand Scrub.

Haircare
Simple shampoo and conditioner or Pantene.

Laundry products
Persil, aloe vera tablets.

Recycling and composting tips
Have a big box to throw all bottles, plastics and papers into – just got to keep it neat until collection day.

Gardening naturally
Am about to start a vegetable patch. Too early to comment but it will be organic.

I'd also like to recommend...
... not eating dairy or wheat. Also, chew well. Don't eat on the run. It is so important to be relaxed when you eat. Organic wine for reduced 'day-after' effects. Having treatments whenever you can find the time and money. Use manuka honey on burns. Surprisingly, hot water with lemon and honey is a slimming drink. If you have colitis or any gut problems, take a teaspoon of honey with a pinch of turmeric added last thing at night for ninety nights. If you are too much 'in your head', ground your body by starting each day by massaging your tummy in a clockwise direction with a good oil like sesame massage oil. Do this before you get up. Praying. It works. Get a set of 'Healing with the Angels' cards (Doreen Virtue). Take a card when you need some guidance.

To achieve balance in my life...
I take some time alone or do yoga.

To revitalise my soul I go to...
... our cottage in Dorset, walk somewhere green with trees, go on a yoga retreat.

The one thing I couldn't live without
Love.

Guilty secrets and imperfections
I do find comfort in food. My imperfections are too numerous to mention but include worrying too much about my figure, which drives Johnnie nuts. Self-acceptance is my goal.

If I had a magic wand, I would...
... never desire a glass of wine again.

Seeing All too Clearly

If you could only keep one of your senses, you, like me, would probably pick eyesight. The eyes are incredibly precious organs, so why do we take them so much for granted? It's so important to care for them and there are things we can do to try to improve our eyesight and the general health of our eyes.

A total blood supply to the retina is important, so low blood pressure and anything that makes you anaemic will affect eyesight. Nutrition-wise, vitamin A (betacarotene) is important. It's found in lean meat, fish and eggs. Vegetarians and vegans should eat carrots and orange-coloured fruit and veg and lots of rich nuts such as almonds. And your eyes, like any other muscle in your body, can be trained, exercised and toned. More on this later.

Contact lenses

For me, contact lenses have been the best invention since the wheel. I have very poor eyesight and, even worse, I'm long-sighted. It's worse because as we age most of us become longer-sighted anyway, so I'm done for! I'm incredibly envious of people with great vision. I don't think you guys realise how debilitating it is not to be able to see clearly.

I remember years ago when I was singing with Kim Wilde's band. We'd been rehearsing at a local rehearsal room every day for two weeks. One morning I turned up as usual and walked towards the entrance to the building. There was a car parked opposite me and a group of guys leaned out of the window and did a 'hello, darling' type of shout. I really was not in the mood for strangers heckling me, so I looked straight at the car and told them in no uncertain terms where to go. Then I promptly turned on my heel and stormed into the rehearsal, except that the door was locked and no one had opened up the rooms yet. Imagine how I felt when I discovered that the guys in the car were the band! I vowed to get my prescription checked after that.

When I first tried lenses I was hopeless. I lost them constantly and had a panic attack every time I went near my own eyes, but I persevered and now they're second nature and for me, much better than glasses. If you wear lenses or have considered it, you will have been inundated with adverts trying to sell you 'daily wear' or 'monthly disposable' contact lenses. We're told they're easier to care for, better for our eyes because they're thrown away before they get time to degrade and they work out cheaper because there's usually a monthly payment that includes new lenses and cleaning solutions.

Against just about every optician's advice, I went for 'long-term lenses'. I had my first pair fitted and measured to perfection. I chose high water content, extended wear lenses, since I was going off on a long tour. The theory is that you can sleep in them but I never did. I took them out every night and cleaned them daily. They lasted me at least a year and I had no problems. There was no 'build-up time' and no desperation to get them out due to discomfort at the end of the day.

When the time came to renew them, the 'dailies' and 'monthlies' had become the norm, and my optician again tried to convince me this would be a good idea for me. He gave me some to try and suddenly I was back at square one. I found the actual 'material' of the lens really flimsy and difficult to put in my eye. After a few hours my eyes would start to redden and I was advised to use eye drops (more on that later). I have read lots of conflicting advice on the safety of contact lenses I now have it on good authority from an opthalmist working in a specialist eye unit that the only contact lenses that have ever been 'tailor made' from high grade material to fit the exact measurements of the individual eyes are hard lenses or rigid gas permeable lenses. Personally I've found both of these impossible to wear

It does seem as though that there's a huge profit on contact lenses: they cost only a few pence to make but hundreds of pounds for us to buy. My worry is that the daily disposable lenses are made of poorer quality material. Some people are lucky and they get on fine. I was unlucky and had terrible problems with disposables. I went back to my long-term, high water content lenses, but this is very individual and you should take advice from your optician.

I've found that if I'm relatively careful and clean my long-term lenses daily, they last a good year, which still works out considerably cheaper than monthly disposables, even with the cost of the solutions. But don't mess with your eyesight by risking infection.

You may have seen a headline in the *Daily Mail* in the summer of 2004: LONG-LIFE CONTACT LENS IS THE SAME AS A DAILY ONE. The article claimed that 'millions of Britons who wear disposable contact lenses are the victims of a £250 annual rip-off', and continued:

> Industry insiders have revealed that expensive 'long-life' lenses that are sold to be reused for up to a month (at around £2.40 each) are effectively the same as the daily disposable lenses which sell for 50p each per day. All these lenses are made of the same material in exactly the same proportions – 42 per cent polymer and 58 per cent water – the only difference is that the daily lenses have fractionally different diameters and curves. This has no bearing on whether they can be reused and makes little or no difference to the wearer.

The article went on to reveal US court cases in which major contact lens manufacturers have faced legal action over these issues. One company admitted to the *Daily Mail* that 'there is no medical reason why the daily lenses could not be reused and worn as long as the other brands as long as they were disinfected in the same way'.

When it comes to cleaning, I stick to the 'two-step' solutions. Again, for me, the all-in-one cleaning and disinfecting solutions seemed to irritate my eyes. For what they are, the cost of the cleaning solutions is astronomical. It is, after all, a bit of hydrogen peroxide in water and the saline is a salt-and-water mix. I know in the USA you can buy the saline in a big bottle, considerably cheaper that the small 'vials' that just about everyone stocks here but there are now lots of ranges of one step solutions.

I also make sure I give my eyes a 'rest' with usually one lens-free day a week, when I stumble around in my specs or, if I'm not driving or reading, I leave off any 'correction' for a few hours at least. And a word of warning with contact lens solutions and eye drops, – some contain 'thimerosal', a mercury-based preservative, the same stuff they put in vaccines. (I've even heard that this is used in some mascaras.) Just avoid eye drops if at all possible and ask about the ingredients in your lens solution. Look for the cause of any problem, rather than something to alleviate the symptoms.

Eyesight

Why am I even mentioning this with regard to taking control of your own 'natural living'? Nothing can be done about poor eyesight, can it? Well, actually, I believe if you catch it early enough something can be done. Sadly, it's too late for me: my prescription is around the plus-6s, but it may not be too late for you and certainly not your children.

So what can we do to help our eyesight? Obviously not laser surgery. I know some people for whom that's worked well but, for me, I reckon my vision might be improved but I'd still need to wear glasses, so it seems pointless. Also, to be honest, I'm wary of any intervention that hasn't been around for long. My motto is always stay one step behind the 'bleeding edge' of technology. Laser correction for long sight is a relatively new process, so I think I'll wait around for some long-term data on the other brave guinea pigs who have undertaken this surgery!

And what are the natural options? Well, many years ago I came across an old book from the 1920s, *Better Sight Without Glasses* by Dr William Bates, a renowned American ophthalmologist. It was out of print but interestingly has been revised and reprinted in the past ten years or so. You can now buy the revised updated edition, *The Bates Method for Better Eyesight Without Glasses* by William H. Bates MD (Owl Books).

The Bates method, as it is now known, works on the assumption that the eyes have muscles that move them in different directions and, like any other muscles in our bodies, they need exercising regularly. Looking straight ahead, reading small print and, of course in more recent years, spending day after day staring at a computer screen just won't do it.

Bates developed a series of exercises that include looking straight ahead, moving your eyes only up and down, side to side, diagonally and so on. Each step needs to be performed five times. Those kinds of exercises are fairly familiar and many people do them to relieve eyestrain after working at a computer screen, but Bates also includes some more unusual ones such as 'palming' – placing your palms over your eyes for a few moments, then looking directly at a candle or bright light (and repeating) – and 'swinging' (not to be confused with any dodgy partner swapping!), which involves standing with feet about fifteen inches apart, staring straight ahead and then swinging from side to side – transferring the weight from one foot to the other.

Actually, all these exercises are great fun to do with children. My friend Rowan did them as a child growing up in the early 1960s. Her innovative mother, conscious of her own poor eyesight, lined up my friend and her two brothers and made them do the exercises on a daily basis. Into adulthood two out of the three of them have perfect vision and the third needs specs only now, aged around 55. However, by the time the fourth child came along, her mother was probably too busy and no eye exercises were done. This youngest brother needed glasses from his early teens. Of course, it could be coincidence but Bates would probably argue not. (See www.seeing.org.)

The other 'natural eyesight aid' is pinhole glasses. You may have seen these in health-food shops or in mail order catalogues. They are a pair of cheap plastic glasses with 'lenses' that look completely opaque but are actually covered in tiny little pin holes. Wearing them (indoors obviously, because they do look bizarre!) for a short time each day perhaps to read is said to help greatly with 'training' the muscles of the eyes and helping with focus and concentration. They're around £20. (See www.pinholes.com.)

If, like me, you're blessed with having to wear glasses and contact lenses, leave them off when you can. It makes sense that your eyes will weaken over time due partly to their dependency on the lenses.

And, to end on an up note, glasses can look pretty cool. Just make sure you get ones that suit your face, which is a science in itself. Anastasia or Buddy Holly never had a problem.

The spiritual eyesight improves as the physical eyesight declines

PLATO

Liz

Liz Scambler, 41. Married to Bob (organic farmer) with three children: Ross, 11, Rosie, 10, and Robbie, 7 - otherwise known as the 3 Rs!

Have gone from agriculture to cotton nappies with a spell of teaching in the middle. Founder of Lollipop Advisor Network for all things nappy-related. Now running Onelifeworld www.onelifeworld.com.

Bright and early
Glass of juice to wake me up, usually cranberry and apple, then muck out the ponies with my daughter if she's awake!

Typical brekkie
Special K with red berries and cranberry juice or, if I have time, a bowl of chopped fruit and natural yoghurt.

Lunch
Depends where I am. If the chance arises for a decent Caesar salad then that's definitely a favourite; if I'm the chef, more likely to be a chunk of cheese and an apple with sparkling water if I haven't drunk it all.

Dinner
Quick and easy, e.g. grilled salmon, new potatoes and salad. Yum!

Drinks - water - bottled or tap?
Bottled sparkling water is a treat but our tap water is from a spring and is lovely anyway. Spoilt, I think.

Favourite superfoods I couldn't live without
Baby spinach, raw veggies and Bob's eggs (not necessarily all on the same plate!).

Wild horses wouldn't get me to eat...
... offal of any description.

Vitamins and minerals
Vitamin C, the chewy ones that the kids love.

When I'm under the weather
Mug of hot milk (full-fat, of course - married to a dairy farmer).

Favourite treatments
Full-body wrap with frangipani and coconut milk - gorgeous but don't get it very often.

For exercise
Riding at Land's End Riding School on Westie, who is 17.3 hands and who I consider as my 'other man' that cannot be bettered!

For relaxation
As above, or some quiet music and a glass of red wine.

Save my skin
I use Elemis (www.elemis.com).

Sunscreen
Clinique SPF30.

Favourite beauty products
Elemis body oil.

Cleaning products
Ecover.

Recycling and composting tips
Get the kids into recycling and they are a real help and a good reminder. Get a sticker for the bin which will end up in landfill - check it before you chuck it (mine was courtesy of Devon County Council).

Gardening naturally
Beer is a great slug catcher, sink jam jars into ground and fill with beer.

Babycare
For the kids I make sure they get water with every meal, not juice; fruit ad lib throughout the day - self-service and one 'cooked' meal a day (unless it's hot).

Top parenting tips
Follow your instincts and learn to trust them. Enjoy your children as much as you can - they will be the fastest-growing things you have ever known. When you have a frazzled moment, stop, sit down and do a group hug.

I'd also like to recommend...
... as much fresh air as you can get.

To achieve balance in my life...
Yoga.

To revitalise my soul I go to...
... the beach.

The one thing I couldn't live without
Bob.

Guilty secrets and imperfections
Champagne, if I get chance. Nagging the children about unimportant things, not knowing when to say 'no', drinking too much red wine, not bothering with skincare and forgetting to drink 2 litres of water a day.

If I had a magic wand, I would...
... spend more time at home.

Boing, Boing for Fitness

When it comes to exercise, I must confess I am excessively imperfect. God knows, I've tried. New Year usually starts with resolutions-a-go-go, the first being to justify the hefty gym membership fee by actually going there more than three times before Christmas arrives again. I've tried classes and sports centres, even lived in a house with a swimming pool, but the discipline of a fitness regime has always eluded me.

In truth, I do very little to keep fit. My excuse for this major imperfection is that I have four young children (a fitness regime in itself, you might think), a job (well, several jobs) and, with the best will in the world, I simply don't have time.

In an ideal world, I'd do more yoga. I don't need to tell you all about its incredible health benefits here. Just find yourself a local class and you'll feel the difference in a couple of sessions. It will help you with breathing, balance, posture, stamina and of course stress levels, but, unless its power yoga or Ashtanga, it won't necessarily get your pulse rate up. Pilates is also meant to be very effective, but I must confess that I have yet to try it.

Hopefully, you're less imperfect than I am when it comes to fitness and I'm not going to try to influence you at all. Good for you if you're a sporty type who enjoys keeping fit or even just committed enough to work out because you know you get results when you do. Exercise makes us feel and look better. When I took up running three or four times a week I felt lean, my skin glowed and I had loads more energy. 'Running' may be too impressive a term for what I did, to be truthful. I think the official term is 'fartleking' (yes, you read it right!). 'Fartlek' is a Swedish word meaning 'speed-play'. Another term for it is 'interval training'. It means you run for a couple of minutes, then walk for a couple, build up your time gradually. For me, it was better than starting off fast and collapsing in a heap before I'd even reached the park gates at the end of my road.

One of the best things you can do if you've got a baby is jog with the buggy. If the thought of that makes you reel, well how about brisk walking? Nearly as good and doesn't turn quite so many heads as jogging. I know it seems terribly trendy running round the park with a so-called designer baby in a three-wheeler, but it is a great excuse for a nice bit of 'get fit'. It's definitely preferable to running solo, kitted out in my Adidas, terrified as to whom I might bump into and what they'll think of my wheezing, beetroot-red face (and that's after only one and a half minutes). With my fifteen-month-old, if we walk he usually whinges, but, if I go for it and jog, he shuts up immediately. When it's time for a breather, simply revert to the 'brisk walk' mode à la Mum happily walking baby in the park. No one will ever know! You may not get your heart rate up to quite what you should but at least it's exercise and the buggy makes a great store for your water bottle, tissues, keys and phone. (I've always wondered where serious runners put that kit.)

There are lots of different types of aerobic exercise you can choose from but, from a purely personal perspective, they all have a downside. Swimming is way too wet and plays havoc with your hair, and I also hate the chlorine. Try to find an ozone pool. Ozone purifies by changing the molecular structure of the water so that bugs simply can't multiply. Much better than using heaps of chemicals. In some pools I've been in, chlorine levels are so high that it's overwhelming just breathing the air, and it's rather like swimming in disinfectant. Watch out for regular public pools – they're the worst.

If you yearn for the days when swimming used to mean jumping with your pet dog into the river that ran through your local woods, and if you have the finances to think about building your own swimming pool in your back garden, you won't go wrong with a Natural Swimming Pool. I read about these in the *Ecologist* in 2004, and, I must confess, I'm intrigued. They've been popular on the Continent for a few years now. Lindenthal in Germany has a huge public natural pool measuring 5,000 square metres and they're popular with hotels. Basically, they look like garden ponds and use the organic purifying properties of plants and micro-organisms to clean the water biologically. They use no chemicals, less water, less energy – only a simple mechanical pump and filter are needed – and they provide a natural habitat for wildlife. You'll save money over time, too, because, although the construction costs may be slightly higher than conventional pools at around £300 per square metre, owners of natural pools save a fortune by not needing to buy expensive chemicals and filtration/heating equipment. Of course, you can't heat

Blessed are the flexible for they shall not be bent out of shape.
ANON

the water to the temperature you like your bathwater, but I'm told you aren't chilled to the bone, either, because the material that lines the swimming area heats up quickly and retains warmth.

There are some UK firms that are now offering Natural Swimming Pools, including Fairwater (www.fairwater.co.uk) and Michael Littlewood (www.ecodesignscape.co.uk).

Cycling? Not for me. The expense of buying a decent bike and then another when that one's stolen, plus the hassle of having to change and shower when you reach your destination, is all too much. And I don't want my thigh muscles any bigger, thanks.

Rowing? No, too much like a career. You'll need to live near water and be part of a club working to their timetable.

Aerobic exercise? Well, that's OK as long as you don't have two left feet and you don't mind hobbling about on that plastic step next to that stick-thin coiffured type in leg warmers.

Running? Well I've already said it works, I know, but I find it a chore to force myself to kit up in those expensive gym shoes, warm up and then pound the streets in all weathers, allowing enough time to do my cool-down exercises before getting back into the shower, this time to get clean as opposed to the first one I needed to wake me up.

All of the above can be done as part of a workout session in the gym, If you're going that route choose a 'family friendly' club where its not about 'posing' www.nextgenerationclubs.co.uk.

I don't include dancing in the above list, by the way. It's a fantastic form of exercise and will raise your spirits, but you'll need to dance the night away pretty often to see great benefits. I do have a suggestion, though. Here's an aerobic activity that will do for you everything the above will do and more. There's no downside

apart from the minimal one-off cost of the equipment. There's no aerobic exercise (well, not that you can do alone) that's more fun than rebounding. Yes, you can literally bounce into shape.

I first got my rebounder (mini-trampoline) after reading about it in one of the excellent Leslie Kenton books. That was back in the early nineties. They've since become very popular, though I still think most people think of them as playthings for children. True enough, the kids (and all their friends) love mine. If I'm not careful, they'll commandeer it in their bedroom or leave it out in the rain after bouncing all day. I once caught two of my boys on it at the same time doing 'air guitar' to Rod Stewart's 'Stay With Me'. It did take a battering that day but the amazing thing about rebounding is that it really is for everyone, the kids, Grandma, toddlers – I've never met anyone who can resist the urge if they see it.

Athletes who have injuries or need rehabilitation use them too. You can just bounce up and down, skip, run on the spot, fling your arms around and do lots of 'routines'. There are videos available to get you started, but I wouldn't bother. The wonderful bit is that you can wear what you like and bounce whenever you like. Watch the TV, listen to music or order the kids to tidy up the playroom. When I got it I knew that keeping fit could be fun. It's impossible not to smile while you're bouncing – ask Tigger!

From a physiological perspective rebounding will strengthen your heart and lungs (as long as you get a little bit out of breath) and firm up your muscles because of the unique way your body is subjected to the force of gravity in a variety of ways. It's the only complete vertical exercise where all the organs and even the lymphatic system are affected. This is because the action of bouncing up and down, acceleration and deceleration, brings about continual changes in the forces of gravity

Dancing is silent poetry
SIMONIDES

on your body. It stimulates and exercises every individual cell, which can help with detoxification and result in better skin, higher energy levels and toned-up muscles. When you bounce on a rebounder, your entire body (internal organs, bones, connective tissue and skin) becomes stronger, more flexible and healthier. Both blood circulation and lymphatic drainage are vastly improved. Sounds like magic? Well it is, kind of. You'll feel fantastic with just ten minutes a day. Can't be bad.

Check out sports shops and websites for rebounders, but make sure you get a good quality one. All those years back I bought the PT Rebounder and, believe it or not, it's still going strong. Here's their advertising blurb.

Suitable for all ages and fitness levels rebounding benefits have to be experienced to be believed.

Relieve stress

Raise energy levels

Reduce the effects of ageing

Reduce cellulite

Improve heart rate

Lower blood pressure

Improve sleep

Improve skin texture

AND, most importantly, because it is easy and fun to do you will keep doing it and feel better and look younger

PT Bouncer Rebounder. £79.00. Price includes VAT and delivery in the UK

Diameter: 102 cm (40 inches)

Overall Height: 23 cm (9 inches)

Net weight: 8.5 kg (19 lb)

Max user weight: 140 kg (22 stone)

www.wholisticresearch.com Less expensive ones can be found at other stockists such as Peter Jones, where they cost around £50.

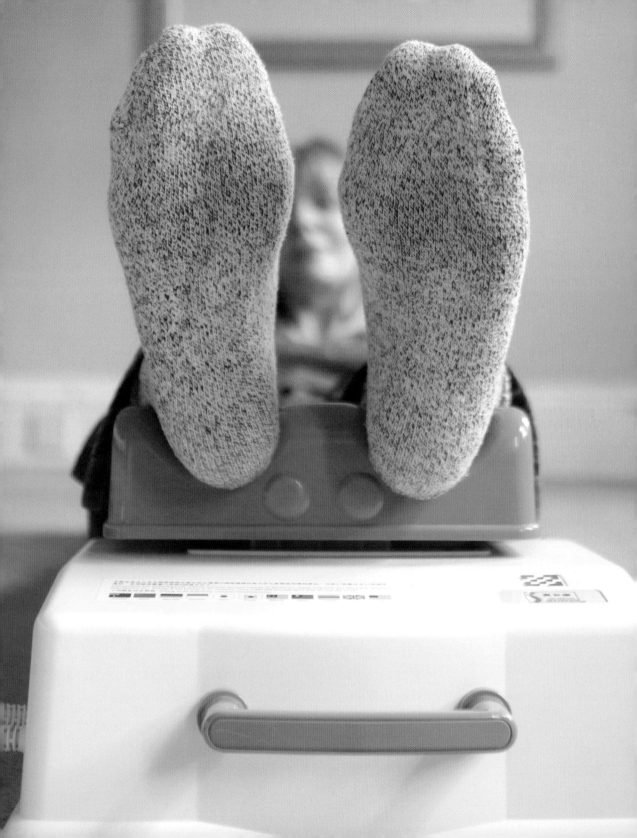

Chi machine

As I've already said quite emphatically, I hate working out. What's more, I can't be doing with that vast array of workout contraptions, gubbins and machinery that we allegedly need to keep fit. A walking machine? Please! Why not just walk? All those expensive gadgets make me feel as if I were in a set for a Jane Fonda workout video from the eighties. But I have been known to bow down to technology very, very occasionally and this little wonder – the *chi* machine – certainly made me do it.

I first heard about this from a listener to *Steve Wright in the Afternoon* on Radio 2. Carl Munson, who runs a healing centre in Devon, heard me singing the praises of the Bowen technique (see 'Touch Therapies'). He is a Bowen practitioner who also finds that he and his patients greatly benefit from the *chi* machine (see 'Imperfectly Natural People'). I'd never heard of it but thought maybe this wasn't just yet another workout contraption that would sit in the corner of a room gathering dust. You know what it's like when you get a hunch about something? Well this idea bugged me and I had to follow it through. I began researching what I think is still a fairly well-kept secret (in this country at least).

The *chi* machine is hailed as an exerciser and massager, a no-effort aerobic workout. Sounds too good to be true, and that's what I thought. I posted a message to my website group saying, 'Anyone heard of this? It's meant to alter your *chi* and help you exercise and relax at the same time.' One very sensible lady emailed back, 'If you want to alter your *chi* why not do *tai chi* classes?' Well maybe that's right but I am, of course (and perhaps like you, good reader), an imperfectly natural person and, where there's a will, there are a multitude of ways. I just ain't gonna make it to *tai chi* and I certainly do not have the discipline for *tai chi*, DIY style. The idea of a machine that can help detox your body, tone you up, help you to lose weight, relax you and help you sleep, you must admit, sounds nice.

So what is it? Well, it's just like a little foot rest that plugs in. My little boy calls mine 'Mummy's body wobbler'! You lie down, rest your ankles on the cradle of the machine, switch on and away you go. Your whole body kind of 'swims' and gyrates. It's a most bizarre but not unpleasant experience. DH (Darling Husband) seemed to enjoy my being on it as well.

It's recommended that you build up gradually towards the maximum fifteen minute time slot, but they do say that two or three sessions a day of three minutes each can be even more beneficial. Now, you see, for a busy gal like me, three minutes is about my limit, so this is perfect. The one I tried and subsequently bought was the one that claims it's the original *chi* machine – the Sun Ancon from Australia.

I must admit that, after the first week or so, I didn't feel much, but, four weeks in, I started to feel a bit more toned up and one day when I actually managed a full ten minutes my calf muscles ached ever so slightly, the way they do when you've been for a jog. They claim that ten minutes on the *chi* machine is equivalent to sixty minutes of brisk walking, so I really felt its effectiveness. They claim,

> The *Chi* Machine's ability to oxygenate, tone and strengthen the body increases the feelings of aliveness and well-being, that is, raises the *chi* or life force, in the bodies of those who use the machine on a daily basis. (*chi* is the Chinese word which refers to the life force or life energy.)

> The massager will help eliminate the body toxins and provide the essential benefits of sports and fitness programs without putting stress on parts of the body such as vertebrae joints, heart and lungs and without depleting body energy levels or causing injury.

Most of the products I recommend in this book are cheap. The *chi* machine isn't. The Sun Ancon is around £300 but, for me, I figured it was cheaper than a gym membership and, so far, I've used it daily. There are cheaper versions available, too. I've seen some on eBay from around £50. I can't vouch for their effectiveness, though.

At Carl's practice, the Newton Abbot Healing Centre, you can have a trial, usually in conjunction with another treatment, or you could have the machine for a week's home trial for around £30, refundable if you purchase a machine.

Anyone from a child to a pensioner can use it, but it is recommended that you don't use it in the first three months of pregnancy.

The chi machine can be used in conjunction with a FIR treatment – Far infra red – not to be confused with a sun lamp ! For treatments and to purchase both the Chi machine and FIR www.integralnutrition.com. Call Sue on 0208 449 9213.

Carl

Carl Munson, 39, director of Newton Abbot Healing Centre (carl@carlmunson.com).

I live in Devon with my wife Rose (a Steiner teacher) and four kids, dog, cat and a few fish. I run a natural health centre, am a massage therapist, health coach and columnist.

Bright and early
Shower, using toxin-free Neways products and shave with shaving oil made with essential oils.

Typical brekkie
First drink is filtered water, then usually a tea with soya milk. Sometimes it's egg and bacon, sometimes a fruit smoothie; more often than not an apple in the car, including pips for vitamin B17.

Lunch
Pittas stuffed with salad leaves plus seeds and salad dressing or a takeaway salad.

Dinner
We eat a lot of green veg - usually organic - either steamed or stir-fried with rice or noodles and small amounts of fish or meat. We like salads sprinkled with roasted sunflower, pumpkin and sesame seeds mixed with fish or chicken on a bed of noodles. We eat a lot of homemade curries, stews and soups and eat together as a family around the table most days which is an important part of our family life.

Drinks - water - bottled or tap?
We are converts to reverse osmosis filtered water or our lovely local Dartmoor bottled water, Clearly Devon, that we buy 19 litres at a time. The kids help themselves and thankfully can taste the difference when they get tap water elsewhere.

Favourite superfoods I couldn't live without
Avocado, apples, InnerLight Supergreens, noni, aloe vera juice and just getting into mangosteen.

When I'm under the weather
I drink plenty of water and jump on my Sun Ancon *chi* machine (oxygen exerciser) for ten minutes. It's a complete state changer that relaxes and revitalises within minutes.

Favourite treatments
Far Infrared SoQi Spa (a dry sauna) combined with the *chi* machine - totally relaxing, utter bliss! Meditation and massage whenever possible.

For exercise
Walking the dog twice a day and working as a therapist keeps me fit. I've just joined a gym, however, as my middle age spread has appeared, combined with the 'Devon dumpling' good-life effect!

For relaxation
Chi machine or Far Infrared as above and meditation.

Save my skin
For skincare I sometimes spray on aloe products and use sunscreen, including aloe. I stay hydrated from the inside out.

Favourite beauty products
Not worrying. Being free of bitterness, resentment and sorrow.

Haircare
Denial and wax!

Cleaning and laundry products
Ecover.

Recycling and composting tips
Our council is hot on this and takes compost away as well as recycling.

Gardening naturally
Keeping it simple and using organic and permaculture principles where possible.

Pets
Feed our aged dog tinned tuna or chicken and olive oil. I think the pet food industry is a scandal about to blow.

Babycare
Can't remember (used to use a real-nappy service).

For the kids
Water, fruit, green veg, fish oil and treats sparingly. They know what to do even if they don't always do it! A good amount of sleep and dealing with unhappiness as soon as possible is essential. We use hugs, arnica, aloe and homoeopathic remedies where possible. Medics are a last resort.

Top parenting tips
Sense of humour – learning to take a joke!
Good discipline, yet freedom to be self-expressed within healthy boundaries. Remember, you are probably doing your best and tomorrow is another day.

I'd also like to recommend…
… the CHAMPION approach. I see health and wellbeing as a 'chain', which is only as strong as its 'weakest link'. The CHAMPION chain stands for Cleanse, Hydrate, Alkalise, Meditation, Passion, Investment, Oxygenation and Nutrition. (See www.healthchampion.co.uk.)

To achieve balance in my life…
Still practising! My wife Rose keeps me 'true', bless her.

To revitalise my soul I go to…
… sleep! Or find God inside through my experience of meditation and searching over the years. 'The kingdom of God is within you.' 'Be still and know that I am God.'

The one thing I couldn't live without
Lack of oxygen, and my wife, would make it very difficult to go on.

Guilty secrets and imperfections
Beer, chocolate, staying up too late, too much time on the computer and a horrific lack of focus. Life is just far too interesting to get trapped in one little rut!

If I had a magic wand, I would…
I really can't complain. Life is good! Financial freedom would be a real bonus and a wand waved over my wallet for financial self-discipline might help.

Soul Searching

One of my old boyfriends should have been a therapist. It was an awfully long time ago, but I must have been at least *sympathetic* to the idea of counselling, because he steered me into a kind of DIY therapy, which I think is the essence of most counselling – helping you to help yourself. He made me set 'goals'.

Goals are important – there are no two ways about it. Probably you, like me, hate the whole idea of positive affirmations. Staring into the mirror and saying over and over 'you are beautiful' just doesn't do it for me. I would just lose it, hit the mirror and yell, 'No I'm not: I'm knackered and I've got bags under my eyes.' Then I'd crack the mirror and berate myself for giving the whole household seven years of bad luck. Setting goals and identifying what it is you actually want is very important.

I have a lot to thank my ex for. He supported me through a time when I had very little work and was striving to find success in the overcrowded world of the music industry and the media. He wouldn't let me sit about, though: he used to get me to write pages and pages of stuff about what I really wanted, why I wanted it and how I was going to try to go after it. Usually, by the time I'd exhausted an idea on paper, I was starting to wonder whether I really wanted that particular thing after all.

As many self-help books will tell you, lots of us are uneasy and dissatisfied with our lot, but, when asked what we want, we have no idea. You've probably heard the saying that many of us spend our lives striving to reach the top of the ladder only to find that, when (if) we reach the top, the ladder was pitched against the wrong wall. My boyfriend really believed you must be clear about your dreams and, if you aim for nothing, you'll probably achieve nothing. If you set clear goals and do what's necessary, you'll probably only fall just short of them. In other words, set a list of eight goals, and you will probably actually achieve five or six of them.

I made my list of seven or eight 'dreams' and then wrote a supporting page as to what I could do to make these things happen. I didn't read it out loud but I did look at the list most days and I did try to put some of the intermediate steps in place. It was fascinating when I came across an old notebook years after I'd done this exercise for the first time. A tatty bit of paper flew out and I saw it contained the first list of goals I'd ever written under duress from my sensible boyfriend. He'd said it was OK to 'dream a little', not to restrict yourself. You should put on the list things you really want and you must state them in the present tense – 'I *am* successful' etc. – as if it had already happened.

> "Dance as though no one is watching you.
> Love as though you have never been hurt before.
> Sing as though no one can hear you.
> Live as though heaven is on earth."
>
> SOUZA

That's very important for the unconscious mind, which doesn't differentiate between real and imaginary. He told me to be very specific.

Well, on that bit of paper, alongside a few 'wants' (too personal to mention here) was the line, 'I am presenting my own show on national radio.' I had dreams of presenting on Radio 1. In reality, where was I at that point? Well, I was what they endearingly call the 'traffic crumpet' doing a few reports on local radio, the 'Stray dog on the B3352' sort of thing.

When I came across this bit of paper five or six years on, Richard Branson's new Virgin Radio had just launched and I had my own show. Goal achieved!

Second on the list, which was in no particular order, was, 'I am a successful singer/songwriter and will tour as a support act for a well-known artist.' But was the reality there? I'd always loved singing and earned a living with my voice, but I'd never written my own material, and doing live shows as a support artist was notoriously difficult, unless you had a major record deal, which I didn't.

Five years on? I had toured the world singing backing vocals with Wham! and George Michael; I sang with, among others, Boy George, Kim Wilde and Natalie Cole; and I had my own hit record in the UK called '7 Ways to Love', which reached Number 8 in the charts. Seeing myself on *Top of the Pops* was a bit of a shock, though: it was like, 'How did *that* happen?'

Things to do with my personal life had equally come to fruition. I shocked myself, actually, because each of the seven things I'd written on that list had come into being. Why? Because I really wanted them. I do believe that, if I hadn't put some time into correctly identifying what I wanted, they might not have happened.

Goal setting and affirming what you really want is something you can easily do for yourself, but it also plays a part in professional counselling or therapy.

Therapy is no longer the dirty word it was thirty years ago. Back then only people with serious psychological disorders or people who felt sorry for themselves went to see counsellors. The general consensus of opinion was that, if you were having any kind of emotional 'mental' problems, the best answer was to 'pull yourself together' (a popular philosophy with blokes!). As a nation, we laughed at the Americans with their fascination for visiting their analysts for years on end. Now things have changed to a certain extent, but I still believe long-term analysis is a very bad idea. I have a girlfriend who was unhappy, in and out of relationships of the one-night-stand variety, unable to function at work and at home, and I found out she'd been seeing a therapist, the same counsellor every week for twenty years! Was it working, then? Clearly it was for the therapist!

When I first developed an interest in holistic health, I quickly realised that spiritual and mental wellbeing was a huge part of it. Our minds are as important as our bodies, if not more so, in terms of our general health and wellbeing. I bought a veritable library of self-help books and did find some of them useful. They helped me to identify my own personal anxieties and 'patterns', to recognise that I was not alone, and they gave me some simple strategies to help myself overcome some of the more irrational fears and worries. At some point, though, I realised I needed more personalised help. For me it came in the form of a hypnotherapist.

Hypnotherapy

A girlfriend told me she'd finally got a grip on her compulsive eating problems and taken control over her nutrition and her weight after seeing an excellent counsellor/hypnotherapist for around ten sessions. Although my problems were of an entirely different nature, I took the recommendation and went off to see this lovely lady named Petra. This is one area where I must say it's imperative that you get a personal recommendation. Ask around. If you really can't get referred, go to an accredited body to find someone, then make an initial free-consultation appointment just to check them out. Make sure you feel very comfortable in their presence, as you may well be sharing your innermost thoughts and secrets. Often CD's can be beneficial too. Glenn Harrold author of 'De-stress your life in seven easy steps' Orion books come with a great CD www.hypnosisaudio.com.

Unless you have a mental illness, you will not need the type of psychiatrist who is a medical doctor and has taken further training in psychiatry. They will diagnose a problem and may refer you to another therapist such as a psychologist or other professional. Psychologists, usually have a psychology degree, which they supplement with a vocationally based training course to become a clinical psychologist, an educational psychologist or another type of psychologist.

A psychotherapist is trained to work with people who have deep seated emotional problems and a counsellor is someone who practises one or more types of therapeutic intervention.

Hypnotherapists are sometimes one of the above who have taken extra training in the use of hypnotherapy and visualisation, whereas a coach tries to help a client set and achieve their own personal goals, and they may have little or no training. The training and accreditation for all of these, apart from, of course, the psychiatrist, can vary enormously and, yes, there can be charlatans. That's why working out the best type of help for you and getting a recommendation is so important.

When I first went along to see Petra, she asked me a few very pertinent questions to start the ball rolling. I soon became aware that there were a bunch of fairly deep-rooted beliefs and issues that I really needed to deal with and, over the course of a few months, she really helped to calm me down and sort me out. Petra used similar techniques to those used by my old boyfriend, but hers involved visualisation. She would ask me to write down what I wanted, again in the present tense as if it were already happening, then visualise it in detail.

The power of the mind is incredible. I used the technique to get the birth I wanted for my second son (I wanted a water birth). I'd already had one very long, difficult labour, so that might not have been a natural consequence for me, but I made it happen. I was absolutely determined. Another girlfriend had an amazing experience with Petra's 'write it down and believe it' technique. She was a widow and felt ready to meet another partner. Petra asked her to describe the man she wanted. Of course, she said the usual: 'Oh, handsome, rich, kind.' Petra said, 'No, now be specific.' She thought carefully, then she wrote her wish list. A few weeks later, two separate friends on different sides of the world rang her to say it had been on their mind that she must be introduced to a friend or colleague of theirs. The UK contact invited them both to dinner and one year on they were married. Her new partner fulfilled, to the letter, everything she'd listed in detail.

'Wow!' you're thinking. 'That's it? I just need to write down, "I am a gorgeous film star and married to Brad Pitt" and it will happen?' Now don't get silly! You can daydream but your goals must be grounded in realism. It's unlikely you'll make it as an Olympic swimmer if you don't like getting wet. Petra taught me a few techniques, too, so that now, when something is kicking off or I know I'm repeating old patterns, I can usually 'Petra myself' and ask, 'What would she say about this situation?' If I could, I'd shout her name from the hilltops and her door would be beaten down in the rush, but sadly she's now retired.

Life coaching

Much more common in recent years is the phenomenon of life coaching. This is certainly not for you if you have any emotional baggage that needs dealing with. It's more a positive approach to help you to help yourself and it is good for people who want strategies to help them get the best out of their relationships, work or personal life. It's usually short-term and can be done on the telephone, but it does require you to put some effort in and complete whatever goals or tasks you've set for yourself.

If all of the above leaves you feeling overwhelmed and you hate the idea of telling a professional your personal details (that's you, boys!) maybe you just need a friend with a listening ear. There have been many occasions when I've needed to talk something through and I've 'booked' half an hour with my dear friend Rosi. Getting her perspective on my problem usually helps me see it in a different light and then I can move on. I can then do the same for her when she's in turmoil. Generally, it's so much easier to sort out someone else's life than your own. The old expression 'can't see the wood for the trees' comes to mind. What we need to do sometimes is clear out some of the rubbish to see what's really there.

Life coaches can help you with these kinds of goal-setting techniques and can support you in reaching them. In her excellent book *Behind with the Laundry and Living off Chocolate* (Crown House), Lynette Allen gives lots of tips for busy women, and I must confess to an involvement. I narrated the audio version of the book and also added a few experiences of my own as to how visualisation and goal setting have worked for me. There are also specialist life coaches. I was offered a few trial sessions with a 'parent coach'. I found it very helpful to reassess my values when it came to my children and it did help me put into practice some of the ideas I came up with during the sessions. It links to feng shui, too, in a funny kind of way, as our environment affects the way we think and sometimes, by putting things in certain places, we can direct energies and thoughts and change the dynamics of a situation. (See the chapter 'Dump the Junk – Space Clearing for Mortals'.)

Some great, now deemed classic, books on visualisation and helping you set your goals and achieve your dreams include: *Feel the Fear and Do It Anyway*, by Susan Jeffers (Arrow); *The Journey*, by Brandon Bays (HarperCollins); *The Rainbow Journey*, by Dr Brenda Davies (Hodder and Stoughton); *The Seven Spiritual Laws of Success*, by Deepak Chopra (Bantam); and, mixing psychotherapy with spirituality, *The Road Less Travelled*, by Scott Peck (Arrow).

> There are no short cuts to any place worth going
>
> ANON

Spirituality

Talking of spirituality, I believe you've gotta have faith!

Your needs will be different from mine, but all I'd say is, when it comes to holistic living, remember your soul. Your conscience will tell you if you need a spiritual overhaul and, to a certain extent, we all have a spiritual immune system that needs building just as much as our physical one.

Don't panic here, gals. I am not about to try to convert you! I believe faith is an entirely personal quest and you absolutely do not need tips from me - save to say that this is a book that deals with the body and the mind and throughout I've tried to give you my perspective on things and tell you what's worked for me, so it would be remiss of me not to mention my own Christian faith. Don't think for one minute that I see myself as an evangelist or that I'm even a shining example of Christianity. I certainly have many imperfections in that department. It's just that, when it comes to the mind–body connection, I do have a belief, a faith, and I think that impacts on my general wellbeing.

I can't go into details of a road–to–Damascus–style conversion either. I was just a child who liked showing off, so Sunday school held a great attraction for me, getting to sing and win prizes. As I got into my teens at a time when many of my friends were going off the rails and joining the 'church of the backsliders', I was fortunate enough to have a fantastic boyfriend who was part of a really happening church youth group. That in turn got me interested in gospel music, Christian events and, eventually, in a personal faith.

Over the years, of course, I went through times of disillusionment, and there were periods when I didn't set foot in church or think about it from one year to the next. But the funny thing is, I reckon it wasn't all up to me. I believe God held onto me and found ways of bringing me back into the fold, if you like, even out of the blue giving me my very first radio show, playing predominantly Christian music on *The Gospel Hour* on GLR, now BBC London, at a time when I was at the height of 'questioning' everything. I'd wanted to work in radio but had never even considered the idea of playing gospel!

Maybe you're a pagan, a Buddhist or maybe agnostic, but one aspect of faith that I do highly recommend to everyone is prayer. That, of course, is not exclusively an activity for Christians. You can pray to whichever god you choose, or just to the universe, but prayer is an interesting phenomenon. There have been numerous studies that suggest that people who pray are healthier and live longer. You may equate this with meditation and of course the act of quietening your mind will reap great rewards, but prayer is slightly different in that often, but not always, it is petitionary. Often we ask for something in prayer whether for ourselves or others, rather like the goal setting and visualisation I've already discussed. There's a theory that everyone prays at some time in their life, even if it's only a crisis prayer: 'Lord, help me!' Incredibly, more often than not, prayers are answered, not necessarily in the way we've asked but answered nevertheless.

Many years ago, I met a really helpful 'spiritual counsellor'. I was in a difficult relationship at the time and feeling tremendous amounts of anger and frustration, which, somehow, didn't seem to fit with being a Christian. I couldn't even find the words to form a prayer that might help me through that dilemma. This lady showed me that in faith, as with any other aspect of life, we are all at a different stage of our journey. It sounds terribly simplistic but she helped me to find a way to use visualisation - a technique that works for me because I am very visually oriented - to talk to God and find the peace I so desired. At the time, I wasn't a member of a church and really felt quite disillusioned with Christianity generally. She encouraged me not to feel pressurised to take part in anything but just to go and take what I needed for a while.

> " Ask and it shall be given to you; seek and ye shall find: knock and it shall be opened unto you.
>
> MATTHEW 7:7 "

For the next six months, I went twice a week to St Albans Cathedral, Hertfordshire, and soaked up the atmosphere. I felt the presence of the 'old souls' in the walls and just breathed in the incense and let the incredible sound of the choral singing wash over me. It was 'bells and smells' at its best and, when I'd given my soul time to recuperate, I was ready to pray again, ready to participate, be part of a church and to offer my contribution.

Check out the section on retreats for more spiritual rejuvenation or, if you'd like a bit of daily inspiration and support from a liberally Christian point of view, look at www.vurch.com. For more 'alternative' Christian ideas and support, try www.moot.uk.net.

Hatty

Hatty, 31. Five children. Concerned about the impact our disposable, ultrahygenic and overmedicated society has on the world around us, hoping some of this philosophy will rub off on at least a couple of my children!

Bright and early
Run a bath/shower, children usually up (to get in some time in the bath/shower because the water heater isn't on during the day), pour a pint of orange juice, get children to get their own breakfast (toast/sugar-free cereal and pure juice or water).

Typical brekkie
Orange juice and toast if I can face the toast.

Lunch
Usually sandwiches for the children and fruit for me (they snack on fruit during the day), soup and crunchy/garlic bread.

Dinner
Organic veg if I can get it, with pasta dish, jacket 'tatties' and salad. Salad with home-made burgers, organic sausages. Toad in the hole.

Drinks – water – bottled or tap?
Tap water – the amount we drink I cannot afford bottled. Pure juice, I allow 1 litre for myself in the morning of orange, the children have 2 litres of either apple or orange a day and the rest water.

Favourite superfoods I couldn't live without
Carrots, apples, sharon fruit, melon, pineapple, garlic. We eat large amounts of these each week.

Vitamins and minerals
I don't.

When I'm under the weather
Vitamin C, fish oils.

Favourite treatments
Recently discovered the benefits of liver/gallbladder flushing, also chiropractic.

For exercise
A walk in the woods, by the sea or over the hills.

For relaxation
Feet up with a book.

Save my skin
Aloe vera, coconut oil.

Sunscreen
Hat and baggy clothes.

Favourite beauty products
Exfoliation mittens for body and cloth for face. Aloe vera or coconut oil to moisturise.

Feminine care
A menstrual cup. I have found it invaluable in reducing the amount I lose during my moon and it reduces pain. Washable sanitary towels/pantyliners also reduce waste in the environment and are more comfortable for me.

Cleaning and laundry products
Bicarb, lemon and vinegar are all fantastic and cheap! For washing, salt, bicarb – both work well on stains.

Recycling and composting tips
Make it part of the family.

Gardening naturally
I use the contents of my menstrual cup as a plant food, they love it.

Pets
Feeding them fresh food whenever possible has led to our having very strong animals.

Babycare
Breastfeeding, cloth nappying. Not using chemical soaps on their delicate skin, not washing hair with anything other than water, being educated at home.

For the kids
I make sure they get fruit, water, fresh air, enough sleep, lots of cuddles.

Top parenting tips
Go with your heart; be educated; make you own choices based on evidence you have researched.

I'd also like to recommend...
... homoeopathy, having the courage of your convictions.

To revitalise my soul I go to...
... Ireland.

The one thing I couldn't live without
Books.

Guilty secrets and imperfections
I'm human.

If I had a magic wand, I would...
Listen to my instinct right from the word go!

Pregnancy and Birth – It's Not a Disease!

Don't get me started, as this is my favourite soapbox subject. How long do you have? For those of you for whom this is relevant, read on (everyone else can skip to the next chapter).

Having a baby is one of the most fantastic things you can do, as those of you who've done it will know. Well, it *should* be one of the most fantastic things!

I'm so passionate about this stuff and, as I was writing this chapter, my laptop memory was soon flashing 'overload' and I came to the realisation that this was a whole book in itself – so watch this space!

Women have been having babies for millions of years and what was a perfectly natural event has, in the past fifty years, been turned into a medical condition and one that requires the infinite wisdom of scientists and doctors. I say, 'No – mother knows best!' Pregnancy is not an illness but it can throw up (sometimes literally!) some miserable symptoms. Similarly, birth should be a natural process but, over the years, intervention and 'medicalisation' of the birthing experience has become the norm.

My second book, *Imperfectly Natural Baby and Toddler* is dedicated to these issues as well as early parenting so I can't cover it all here. However, what I would say in this book to those of you about to embark is: remember these things…

As with everything in this book, the key word is 'holistic'. Look at the whole picture and remember that it's your and your baby's birth, not the doctor's or hospital's. You're in charge. Go with your own instincts. If you want a water birth, prepare for that; if you want a home birth, know your rights and insist on one – it can be an immensely positive experience.

I do believe a good pregnancy and birth is often about the amount of preparation you put in. Learn as much as you can about natural birthing, although I prefer to call it 'gentle' birth and embark on a holistic birth-preparation programme. Seek and follow advice from a preparation programme for natural birth (see website recommendations), as it will help you find a drug-free and 'inspirational' birth. There is much that you can do to help prepare yourself mentally and physically for the birth of your baby. Depending on your finances, time and your individual needs, this holistic preparation could in-

"

If I had my life to live over, instead of wishing away nine months of pregnancy I'd have cherished every moment and realised that the wonderment growing inside me was the only chance in life to assist God in a miracle

Irma Bambeck

"

clude reflexology with a prenatal special- ist, massage, prenatal yoga and help with nutrition (sadly, it's not necessary to eat for two, or twenty-two for that matter).

You can also try Ayurvedic herbs (to be used under supervision only) and the regular application of specially formulated oils to help with stretch marks and keep- ing the perineum intact as, let's face it, you won't want to be sitting on a rubber ring for three weeks after the birth. The absolute guru of this is the woman who helped me through the labour of each of my children, Dr Gowri Motha. Get a copy of her book, *The Gentle Birth Method*, and go to www.gentlebirthmethod.com for all the lowdown and her excellent products.

Also famous for her clinic and pregnancy shop is Zita West. To see her products check out. www.zitawest.com.

You can also contact the Active Birth Cen- tre at 25 Bickerton Road, London N19 5JT. It was founded by Janet Balaskas, author and arch advocate of empowered moth- ers, who coined the term 'active birth'. The centre offers a programme of yoga classes for pregnancy and post-preg- nancy, antenatal classes for couples and a full range of treatments. They also hire out birthing pools for home births nation- wide and have a well-stocked shop and mail order business to cater for everything you'll need before and after the birth. (See www.activebirthcentre.com.)

Any books by Janet are worth getting hold of, especially *New Active Birth* (Harvard Common Press) which is out now. In the past, Janet has also written books with Dr Yehudi Gordon, who, while being one of the world's leading obstetricians, has one foot firmly planted in the ideal of natu- ral birth and integrated holistic care. He was present at the birth of my first two boys after a friend recommended him to me. (She reckoned he'd been doing yoga positions throughout her labour to help create the calm environment!) His excel- lent book is *Birth and Beyond: Pregnancy, birth, your baby and family – the definitive guide* (Vermillion).

Fortunately, there are many more holistic- birth centres popping up all over the UK. Ask around to find one near you.

Be aware, though, that intervention cre- ates intervention, which is possibly the most important rule. Don't let anyone interfere with the natural process unless you know the baby could be at risk. Babies will be born when they're ready. (I have a friend who recently had an inspirational home birth at 44 weeks.) Many horror stories are the result of hospitals rushing things to suit *their* timetables, not yours or the baby's.

You may be very new to all of this. Believe me, so was I with my first baby. I hadn't planned on having children at all and the doctor diagnosed Sonny as an ovar- ian cyst! I read everything I could find on natural pregnancy and birth and made my choices from there.

There's a great book and DVD giving you all the basic information you need, plus prac- tical tips on pregnancy, birth and looking after a new baby: *Help! I'm Having A Baby* can be ordered from 01637 831001 or visit www.babiesdirect.com.

And, thinking ahead, breast is best – that's it! My absolute passion, but more on that in *Imperfectly Natural Baby and Toddler* (Orion books).

Sleep with your baby for at least six months and avoid like the proverbial plague anyone who recommends 'controlled crying'! Read Deborah Jackson's fantastic book *Three in a Bed* (Bloomsbury), and, if you're into the more philosophical or cultural background to this subject, read *The Continuum Concept* by Jean Leidloff, a book that is truly capable of changing the world.

'Babywearing', or carrying your baby in slings, keeps them safe and secure in the knowledge that you are there. The horizontal ones are great for newborns (see www.kari-me.co.uk and www.freerangekids.co.uk). They've been inside you for nine months and they still need to be close. Buy a pram or a buggy but use it to carry the shopping.

When you address the thorny subject of immunisation, get informed. Don't be rushed into a programme of vaccinations from eight weeks. Get every bit of unbiased information you can lay your hands on and make your parental choices. (I can see the professionals queuing up to lecture me now!)

I could go on about interim health checks, nurseries, schools and the alleged Holy Grail we call education (see *Those Unschooled Minds* by John Holt).

natural
alternatives

Let Food Be Your Medicine

You and I know there's a wealth of information out there on healthy eating, so I can't cover everything. It's a very individual thing, but most of us know that, to a certain extent, we can control our health and wellbeing with our diet. I'm just going to share briefly with you what I've learned over the years. True enough, I break many of my own ideals but, in a perfect world I would.

Never eat processed foods

I believe that processed foods should carry a government health warning, in the way that cigarettes do. It's not rocket science to see that a TV dinner is not going to be as nutritious as Mum's home cooking. The really worrying bit is the harm it could be doing to us.

The food industry in general seems always to steer us toward the less-than-healthy options. Have you noticed that the Supermarket '2-for-1' offers we are encouraged to buy are, in most cases, promoting the junk food end of the range? Advertising campaigns for processed foods are huge. Children's television is bombarded with commercials promoting unhealthy eating, although, as I write this, the UK government has produced a White Paper urging manufacturers to agree to a voluntary code of regulation limiting the advertising of junk food during children's TV hours. The White Paper also suggests some form of colour labelling indicating 'product healthiness'. Somehow this prospect doesn't fill me with delight. It seems full of half-measures. Many had hoped for a ban on the advertising, and the labelling seems open to manipulation, but I suppose it's a step in the right direction.

You will remember the Sudan 1 scare in early 2005 (for more, see 'Save Your Skin'). We all scanned that food list in horror, wondering what we'd been eating and feeding our kids for the last few years before we realised it contained the harmful chemical found to cause cancer. If you're reading this book you probably patted yourself on the back at first and thought, 'Well, I never buy pot noodles, chicken drumsticks and so forth – I'm far too healthy.' But you, like me, probably got a shock when you realised the list included what we thought were fairly innocuous 'convenience' foods, including some brands of vegetarian three bean bake, cheese and tomato pizzas and Worcestershire sauce. Most of us also realised we'd probably had more than our fair share of that naughty chilli powder in a takeaway curry. So we all removed the offending items from our shelves – but didn't it make you think of the wider picture?

What about all the other preservatives and chemicals we consume in the name of convenience? What about these potentially dangerous substances that are so prevalent in all we eat that they just don't hit the headlines any more? Even allegedly healthy options sometimes come under the 'processed' banner. There are many people who still believe margarine is healthier to eat than butter, even though there is a wealth of information about the risks of consuming hydrogenated oils. We pride ourselves on our sophisticated, readily available and varied nutritional habits, but the truth is that, in the West, we have more heart disease, more cancer, more diabetes and more obesity and, maybe not by coincidence, we consume vastly greater amounts of chemical-laden and processed junk food.

There have been several studies proving that in wartime Britain the average person had a healthier diet than we do today. This seems incredible at first because people certainly were not eating 'superfoods' and they'd never come close to a millet-and-quinoa pilaff, avocado-and-grapefruit salad or tofu-and-sprouted-seeds beany burger. Food was rationed and, yes, that's the key. Most people ate less and exercised more (not in the gym but cycling, walking, gardening and just working hard). People

grew their own vegetables organically (even though they didn't think of it that way – it was just that there simply weren't many pesticides and chemicals available) and baked their own bread or bought it at the local bakery. It would usually have been wholemeal and would contain no chemical preservatives.

Each person's ration book allowed only limited amounts of tea, coffee, sugar, butter, dairy produce and eggs per week, so no one had the opportunity to be overloaded and, apart from the odd tin of corned beef and box of powdered egg, there was very little in the way of heavily processed food. Certainly, no one arrived home from a hard day at work to a microwaved ready meal. In a funny kind of way, our parents and grandparents were living organically and holistically without having to think about it. That was just the normal way of life.

I try to take my lead from that kind of nutritional lifestyle, though my imperfect status does allow me the occasional quick meal from the freezer. It's easy to get into the habit of cooking from scratch. It really doesn't take very much longer. You can be clever about it and make huge casseroles, soups and stews that you can span over a few days. It's all just a change of mindset – and it's easier. Not as imperfect as I am, my friend Lynda would not contemplate buying a takeaway pizza. When she makes one it's nicer, much healthier, takes about the same time as driving to the takeaway and back and the kids still get their treat.

To eat is a necessity, but to eat intelligently is an art.

La Rochefoucauld

Go organic

I may be in danger of sounding like my mother here but it's official: strawberries do not taste the way they did in 'my day'. I had mistakenly thought that this was simply a by-product of getting older and the almost sublime orgasmic sensation of biting into a fresh strawberry (or peach, as I vividly remember), was something that no longer impressed my jaded mature taste buds. Alas, no, I was right the first time: they just don't taste that good. The mass production, the chemicals, pesticides, the long storage and the sci-fi processes used to prolong the fruit's life have all contributed to a deadening of its very life essence. Most fruit and veg have less vitamin and mineral content and contain more environmental toxins and pollutants than fifty years ago. And, in case *that's* not bad enough, it tastes worse. That's progress, I suppose.

Most of the fruit and vegetables we buy look perfect and last for ages. It's not always so with organic produce, though, strangely, I somehow feel that proper, fresh organic food is more 'alive'. I'm always suspicious of food that lasts too long. Have you ever tasted an irradiated strawberry? That experience almost put me off strawberries for life. Not to put too fine a point on it, it felt as if I were eating 'death'. It was that bad. Of course they *looked* fresh and lovely, which I suppose was the main point, but you could almost sense that nothing of the fruit remained but some mummified molecular bastardisation in the *shape* of a strawberry.

The life force had gone. Even without the 'nuking' process, fresh and especially soft fruits have been suffering a gradual decline over the last thirty years. Yes, they're all bigger, with fewer imperfections, but often they taste, well, just useless.

Organics are a light on the horizon. We may not get to relive that childhood experience of biting into that freshly picked apple but we can certainly get nearer to it.

Now, there's 'organic' and there's 'organic'. I just don't trust the mass-marketed supermarket organics any more. They all quickly jumped on the bandwagon with their organic ranges, but I don't think their hearts are in the right place. If, like me, you've been gravitating towards the organic shelves in supermarkets since the off, have you noticed how they have been gradually phasing out stocks of independent organic suppliers and replacing them with their own brands? An independent organic company that would supply, say, canned beans of all varieties, would suddenly find that their cans of kidney beans, for example, were no longer on the shelves, having been replaced by the supermarket's own brands. What a coincidence that this happened to be their most successful bean product in the range! Without the supermarkets buying these small independents' 'big sellers', the survival of the independent is undermined. Before too long, all you will see is own-brand organic products on the shelves and, hey presto, job done. No more independents.

There are lots of little companies whose products I'm finding more difficult to get at the supermarkets – companies such as the utterly brilliant Whole Earth (recently prevented from calling their marmalade 'marmalade' because it doesn't contain enough sugar!). It's worth searching high and low for their stuff. If you're going to eat baked beans, you'll find that Whole Earth's are just the best. You can actually taste the bean, instead of goodness knows what, laden with artificial sweeteners. Other companies, such as Suma, Biona, Doves Farm and Seeds of Change, all do really good stuff, so support these smaller companies if you can. Supermarkets know that it makes good sense to respond to public opinion, so ask for them by name at Customer Services. Complain if the only option is the own-brand variety, or, better still, shop at a health store – they need your support.

If you live in London or Bristol and you're close enough to get to Fresh and Wild, rejoice! I wandered into one almost by accident in Soho one evening (yes, I know it sounds incongruous) and just could not believe the array of fresh organic vegetables, the deli and the café. All manner of healthy groceries were on offer and there was another floor stocked full of natural, chemical-free toiletries, beauty products and household goods, and a fascinating selection of books. Planet Organic is also brilliant, but hopefully you'll be able to tell me about your local and we can compile a list of fab health shops.

A great book to have to hand is *The Organic Directory* (Green Books). It is a fantastic annual publication with details of organic food manufacturers, wholesalers, restaurants, vegetable box schemes, organic farms, B&Bs, educational organisations and much more.

What about the various organic certifications? I always look for the Soil Association organic accreditation. They are the most recognised body and they insist on far more stringent testing than some of the other organisations.

There's little doubt now that the organic movement is starting to play a significant role in world trade. Interestingly, I read that the Japanese are the largest per capita consumers of organic products in the world, but the USA, Europe, Australia, New Zealand and Southeast Asia all have fast-growing markets, too. If you're sourcing organics abroad, check out their certification programme. In the USA, look for a symbol containing the words 'USDA organics'; in Japan 'JAS'; in Australia 'BFA'.

Back in the UK, when it comes to fresh produce, again, I'm a little wary of the so-called organic fresh ranges at some supermarkets. Why do I always get the feeling that this is the oldest, mankiest fruit-and-veg in the shop, there by the skin of its teeth on some very basic 'absolute minimum requirement' for organic certification? Why not cut out the middleman and, wherever possible, source your organic fruit and veg locally?

It's not only the way a plant has been grown that affects its nutritional value but how long and where it has been stored. I'd always recommend growing your own. Then you know exactly how fresh it is. Oh, how I wish I could find more time and commitment to do this. It doesn't take much, to be honest, if you're happy with a few home-grown potatoes, some spinach and runner beans, but, if you're as imperfect as I am, you won't harvest enough to feed the family and the winters will be bleak. So find a local organic supplier. Find out where their food comes from and get it as 'farm-fresh picked' as possible.

I found Riverford Organics to be a great supplier. They grow most of the food they sell on their own Buckfastleigh Farm in Devon (0845 6002311) and distribute it across the UK. Their food can be delivered locally to most areas and you can order from their huge list of produce or just take pot luck with a weekly organic vegetable box. In 2005, they won a DTI Regional Commerce Award for their excellent franchising scheme. It means you know where the food is coming from but it's still delivered to your door shortly after it's picked.

The great thing about organic box schemes is that you eat what you're given. It's a great way to get you out of your usual pattern and into a more natural, seasonal approach to eating by trying different fruits and vegetables. My medium-sized box for the last week in October included potatoes, carrots, onions, cauliflower, Crown Prince squash, a gourmet bag (salad leaves), green and red curly kale, leeks, celery, Brussels sprouts and tomatoes.

You know it's 100 per cent UK-grown and very fresh. Cauliflower isn't something I would normally choose but, just because it was there, I made a fabulous traditional cauliflower cheese that went down a treat. I certainly wouldn't buy a squash because no one knows how to cook them, but Riverford and many of the organic suppliers provide you with information on the seasonal produce, some tips on how to cook them and even recipe ideas. So, when I've finished typing this, I intend to make squash and lentil soup with chilli and fennel seeds. Fab. They also do excellent organic eggs, milk, yoghurt and a wide range of grocery items. (Go to www.riverford.co.uk to find your nearest distributor.)

For other full ranges of organic fruit, veg and general supplies, see www.local-farmers-markets.co.uk. If you can get together and form a little cooperative with friends or neighbours, you can save a lot of money by buying wholesale. Try www.infinityfoods.co.uk. Or check out the bulk buying section on my own forum www.imperfectlynatural.co.uk.

A great way of finding out about organic food suppliers in you area is to look out for an organic festival. There are usually lots of local and nationwide companies at these events with products to buy and lots of samples to try. (Refer to www.soilassociation.org.)

Dairy

Dairy products have had a bad press recently, too. It's a good idea if you're on a detox diet or feeling 'mucousy' (charming!) to leave off dairy for a few days. It's amazing how different you feel. In general, though, I think this is an area where organic food is really important. Always insist on organic eggs (not just free range). The best I've ever eaten are straight from under my friend's chickens. 'Blind-test' a fresh organic egg against a supermarket free range one and I defy you not to taste the difference immediately.

It's a similar story with milk: organic milk contains almost three quarters more of the wonder nutrient Omega 3 than conventional milk, and the same goes for yoghurt. (Obviously, buy the live, unsweetened variety to get the full probiotic effect.)

Years ago, we went to a lovely little guesthouse in Suffolk where the proprietor had the best yoghurt that I'd ever tasted for breakfast. She had brought back a live culture from Thailand (it had been in existence for at least twenty years) and had made her own ever since. She gave us a little dollop of the starter culture in some milk to take home and we made jokes about its 'throbbing' on the three hour journey. It needed to be strained and left in milk every day and for a while we also had yoghurt that was the talk of the town. Sadly, we went away for a few days and hadn't really asked anyone to look after our 'pet', so we let it go. The moral of the story is to get the most 'live' yoghurt you can find.

The best organic live yoghurt I've found on the supermarket shelves is made by Rachel's Dairy. Try it with porridge oats and a handful of sunflower and pumpkin seeds – it's delicious.

> Let thy food be thy medicine and thy medicine be thy food.
>
> HIPPOCRATES

Superfoods

You know what I mean: it's a buzz word for health freaks but important nevertheless. So-called 'superfoods' are those special foods that heal, that contain all the valuable vitamins, proteins and minerals we need to give us a sense of physical and mental well-being. The obvious one is garlic, the king of superfoods, so cheap and readily available that we often forget about it. Garlic is a key component of the Mediterranean diet and we know it is good for our health, being antibacterial and antiviral. It can be used in medicine to treat major infections and a study last year claimed it can reverse the signs of heart disease and dramatically reduce the build-up of fatty acids in the arteries.

Other superfoods include onions, peppers, beetroot, cabbage, spinach, apples, oranges, apricots, hemp seeds, pumpkin seeds, olives, more recently Goji berries and the lesser-known quinoa – a seed grown in the Andes for thousands of years. It's fairly new to us but it is said to have more protein than any other grain and is very rich in vitamins and minerals, particularly calcium, and provides all the essential fatty acids. I've collected together the personal choices of a number of friends, who outline their favourite superfoods (see 'Imperfectly Natural People').

Meat, poultry and fish

As you might have guessed, I'm a veggie, though not really, because, occasionally, I eat fish. So I'm certainly not going to lecture you about that. As you'll see from 'Imperfectly Natural People', several of my colleagues and friends love meat, and I must admit that before I gave it up there was nothing I liked more than a rare bit of cow's derrière. It's a personal choice and there are some nutritional benefits to be had from eating meat that you have to work hard to replicate if you become a vegetarian or a vegan, including some of the B-complex vitamins, for example.

I do feed my kids meat though. I found a local organic butcher and everything comes from there. I even trust the hamburgers. If you can find one, ask if they buy direct from the people who farm the animals that produce the meat and poultry, then you'll also know how they've lived and been fed. These people are passionate about their organic status and will usually be more than happy to tell you all you want to know.

Maybe you have a local butcher who offers organic meat and can tell you exactly where it comes from. If not, look for the several mail order companies who specialise in meat. You could try www.savethebacon.com, who call themselves the 'farmers' market on the web', Higher Hacknell Farm (www.higher hacknell.co.uk) or Sheepdrove Organic Farm (www.sheepdrove.com). I've also just discovered the excellent Soil Association-accredited www.organicbutchers.net. Exactly what it says on the tin: order from their affordable selection of fully 'traceable back to the farm' organic meat and they'll deliver to your door (0800 085 1340).

For organic fish, it's much more difficult of course. Deep sea fish ought to be organic by its nature, but in recent years we've heard terrible scares of toxic poisoning and pollutants. Mercury in the environment collects in fish in the form of methyl mercury and is a recognised danger to us, especially to the nervous systems of unborn babies, which is a bit worrying considering all the advice urging pregnant mothers to eat more oily fish. Trace levels of methyl mercury are found in nearly all fish. My theory is that the bigger, longer-living fish that feed on other fish are more likely to have absorbed greater amounts of toxins such as this. I tend to limit intake of fish such as swordfish and king mackerel to perhaps once a week, especially as I'm pregnant as I'm writing this.

So where do you find organic fish? It's a difficult one. Fish caught in the wild cannot get an organic certification as far as I'm aware, though some might argue that a freshwater lake in a very unpolluted part of the world is about as organic as you can get. Ironically, the organic stuff you'll see in most shops is actually farmed. Organic status for these farms requires that stringent controls be exercised over the use of pesticides, dyes, antibiotics and so on. I'm not sure whether use of chemicals such as these is banned or merely reduced but it's certainly considerably better than a normal fish farm. So get a good fishmonger who's passionate about topics such as this, a local supplier you can trust, and, before you buy, ask where it's from and see if he knows or cares about his sources. Mostly when you see organic, it'll be trout or salmon, though efforts are being made to introduce the organic farming of cod, sea bass and halibut. You can tell organic wild salmon because usually it's lighter (the bright pink colour actually comes from dyes) and much fuller in flavour. I think it's worth paying extra. We had Rick Stein on the Radio 2 show recently and he allegedly gives the accolade of the best trout in the country to www.purelyorganic.co.uk.

After decades of overfishing in the North Sea, herring is now listed by the Marine Conservation Society as one of the 'fish species to eat with a clear conscience'. Nutritionally, they're packed with Omega 3 fatty acids, and there's a Dutch proverb that says that if a herring is around the doctor is far away.

For fresh herring and shellfish try Mitch Tonks Fishworks Restaurants and Fishmongers in London, Bath, Bristol and Christchurch (www.fishworks.co.uk).

For tinned fish try Fish 4 Ever. They produce herrings (fillets only), sustainably fished white- and yellow-fin tuna, sardines, mackerel and anchovies and claim to pack them fresh and cold press them in unheated organic vegetable oil. (See http://organico.homestead.com/fish4ever-products.html.) Stockists are independent health shops and farm shops.

Raw energy

Raw food is packed full of vitamins, minerals and enzymes. It's a shame many of these nutrients get destroyed in the cooking process. A raw food diet is one of my big recommendations for slimming, energy, detoxing, increasing your vitality and protecting yourself against disease.

The cooking process

If you're imperfect like me, it's going to be difficult to keep it up though, so the answer is to get as close as you can to raw. Try a raw-ish 'stir fry veg'. Resist the temptation to add lashings of oil - you need only the tiniest amount of olive oil, say a teaspoon. If you think there isn't enough, it's probably about the right amount. Let it get hot but not smoky and then chuck in the veg. The plan is to just 'sear' the outside and keep the vegetable inside crisp, light and raw. It's the best of both worlds. A dash of tamari near the end of cooking is great but, even better, balsamic vinegar and lemon juice.

Steaming is much better than boiling for 'light' veg. It always tastes nicer and, apart from the old-fashioned steamer baskets, you can now buy the on-the-hob style of steamer units as well as electric ones.

Take a look at your cooking equipment, too. Those very efficient nonstick pans could be doing you serious harm. Some nonstick coatings are made with a complex mixture of perfluorinated chemicals (PFCs). It's widely accepted that PFCs can be dangerous because it has been proved in laboratory tests that they are toxic to mammals. They don't biodegrade and the toxins accumulate in people, animals and the environment. It's difficult to avoid PFCs completely, as they're in electrical goods, furniture, some clothing and rainwear, car engine parts – in fact just about everything manmade! But at least try not to cook with it too often. Replace your nonstick coated cookware with stainless steel or enamel-coated cookware. I've just invested in some heavy but fantastic cast iron pans.

> When diet is wrong medicine is of no use.
> When diet is correct medicine is of no need.
>
> ANCIENT AYURVEDIC PROVERB

I never use a microwave oven. The only time I've ever wished I had one was one Christmas when I'd forgotten to allow two hours to steam the pudding and I knew I could have microwaved it in about ten minutes. (As it happened, we were all too full to eat it anyway, so we cooked it on Boxing Day.) Putting high energy microwaves into food disrupts its cellular and molecular structure and it's hard to quantify exactly the effect that has on the vital force of our foods. Of course, we're told microwaves are perfectly safe and that may be your view, but instinctively most of us, if we admit it, suspect that there's something not quite right about it. I've read of research calling into question not only the safety of the food but of the machines themselves, alongside accusations of the gagging of research findings by the industry. As with many things in this field, there is much contradictory evidence, so you can only decide for yourself. Maybe you want just to limit the extent to which you use them or use them for defrosting only. In my view, a microwaved cup of coffee still tastes terrible and I won't stand near one when it's on.

Barbecues and smoked food

Of course, we all love a barbecue; it's fantastic to eat outdoors and enjoy that wonderful smell of hickory chips and charcoal. But beware of too much meat and fish cooked on the 'barbie'. There are hydrocarbons in the smoke that can disrupt the fat and protein structure in foods. This can create free radicals (yes, the nasty carcinogenic kind), which some say can contribute to tumours in the body. Scary stuff. Don't go completely mad and vow never to have an outdoor cook-up again, but bear in mind certain things. Marinate the food really well before cooking. Be patient and wait until the embers are grey. Don't ever cook while the charcoal's flaring up. In their excellent book *Eat to Beat Cancer*, Dr Rosy Daniel and Jane Sen suggest that 'if we eat barbecue food we should really precede and follow our meal with vitamin C, betacarotene or vitamin E in order to deactivate the free radicals we have taken in'. That's certainly something worth considering.

Seaweed

Without doubt you'll have read about seaweed's healing properties and you may already be taking it as a supplement in the form of kelp, or slapping it on your body for a bathtime treatment, but for most of us the real stuff is just a pile of stinking mush on the beach that allegedly some people eat. The closest most of us have come to seaweed is, at worst, that crispy sugary dish served in Thai and Chinese restaurants and, at best, wrapped around some rice in sushi. But, increasingly, more of us are realising that seaweed in various forms is a wonder food.

It has medicinal properties, too. In an article written for *The Times* in early 2005, Liz Bestic says seaweed was used by herbalists in the past:

Seaweed was used to cure ailments from ulcers to cuts and grazes. Legend has it in Brittany that the earliest seaweed farmers never worried about the cuts they sustained while handling the knotted tangles of seaweed and kelp they were harvesting to make 'pain d'algues' – seaweed bread – because they knew that the wounds healed with little or no treatment. Today NHS nurses still use certain dressings which are impregnated with seaweed to promote rapid healing.

There have been ongoing clinical trials in Japan to discover whether seaweed can help in the fight against cancer. It is thought that there could be elements in seaweed that suppress the growth of tumour cells.

It's an acquired taste, yes, but I think it tastes pretty good and it's good for us, so how does it get from the heaving sand-logged heap on the beach to our plates or into the medicine cupboard? Well, if you know what to look for you can get sea beet between May and December, which makes a good spinach substitute. Samphire, which is a good crisp salad ingredient, is occasionally sold by fishmongers and, for those who want to buy seaweed bread products, a Kent company bake bread using Norwegian Seaweed (www.artisanbread.ltd.uk).

You may have heard of the Welsh speciality laver bread, made from laver, a seaweed found mostly in Swansea. Usually, it is washed, boiled to a pulp then mixed with oatmeal and formed into cakes. It can be fried and served with bacon or cheese. (See www.wales-direct.co.uk.)

It's easy to buy dried seaweed. Most health shops and some supermarkets sell it in 'sheets' or you can buy nori flakes, which can be sprinkled over any salad or casserole. For seaweed foods and supplements, see www.xynergy.co.uk.

Alcoholic beverages

Of course, if you're imperfect like me, you still want a tipple now and again and it scared me when I first realised the hair-raising number of chemicals usually present in the average bottle of wine. The really annoying thing is that currently there is no legislation making it compulsory to list ingredients on drinks, so most wine labels will tell you where the grapes are grown and that's about it. Vegetarians should be careful, too, because often the ingredients include, or certainly the process has involved, the use of animal products.

All is not lost, though. There is an increasingly wide range of excellent organic wines and they're becoming much more affordable. Ask your local off-licence to get some for you, or try to buy them by mail order from The Organic Wine Co Ltd (01494 446557) or Vintage Roots, who also do organic spirits (0800 980 4992; www.vintageroots.co.uk). For organic beer, try Black Isle (01463 811871; www.blackislebrewery.com). There are also two very good books written by wine expert Monty Waldin: *Biodynamic Wines* and *Organic Wine Guide*.

Coffee

When it comes to coffee, much as I love it, it's just not great for you. Most of us will consume about 32 gallons a year. With nonorganic beans, that means about 11 pounds of fertilisers and eight ounces of pesticides will have been used to 'mash up' our annual brew. Scary chemicals such as benomyl, chlordane, carbofurane, DDT, endulfan, paraquat and zineb could all have been used in the production process, though some are banned in certain countries. I prefer my coffee without, so go organic and go fair trade.

Properly certified organic coffee makes a good attempt to follow each stage of the production process. An easily available one that I like is Percol Organic Americana - fair trade of course. (See www.coffee.uk.com.)

Teas

Green tea is very good for you. One of the main benefits comes from polyphenol oxidase, an abundant supply of antioxidants. To be absolutely honest, I'm imperfect on this one. I just hate the taste, though the one I can drink is Clipper Green Tea with Lemon, but, even then, I need a bit of honey to sweeten it. If you can drink green tea regularly, go for it.

There are lots of excellent organic herbal teas and it really just depends on your taste, unless you're using them therapeutically (peppermint is great for digestive problems; chamomile is good for stress and insomnia). As the Law of Sod would have it, Celestial Seasonings, well known for their great range of teas, seem to have discontinued my all-time favourite, Almond Sunset. If you're in the States, buy it there and send me a pack - please! (See www.celestialseasonings.com.)

Clipper Teas do a brilliant range of organic teas and they also do a sensational hot chocolate. The packaging is made from 100 per cent biodegradable, non-chlorine-bleached material from managed sustainable forests, and they use only unbleached tea bag paper. (See www.clipper-teas.com.)

Juicing

There are loads of great books on the benefits of juicing. It's the fast-track way to get your (at least) five portions of fruit and veg every day. It can be totally creative as you can combine just about any fruit, seed or vegetable you choose. Drinking fresh fruit and vegetable juice is the quickest way to absorb easily all the nutrients, phytochemicals and enzymes found in plant food that we need to make us healthy. They are cleansing and give us energy.

Celery juice is said to help asthma and bronchitis and to lower blood pressure. Radish juice controls coughs, soothes sore throats and reduces fever, and pineapple juice helps digestion and cardiovascular disease. Carrot is a bit of a wonder food and fantastic to juice up on its own or mixed with other things. As well as being a great source of beta-carotene and vitamin A, new studies have shown that carrots contain falcarinol, a substance that can help prevent the development of cancerous tumours.

My absolute favourite pick-me-up, though, is carrot and orange juice with the zest of one lemon and a few scrapings of fresh ginger. I came across this gem ten years ago in America. DH (Darling Husband - then boyfriend) and I were on our first holiday away together. Totally lost in a convertible hire car somewhere in the wine country of Marin County, just north of San Francisco, we stumbled on a kind of New Age town called Fairfax and first stop was the juice bar, something you

didn't see much in the UK then. We drank carrot, orange and ginger and it's been a hit in our tent ever since. (Top tip – always keep ginger in the freezer, then grate it like parmesan.)

You can also, of course, try the trendy wheatgrass juice, which is all the rage in juice bars across the States. I must be honest and confess I'm not a huge fan, but I do believe in its health properties. It's one of the richest sources of chlorophyll you can get. It's meant to boost your immune system and protect you against colds and infections. You can grow it and juice it yourself but you may want to gen up a bit from a book and perhaps buy an automatic sprouter (more about sprouting and relevant equipment later).

The truth is that juicing is time-consuming. Buying the fruit and veg, chopping and slicing it, disposing of the waste (into the compost, I hope), cleaning the chopping board and knives and, worst of all, dismantling the juicer and cleaning all the individual components is a long process. If you are imperfect like me you'll probably buy a juicer, use it religiously for a couple of weeks and then find you need the space on the worktop, so into the cupboard it goes. Yes, it's a bit of a faff but, if you make the effort, it's really worth it.

Here's my tip and, believe me, I'm pointing one finger at you and three back at myself: throw money at it. You can get juicers for under £50, but don't. The more expensive ones are much easier to clean, built to last and can be used non-stop. They're reliable and they can handle larger amounts. They also look really flash on your worktop so you're less likely to hide them away. But make sure you get one that does both fruit and vegetables. The Champion Juicer is the one the professionals use. It has just celebrated its fiftieth anniversary and they've sold over a million, so they can't be bad. Get it in white, grey or cream, but it's not cheap at around £299 from the Wholistic Research Company (www.wholisticresearch.com). I also use a much cheaper model from John Lewis. It's a Magimix Le Duo. I must say it works fine.

My next tip is to get lots and lots of your favourite fruits and vegetables and leave them next to the juicer in a huge wooden bowl. Try to keep a wooden chopping board and a decent knife ready, too, so the whole ensemble will look you in the eye as you walk past and, if it could talk, it would say, 'Well, lazybones, gonna get a power-packed glass of live enzymes straight into your gut – or what? Just juice. I'll do it with you!'

Finally, when you've made your morning juice (or a big flask to keep in the fridge and drink later), clean your juicer straight-away. There's nothing more depressing than getting up the next morning raring to whiz up a healthy spirulina juice and finding it full of rotting fruit dregs. Just do it straightaway and – another top tip – keep a nailbrush handy to dig out those awkward bits.

Don't forget you can add seeds to smoothies and juices. You could cheat and buy Nutiva Berry Pomegranate Hemp Juice from www.revital.co.uk.

There are loads of books on the benefits of juicing and some innovative recipes. Check out books by Leslie Kenton and Michael Van Stratton, and any of the excellent books by Jason Vale, the Juice Master, such as *Turbo-Charge Your Life in 14 Days* (Thorsons). www.juicemaster.com.

Old-fashioned homemade drinks

If you can't face juicing, here are a couple of old-fashioned homemade drinks. They're delicious, healthy, require no special equipment, kids love them and you get the added bonus of sneaking in immune-boosting vitamins without them knowing!

I mention Lemon Barley Water in the chapter on 'Natural Cures for Common Ailments' (see page 139) – it takes just 6 minutes to make:

Lemon Barley Water

Put 100g of pearl barley (its labelled as pot barley in some health food shops) into a saucepan, cover with water and boil for about 4 minutes. Whilst the barley is boiling, mix 50g of the best raw, organic sugar with the grated yellow peel of 2 lemons and leave for a few minutes for the lemon to flavour the sugar. When the boiling barley is ready, strain off the water and put it into a big jug, tip the sugar/lemon on top and mix together. Add 1 litre of boiling water and leave to completely cool. When cooled, put through a strainer and add the juice of the 2 lemons. Cool again in the fridge. It tastes divine.

My kids always gravitate towards cordials and juices that are loaded with sugar or artificial sweeteners. Try them on this – another great old-fashioned drink that is really easy to make, although it takes a little longer. This one is so eco-friendly it doesn't even leave anything for the compost!!

No-waste Apple Juice

Peel and core 2 kg of organic apples (sweet are best unless you have a very sour palette). Put the peelings and cores into a bowl and save the rest of the apples (you can make a fresh fruit salad or just eat the chunks). Add a small piece of cinnamon, 2 cloves and half inch of chopped fresh ginger to the bowl. Grate the yellow rind of 1 organic lemon and mix with 80g of the best raw, organic sugar so the lemon flavours the sugar. Add to the apple mix and stir. Pour 2 litres of boiling water over the apple mix and leave for at least 8 hours. Strain, cool in fridge and drink. Yummy!

Dani

My name is Dani Hulyer and I am a 34-year-old Personal Fitness Trainer and Nutrition and Lifestyle Coach. I am originally from Perth, Australia, and have been living in and running my business from West London for the last six and a half years.

Bright and early
On rising my usual routine is to wake up early enough to get a good breakfast in, spend a few minutes stretching and practicing my *Chi* stick exercises.

Typical brekkie
Gluten-free muesli, nuts, seeds and fruit mixed into some natural yoghurt. Occasionally, I will have a boiled egg, some bacon, mushrooms and cherry tomatoes with a juice freshly made from beetroot, carrot and assorted fruit. Probably 95 per cent of my food will be from organic sources.

Lunch
As I am usually on the road for lunch, I try to make sure I get a few seed/nut/fruit bars or a mixed bag of loose stuff into my workbag for snacks. I look for lunch at places that do either organic meals from scratch or salads that I can add some other protein sources to. Good sources if I'm desperate are Pret a Manger ('breadless' salads) and Fresh & Wild (in central London).

Dinner
Typically, dinner will be some form of protein (buffalo, chicken, turkey, pork, lamb and occasionally, fish) cooked in a variety of ways with steamed veggies. I try to rotate my meats on a four day basis and most of them along with the vegetables are obtained from various Farmers' Markets at the weekend. If I have a dessert, it usually consists of yoghurt and fruit with some chocolate 'Nemesis' cake (a fantastic wheat-free cake that we've discovered at the market in Pimlico!).

Drinks – water – bottled or tap?
I only drink bottled 'live' water (direct from the source). The thing to remember with water is that if you don't filter it beforehand (e.g. Brita or similar) then YOU become the filter. Unfortunately, even the water that comes through the filter is recycled, dead water and is lacking the essential minerals that our body needs. Most people do not drink enough water and many alternative and medical practitioners believe that up to 70-80% of our health problems are due to blockages of some sort (circulatory, respiratory, lymphatic, skeletal) or dehydration. Ideally, we should drink the equivalent of our kilogram body weight in ounces of water per day (i.e. a 60 kg person should drink about 60 ounces of water = 3 pints = 1½ litres).

Favourite superfoods I couldn't live without
Green & Black's White Chocolate, chocolate 'Nemesis' cake (!) and avocados and a good mix of dried fruit, nuts and seeds to nibble on all day. Seriously though, I wouldn't be feeling as vital and healthy as I do without such a high percentage of my diet coming from organic sources. The way I justify the added cost is by knowing that when my body is getting the nutrients it requires, it doesn't crave other sources (usually non-foods)... basically meaning I eat less (or rather I eat what I need)!

Wild horses wouldn't get me to eat...
Processed foods (unless I'm really desperate). Basically, I know that it will take all the good nutrients in my body to deal with the toxic effect of the processed rubbish (non-foods) and that I will just crave more food until my body feels that I have obtained the nutrients it requires.

Vitamins and minerals
With the knowledge that not all fruits and vegetables are picked at their optimum nutrient-density time and are often stored for long periods before sale, I believe even those who get 7-10 servings of 'fresh' produce a day are still missing out on essential micronutrients. In the last few months, I have discovered Juice Plus+ capsules and have

enthusiastically promoted the product with all my clients, family and friends. From my own experience, I have noticed an improvement in energy levels, fewer sugar cravings, increased mental clarity and my skin is feeling clearer and softer. The only other 'supplement' I take is Propolis drops during the winter and a varied combination of oils rich in Omega 3 fatty acids (hemp oil, avocado oil, or one called the good oil).

When I'm under the weather
I stay in bed, drink lots of water and try to eat as much as I can to battle whatever it is that is trying to attack me! Chocolate sometimes helps of course!

For exercise
You name it and I'll either have a go at it or show you how to do it!

For relaxation
I try to practice deep abdominal or Pranayama breathing, some yoga stretches, or walk in a park or along a beach to breathe in some natural energy.

Save my skin
Products from Dr. Hauschka (biodynamic) – Rose Day Cream, Body Cream and Hand Creams; Green People – Aloe Vera Shampoos & Conditioners; an Australian brand called Aesops – Jasmine Face Moisturiser and a cleanser;

Sunscreen
Korres Factor 15 Facial Sunscreen and a lip protection lotion.

Favourite beauty products
Dr. Hauschka and Aesops.

Haircare
Green People or Jason's (organic)

Cleaning products
Usually products from Ecover.

I'd also like to recommend...
Any online organic food and product delivery system (e.g. Abel & Cole, www.organic delivery.co.uk), Farmer's Markets; knowing how to use a Swiss Ball, Foam Roller and a Medicine Ball to stretch and strengthen any body part as required!

To achieve balance in my life...
I try to incorporate some quality time by myself - stretching, breathing, reading, whatever. I also try to get home to Australia once every 18 months or so. This is good to re-establish my accent!

To revitalise my soul I go to...
A beach or a mountain as far away from my normal life as possible. The Italian Dolomites or Canada are great for the mountain aspect and for beaches, I'll take just about anything clean, warm and sparsely populated!

The one thing I couldn't live without
Family

Guilty secrets and imperfections
I've already mentioned chocolate haven't I? A few of my imperfections are well hidden by having good posture!

If I had a magic wand, I would...
Eat according to my 'Metabolic Type' even though it means cutting out a lot of the food I feel I don't have a problem with, and making sure I do my *Chi* stick exercises and some stretching every day.

Sprouts

No, not the soggy green things you overboil for Christmas dinner, but sprouted seeds. Sprouted seeds are one of the most amazing wonder foods. You probably remember when you were a child covering a little jam jar of water with muslin and growing your own little seeds or making mustard and cress on a little bit of soggy felt. Well, it's all the same principle and it's so worth doing.

Sprouted seeds are one of the most concentrated sources of vitamins, minerals, amino acids, proteins and enzymes. They cost next to nothing, they're organic and you can add them to salads and sandwiches all year round. Make sure you buy organic seeds to sprout of course. The easiest to start with are alfalfa, aduki beans and mung beans, but you can also sprout broccoli seeds, brown and green lentils, red clover seeds, rocket seeds and unhulled sunflower seeds. Usually a bag of organic seeds will cost between £1 and £3, but of course they make a huge volume of sprouts. You don't even need any special equipment to start sprouting other than a jam jar and a bit of muslin.

One great tip is to keep two of those little plastic cartons with lids that you get when you've had a Chinese or Indian takeaway (admit it, you've had one recently) and recycle them. Wash them out thoroughly and dry, then line the bottom with a piece of damp kitchen towel or muslin. Put a layer of alfalfa seeds in one and mung beans in the other (make sure you buy the organic seeds intended for sprouting), pop the lid back on and leave on the windowsill. Tip the water (the condensation that's appeared) back in (or rinse it out if there's lots), shake around and, within two days, you'll see sprouts. Within two more days they'll be ready to be well rinsed and eaten with salads.

Often, people buy a professional kit. You can get a glass sprouting kit comprising two or three 0.75 litre glass jars with stainless steel mesh tops, drainage rack and glazed ceramic drip tray. Then you just rinse the seeds twice a day and invert the jars. The kit costs around £30. If you want to spend a bit more, get a Freshlife Automatic Sprouter. This is an ingenious thing that pumps water from the base to sprinkle over the two trays of seeds or grains growing in a big barrel above, keeping them fresh and watered without your needing to do anything at all. It will also grow wheatgrass and costs around £73. Find out more about the above and lots more sprouting kits and organic seeds from www.wholisticresearch.com.

The great wheat debate

Either you or someone in your family or close friends will be allergic or intolerant to wheat, I can assure you. Alarming, isn't it? It's hard to believe that such a staple food and one that has dominated our diet for so many years can be bad for us. I have a girl-friend whose stomach blows up as if she were five months pregnant if she takes one bite of a bread roll, and another friend who, after many years of headaches, bloating, irritable bowel syndrome (IBS), wind and acne, has finally cut out wheat and is glowing with health and vitality.

Wheat contains gluten and often it's that protein that is the baddie, as it can be very difficult to digest. I think that all of us have some level of intolerance to gluten; some just cope with it better than others. Many people feel better when they exclude it from their diet, even for a short time. This is not to be confused with the very serious gluten allergy, coeliac disease. Sufferers from that condition really must avoid gluten completely and for ever.

I don't believe the solution is as simple as suggesting that everyone give up all bread products for ever. I think one of the problems is the way bread is now produced. Go and look at the ingredients of the average so-called 'healthy' loaf on the supermarket shelf, whether brown or white. Even one that claims to be free from artificial preservatives and colourings is likely to contain a heap of stuff apart from wheat flour, yeast and gluten, including hydrogenated vegetable oil, salt, emulsifier, spirit vinegar, mono- and DA glycerides of fatty acids and treacle or sugar/sweetener. No wonder a loaf lasts for up to a week.

I find the best way is to get a breadmaker and make your own wholegrain or even mixed-grain bread. In Karen Kingston's Book *Creating Sacred Space with Feng Shui* (Piatkus), she says,

> Everything is alive. Pure energy is all around us even if we cannot see it. Kirlian Photography (photography which shows up the auric field) offers proof to clinical western minds of the existence of energy fields which emanate from all things. I once saw a Kirlian photograph of a slice of white processed bread alongside a slice of organic brown wholegrain. Around the white bread there was a flimsy excuse of an energy field, whereas the brown bread's emanation was so strong, vital and many times bigger. Processed food loses so much of its vitality.

The great advantage of having your own breadmaker is that you can experiment with different types of wholegrains. Spelt is an ancient grain that is more easily digestible by many people who are intolerant to wheat. You can also make your own wheat- and gluten-free bread but you'll need to be a bit more creative with the recipes. Sweeten it with honey instead of sugar and chuck in lots of hemp/poppy/sesame/pumpkin/sunflower seeds to increase your essential fatty acid intake and make it taste of something, otherwise it can be quite bland. I always use honey or molasses to sweeten any bread I make instead of sugar, and organic unsalted butter instead of margarine, and I usually reduce the amount of salt quoted in the recipe. Also, go to the health-food shop or organic supplier to buy your grains and try to get organic yeast. Bear in mind, too, that homemade bread has none of the preservatives of the shop-bought stuff, so you'll need to keep it in an airtight container and eat it within two days.

If your imperfections stretch to just not coping with a breadmaker, or for those times when you've run out of yeast or other ingredients, the good news is that there are some great alternatives available in the shops. Look for the Terence Stamp range (yes, the actor with the gorgeous blue eyes) of wheat- and gluten-free foods. Try to find a local bread shop that will make 100 per cent rye bread, since many of the supermarket brands are only *part* rye, part wheat and gluten. Try pumpernickel bread, hemp, buckwheat and, if you can find it, a ready-made spelt loaf.

Of course, wheat is not present only in bread. What about crackers, biscuits, pasta and cereal? The fantastic news is that even in the last couple of years the alternatives are much more readily available and usually excellent. My favourites include Orgran Rice and Corn Pasta, Nature's Path Organic Millet Rice Flakes and Nairn's wheat-free biscuits.

Most supermarkets now also have a gluten-free section offering chocolate bars, biscuits and cakes. These are wheat- and gluten-free but that doesn't necessarily mean they're particularly healthy. They are often highly processed and contain high levels of salt, sugar (or sugar substitutes) and flavourings.

When it comes to cereals there are some good ranges of organic muesli but it's very easy to make your own with organic oats, fruit and nuts and seeds.

Muesli

2 cups oats

1 cup oats, dry-toasted

1 cup each of chopped almonds, desiccated coconut, chopped apricots, raisins

Gluten-free muesli

1 cup each of millet flakes, brown rice flakes, dry toasted buckwheat flakes, chopped hazelnuts, sunflower seeds, chopped apricots and raisins.

Oats are good, so porridge for breakfast is fantastic (add fruit, nuts, seeds and yoghurt if you like) and cook with rice milk so you have a dairy-free porridge that doesn't need sweetening. Oats are still best avoided if you have a definite gluten sensitivity, so remember that while you're knocking up flapjacks sweetened with honey and raisins.

Rice cakes, rye crackers and corn cakes (organic and unsalted if possible) are good for snacks with hummus. Use brown rice instead of white and, for some really interesting alternatives to rice and even couscous (which we tend to forget is a wheat product), try quinoa. It's something of a well-kept secret, that one, as we've already seen under 'Superfoods' above. It cooks in no time and can be eaten instead of rice and pasta, or can be added to casseroles and risottos. You can do the same with millet and buckwheat.

Sweet stuff

Trust me, I'm no domestic goddess. I have to pay the lovely woman who runs the local café to make me wheat- and gluten-free lemon cakes. She's just set up a mail order company offering a complete range of breads, cakes and treats. (See www.glutenfreebakery.co.uk.)

But, when my kids (and I) crave something sweet and I'm trying not to be too imperfect, one of my favourite things to knock up is what I call 'Sweetie Balls'. I must give the credit here to Carol Vorderman. In *Detox for Life,* she calls them Marzipan Balls. All you do is grind almonds finely and knead with honey and water to a smooth paste. Form small balls and roll them in ground cinnamon. These are so easy to make and everyone loves them (so long as you don't have a nut allergy obviously). I've even made a load of balls, divided them into sixes or eights wrapped in that iridescent cellophane stuff and tied it with a ribbon – and that's my healthy contribution to the church fête cake stall. It's the closest we come to handmade chocolates.

Because I'm imperfect I must confess that my kids do eat actual sweets, too. I just can't be perfect enough to keep them away from the little treasures, but I make sure that, 98 per cent of the time, the sweets are organic and free from the really hair-raising colourings and chemical additives. Health-food shops do a good range of treats. Candy Tree make excellent corn syrup candies. They are proper round lollies on a stick so the kids think they're getting the real deal. Just Wholefoods make VegeBears, organic, gelatine-free fruit jellies and fruit gums. There's also some excellent organic liquorice made by Free Natural. In case you have difficulty finding any of this stuff, to my great delight I've found the Organic Sweet Shop, a mail order company set up by a guy who was desperate to get hold of this stuff for his own family. He does the widest range I've ever seen, plus organic biscuits and little individual bars of Green & Black's chocolate. (See http://stores.ebay.co.uk/The-Organic-Sweet-Shop.)

Talking chocolate

I really should have listed it among the superfoods. It's so emotive and powerful and, of course, I'm not going to suggest we all eat loads of chocolate, but I'm not going to say give it up, either. It's well documented that it lifts our spirits and improves our sense of wellbeing. The key is: don't guzzle the whole box. I also think there's a huge difference between eating your average sugar, fat and chemical laden 'choco' bar from the local newsagent and eating a square or two of really high quality chocolate.

The Europeans are good at this. French chocolate is, by and large, far superior to ours and, even if you buy a household name brand over there, you'll find it tastes less sickly sweet. They just won't stand for it. Have organic chocolate if possible and the higher the cocoa solid ratio the better it is. Green & Black's are the market leaders here. They do a wonderful organic, 70 per cent cocoa, dark chocolate and you need only a couple of squares to feel you've had a treat. They also do great organic milk chocolate with added ingredients such as ginger and mint. All their products are ethically traded too. (See www.greenandblacks.com.)

Dieting makes you fat

As a rule, I don't believe diets work. You would be pressed flat if you lay under the stack of books in my house about losing weight. I've been up and down like a yo-yo for many years and tried most diets. It's a very individual thing and I can't tell you what to do. They can be a quick fix or a fast track, but it's what happens when you resume normality that matters. What's your lifestyle? How healthily do you eat? Do you eat what, for you, are the right foods? Do you exercise? Usually, unles your mindset has changed, you'll go back to all your old habits and the weight will pile back on.

I've already referred to the fantastic Carol Vorderman's *Detox for Life*, and there are many books on the subject. She is well documented as saying that she tried many diets and nothing worked until she came across the detox concept, realised that food is linked with emotions and that we can't just starve ourselves. Afterwards, she changed her way of eating for good.

Everyone needs to be in tune with their body and aware of its unique needs. What you put in for fuel and for enjoyment purposes should feel right to you. Only you know when you're overloading or feeling bloated or lacking energy. One of the best tips I found was from Leslie Kenton. She suggests controlled fasting. It's a fantastic way to detoxify your system, cleanse it and then start again. When you fast for a few days you give your body a chance to recuperate and, when you start eating again, it's incredible how you actually notice what you're putting in your mouth. There's no way you would break a fast by eating a fry-up, so it gives you the opportunity to really taste your food and notice its effects.

The word 'controlled' is important, though. It's a hugely bad idea just to stop eating. That will certainly make you ill and very miserable. Experts reckon on starting with a two day fast. Try to do it over a weekend or a couple of days when you can relax. It's hard to carry on at the usual full pace when your body is detoxing. The day before you start, have light meals, as unprocessed as possible, no alcohol, tea or coffee, preferably just fruit and veg and maybe some rice or grains.

Ease yourself into the detox slowly, and have lots and lots of water to sip throughout the day. Drink a whole glass whenever you feel real hunger pangs. Make sure you have time to rest, take energising walks and lots of showers and baths. Book a massage or some other treat if that's possible and be prepared to feel pretty dodgy for a day or so. You may find you get a headache and a weird taste in your mouth – it's quite normal. You may even feel nauseous and probably quite tired for a while, but you should get to a point where you kind of 'break through' and start to feel fantastic. It probably won't be till the end of Day Two, but that's when you won't want to lose that feeling, so, when you break your fast, it must be with fresh fruit. Introduce heavy foods very slowly and you'll probably find you just don't fancy that stodgy dinner any more, and feel much better with a light meal of vegetables and rice. For further information, I'd recommend reading *Endless Energy* by Susannah and Leslie Kenton (Vermilion).

This is just a bit of fun, one of those emails that do the rounds:

The Stress Diet

This is a specially formulated diet from the USA designed to help women cope with the stress that builds during the day:

Breakfast: 1 grapefruit, 1 slice whole-wheat toast, 1 cup of skimmed milk

Lunch: 1 small portion lean, steamed chicken, 1 cup spinach, 1 cup herbal tea, 1 Hershey's Kiss

Afternoon Snack: Rest of the Hershey's Kisses in the bag, 1 tub Häagen-Dazs ice cream with chocolate chip topping

Dinner: 4 glasses of wine (red or white) 2 loaves garlic bread, 1 family sized supreme pizza, 3 Snickers bars

Late night snack: 1 whole Sara Lee Cheesecake (eaten directly from the freezer)

Remember – Stressed spelt backwards is Desserts.

Send this to four women and you will lose 2 pounds. Send this to all the women you know (or ever knew) and you will lose 10 pounds. If you delete this message, you will gain 10 pounds immediately.

That's why I had to pass this on. I didn't want to risk it, so my weight loss will depend on how many people read the book! Remember, it is called *Imperfectly* Natural Woman!

Essential fatty acids and dietary supplements

In a lovely ideal world, we wouldn't need supplements to our diets at all, be they vitamins, minerals or essential fatty acids (EFAs), but we all know the reality: diets today are, shall we say, less than perfect. I see supplements as a kind of damage limitation.

It can be totally overwhelming when we walk into a health-food store and see the huge range of vitamins and minerals available. We'd be rattling if we took one of every variety. It is very difficult to know exactly what our bodies need. If you can see a nutritionist you can be tested to determine which minerals are lacking, or you can send off blood and hair samples to give a clearer picture of what's needed; but, as a general rule, (and this is a sweeping statement) I'd say listen to your body and your own intuition. If you're feeling under stress or reckon you're about to get ill, up the ante a bit and take some protective measures. (See the chapter 'Natural Cures for Common Ailments' for what I take when I've got a cold coming on.) The rest of the time, get a good book on vitamins and minerals and see what you think appeals. An excellent manual is *Vitamins and Minerals* by Eleanor Stillwell published by PRC Publishing, part of Chrysalis Books.

As a rule of thumb I'd suggest you consider taking a good multivitamin tablet every day, some vitamin C (more when you're fighting an infection) and the one I recommend for all of us, particularly women, essential fatty acids.

EFAs are naturally occurring, unsaturated fats, some of which are not produced by the human body. There are two very important ones, Omega 6 and Omega 3, and without these, many bodily functions would not be possible. Our bodies use linolenic acid to make another two EFAs, docosahexaenoic acid (DHA) and eicosapentaenoic acid (EPA). These are found in fish oil as well.

One of the major roles of EFAs in the body is as structural components of cell membranes. EFAs are also vital for the formation of hormone-like substances called prostaglandins, which are crucial for a variety of functions including steroid hormone production. I trawled the Internet in my quest for EFA info and found only good news and long lists of the benefits of this stuff. 'Essential' is the operative word here. That's the technical bit. In short, your body loves EFAs, found in fish oils and in low levels in animal products such as liver and kidneys, but how much herring, mackerel, sardines and fresh tuna can you eat? And how full of toxins are those foods, anyway? Apart from that, when was the last time your other half or five-year-old asked for liver? It's a difficult one.

Are EFAs just more fat? Well, no. Our diets are loaded with fat, but the wrong kind. The saturated variety does nothing to improve overall body function except storing fat deposits. I've struggled to get EFAs into my kids. One flatly refuses to eat oily fish and the other one will manage one spoonful of tuna twice a week if we're lucky.

There have been so many reports recently that suggest we need these EFAs to help with brain function (even to help with depression and Alzheimer's disease). Recent research even suggests that DHA in the diet of our ancestors was an important factor in the evolution of human intelligence. Children who are given supplements on a regular basis consistently perform better in IQ tests and it also has a positive effect on children with learning difficulties and behavioural problems. It is confusing, though, working out your DHAs from your EFAs but the excellent website www.dha-in-mind.com explains it well.

Intake of DHA and EPA has declined in the UK and other countries with a Western diet over the past fifty years. This is shown by levels of DHA in breast milk, which are much lower than they used to be. We are eating less fish and offal. Modern farming practices have led to a reduction in the DHA levels of eggs and meat and we now eat more food that is high in another Omega family, the Omega 6s. Experts now advise us to redress the balance and eat more Omega 3s, including DHA.

So we know we need it but how do we get it? The obvious source is oily fish and fish oils, though there are concerns about fish nowadays. The seas are so polluted, and these types of fish seem to absorb pollutants such as mercury more readily than others. The problem with fish oil supplements (e.g. cod liver) is that it is not always the 'purest' or the most complete mix of the oils. We're a bit more sophisticated now when it comes to how our fish oils are processed and I'd recommend getting a fish oil supplement that's been through a purification process. Check with your friendly health-store person rather than pick the standard supermarket cod liver supplements. The best I've found are called Morepa, which come in capsules and even mini-capsules (www.minami-nutrition.com). You can buy them from www.healthyandessential.com/shop/.

But what if you're vegetarian? A good source is hemp oil and flaxseed oil. They taste great on salads and have a real earthy flavour. Don't use in cooking, though, because the heat process destroys their goodness.

I've recently found a fantastic oil, and at a good price. The Groovy Food Company decided that a really good option for veggies was needed and so produced Cool Oil, a blend of organic seed oils - flax, hemp, pumpkin and evening primrose. It provides Omega 3, 6 and 9 in a 2:1:1 ratio. I was even more delighted to see it in Sainsbury's, which is great news for the cause, since it's a major obstacle for the innovative independent producers to get their stuff to the 'mass markets'. The suggested daily intake is around 1 tablespoon a day, which is not difficult because you can drizzle it over salads, spoon it over casseroles and use it in 'smoothies'. Keep it in the fridge and, once opened, use within six weeks. (See www.groovyfood.co.uk.) Udo's Choice is the market leader but has a heavier

flavour (and isn't cheap) and it's also available in a tablet form.

What about DHA-fortified foods? I've seen them appearing recently. Normally, I hate that word 'fortified'. It usually means throw something in that you want to brag about to make your otherwise fairly unhealthy product healthy. But I must confess that I'll try anything to 'get some in' when it comes to my children. Believe me, I've given my kids 'liquid EFAs' (essential fatty acids in liquid form) in vanilla flavour, lime and tutti-frutti; I've called it special astronaut juice and then watched them go into orbit after they've tasted it. I've tried sneaking a bit into their dessert only to be told, 'Mum, this pudding tastes of rubber and acid.' (I know they only mean to be honest!) A range of DHA-fortified foods is now available and marked with a DHA logo. You can get a 'good health loaf' for women and 'healthy eggs', so are these enriched foods actually 'get-downable' or do they taste of fish? Please, I don't want fishy eggs!

The manufacturers claim that the DHA-rich natural oil that is added to enrich foods is in the form of tiny droplets, each of which is protected by encapsulation. The result is tasteless and odourless and does not affect the flavour of the food while delivering the benefits of DHA.

So in my imperfect state I've resorted to buying a DHA-'fortified' drink to supplement my fussy boys until they're of an age when they just understand they must take this capsule or have a spoonful of this oil and be done with it. You're dying to know what this drink is, I know. It's called Supajus, 'the think drink', and it's a 250ml carton of orange juice enriched with Omega 3 DHA. Apparently, they use pure tuna oil from the southern Pacific Ocean.

Supajus claims to contain half the recommended daily allowance needed (up to 1mg), so we still need to eat healthily – but it is a start. One thing is for sure: you can't taste the fish oil at all. It just tastes like regular concentrated orange juice. It also gives 100 per cent of the recommended vitamin C intake for children. I'm not shouting this from the rooftops as a 'superfood' but I am recognising that in this imperfect world imperfect parents like me probably do need this imperfect drink to supplement the imperfect diet of their imperfect kids. Supajus costs around 79p for a 250ml carton from health-food stores and some school vending machines. (See www.supajus.co.uk.)

They now also offer an apple and black-berry flavour which is great.

For veggie kids, the Groovy Food Company offer a 'yogpot' – a yoghurt with the Omega oils sneaked in. Excellent.

Nuts and seeds

What we haven't mentioned yet is the wonder that is a bowl of nuts and seeds. I don't mean salted peanuts but pretty much anything else will do.

Mixed seeds are really a wonder. Try to eat a bowl every day if you can. It's so simple. Get a little coffee grinder (use a separate one unless you want coffee-flavoured seeds) and grind up a handful of sunflower, hemp, pumpkin and sesame, add a few linseeds and sprinkle the mix over cereals and yoghurt. Hempseeds are fantastic www.yorkshirehemp.com.

For savoury snacks, you can't do better then a bowl of toasted seeds. Heat up a frying pan with a dash of olive oil and when it's hot, throw in any mix of seeds (all of the above work great), then drizzle a bit of tamari over them. Lightly toast until browned, cool and eat by the handful or as an addition to salads and sandwiches. They taste great and give you a real boost of the essential Omega 3 oils.

A brilliant book that explains all the benefits of eating more EFAs is Dr Basant Puri's *The Natural Way to Beat Depression* (Hodder & Stoughton). He has been able to identify physical changes in MRI scans of brains after patients suffering from depression have been taking fish oils for about a month.

To end on a technical note, all reports I found said that there are no known side effects from eating EFAs.

Manuka honey

I've never been a huge fan of honey. Sure, I've had it with lemon when I've been full of cold and I've forced down a spoonful after a terrible hangover (trust me, that one didn't work!) but having children was what got me looking again at this amazing foodstuff. When I was searching for a healthier alternative for Buddy (second child), who has an incredibly sweet tooth, the guy in my local health shop recommended manuka honey. "It's also antiseptic," he said, "and brilliant for sores and wounds."

Well, I knew of honey as a contraceptive aid (remember the craze of the honey cap in the eighties?), so it didn't surprise me that it was useful for more than just eating, and I tried to find out more. The last day of term came at Buddy's kindergarten and all the mothers were contributing homemade cakes and goodies for the party. Now, these were maybe not a holistic but certainly a wholesome bunch of caring parents, ones who perhaps, given the opportunity, would prefer not to feed their kids burgers, chips and ice cream. What could I provide that was a treat but would spare me the looks of thunder from some of the more, shall we say, 'dedicated' mums? Answer: the aforementioned 'Manuka Honey Sweetie Balls' (see 'Sweet stuff' above). Basically, you finely grind some almonds, mix them up with the honey and roll into little balls. Then coat in cinnamon powder. The kids could not get enough of them, and nor could the mums!

I also spread manuka honey on toast and rice cakes and use it in cooking for flapjacks and homemade bread, and you can make a great manuka honey smoothie by blending 2 teaspoons of manuka honey, half a banana, half a cup of chopped papaya, 1 cup semi-skimmed milk or rice milk and 3 teaspoons of natural yoghurt, which turns it into a fantastic hangover cure!

Manuka honey comes from bees that use pollen from the manuka bush (*Leptospermum scoparium*), which grows wild in the lovely land of New Zealand. That part of the southern hemisphere is one of the least polluted areas on earth, so we're talking happy bees here. The Maoris have used the honey for generations, both externally and internally, and modern medicine is now reconsidering such uses in the light of new research into the properties of this amazing stuff. I've read about its use in hospitals, where it has been applied directly to wounds, a process known as apitherapy (from '*Apis*', which is the honeybee genus).

In the shops, you'll see it marked 'UMF', which means 'Unique Manuka Factor', and it's a kind of industry-standard grading. The honey is tested for its antibacterial properties and awarded a grading, usually between 5 and 15. It's then deemed 'active'. The best stuff, used in apitherapy, will have a grading above 10. Get the highest UMF rating you can afford, and always get 'active'.

Just to get technical for a bit, all honey has antibacterial properties. This comes from the natural process of producing hydrogen peroxide from enzymes in the honey. However, the effectiveness of this is quickly diminished by heat, light or even contact with bodily fluids. Active manuka honey is known to have extra antibacterial properties, separate from the hydrogen peroxide effect, hence not just any old honey can be used in apitherapy and not even all manukas achieve active status. So this really is a 'rare' honey. It's actually the nicest honey I've ever tasted. Almost like a natural sweetie on its own but without the E numbers. It's expensive, but definitely worth it.

I've also applied it directly to burns and, when one of my boys had a splinter in his foot that became infected, we left the toxic bottle of antibiotics on the shelf and just waited for a few days while we tried applying active 10+ manuka honey. It cleared up within two days. I also have a friend who wishes to remain nameless who applied it to his painless haemorrhoids – cured! A bit sticky but much better than over-the-counter 'pile cream'.

Active manuka honey is fantastic to eat, and for information on its therapeutic properties, check out www.naturesnectar.com, www.medihoney.com For great honeys from around the world see www.rowsehoney.co.uk www.medihoney.com For great honeys from around the world see www.rowsehoney.co.uk.

Water filters

Are you, like me, old enough to remember when drinking a glass of water meant going to the tap and gulping it down? Buying a drink at a shop or café usually meant a bottle of lemonade or cola and the idea of bottled water was, well, simply ridiculous. How things have changed! Since we were all warned many years back that tap water is bad for us as a nation, we've spent millions of pounds on expensive bottled mineral water that costs more than petrol and can cost a fortune in treatments because our backs and shoulders have been put out by lugging six litres of it back from the supermarket!

Bottled water companies have indeed triumphed. British sales alone are worth around £2 billion a year but are we buying it because it tastes better, is convenient to carry around or because it's better for our health?

There is no doubt that water is essential to us and we need lots of it. The eight glasses a day that we are currently advised is the recommended amount is, to my mind, the minimum. Of course there's the hazard of needing to pee all the time but it's interesting that, once you start drinking lots of water, your body seems to adjust after a day or so and you don't need to go the loo quite so often. I have several friends who swear by drinking loads of water as their main aid to losing weight.

Always drink water at room temperature though, since icy cold water is a shock to the system. It chills the stomach, which then makes us absorb nutrients less effectively.

So what kind of water should we be drinking? We all know it's pointless buying a bottle of 'table' water. It isn't natural and contains no minerals. Remember the episode of *Only Fools and Horses* where Del Boy discovers an ancient well in the garden? They decide to bottle the water from it and call it 'Peckham Springs'. Of course it turned out to be no more than a burst water pipe so in fact Del was rebottling the water from the local water authority that was already going into his kitchen tap!

My friend Rod in Cornwall is lucky enough to have a genuine well in the grounds of his home. He took samples from it, got the water tested and accredited, and now he has his own pure spring water 'on tap' in the kitchen. Oh, lucky man!

So what are the minerals in bottled mineral water? Usually, calcium, magnesium, sodium and sodium bicarbonate, but the levels will vary depending on where they spring from – literally. The mineral water companies and the National Mineral Water Association would have us believe that their water tastes better and has great health benefits. The World Health Organisation, many GPs and of course your local water authority would disagree and suggest that mineral water is no better for you than tap water unless you have a low dietary intake of certain minerals. In which case you could benefit from drinking water with high levels of a particular mineral, but that of course might not taste as good. It also starts to prompt the question, 'Hold

on, then. If I need certain minerals, can't I supplement my diet in other ways?'

This is where I was a couple of years back. Since I was a student, I've bought bottled water. I've always lived in hard water areas, where the tap water tastes fairly disgusting, furs up the kettle and needs a huge amount of soap to create any kind of lather for washing. So I committed to buying bottled water and I've been breaking my back carrying it home ever since. In the early 1980s, I used to sing backing vocals in various pop groups. Once, I was on a tour with Mari Wilson (remember her, with the huge beehive?), and we found ourselves in a remote area of Scotland. Desperate for some supplies, we stopped the minibus at a tiny village shop. In we walked (we're talking extremely big hair here, as was the group's on-stage requirement) and my request for a bottle of Perrier was met with a dumbfounded silence. Only then did it dawn on me that the shopkeeper didn't think I was from another hairy planet at all, but was trying to figure out just what on earth it was I wanted. 'It's fizzy water,' I said. Another short silence. 'Panda Pops?' she asked. When I asked if she had any still water, she said, 'Yep, in the tap.'

At the time, I thought *she* was the one who was nuts, but in recent years my views have changed. It's only when I took stock one day that I realised how much I was spending on this stuff and, in fact, how many empty bottles I was throwing away, adding of course to the growing plastic mountain. The problem is that, once opened, mineral water will lose its freshness very quickly and actually becomes a breeding ground for bacteria. I was buying a large plastic bottle of mineral water, having a couple of swigs and then leaving it in the car. There it would sit in the hot sunshine for a couple days breeding bugs and generally 'going off'. Also, I began to wonder, even before it got cooked on my dashboard, how long this stuff had been lurking on shop shelves.

A few years ago, I decided to ask around and found there were several alternatives to bottled water. One is magnotherapy. The beneficial properties of magnets have been known for many years. Magnets can treat everything from joint pain to stress, usually by increasing the blood flow (see www.ecoflow.plc.uk and www.magna-health.com), but I hadn't realised its effects on drinking water. When a jug of tap water is placed on a special 'coaster', the coaster will magnetically treat the water and affect its taste. Vitaflow is one of the better makes but there are several systems around. You can also buy a magnetic wand that is placed in a glass or a jug of water for ten minutes and is said to ionise it and leave you with softer water with a much – improved taste (see www.worldofmagnets.co.uk). Ecoflow also make water conditioners. www.ecoflow.plc.uk.

> "In time and with water, everything changes.
>
> LEONARDO DA VINCI

Filtered water is of course the option many people use instead of buying the bottled stuff. The problem we all know with our tap water is not what it contains 'naturally' but what's been added. Well, in some areas it's fluoride, which, needless to say, I'm hugely against, but in every case there will be chlorine and chemicals to aid purification, plus, some critics say, traces of pesticides, heavy metals (such as calcium and lead), nitrates and even asbestos, as well as fair amounts of bacteria.

I started to wonder whether at least part of the time I could use a water filter system to remove the 'nasties' from my tap water, except that I wouldn't be having any added minerals. But obviously I could get minerals with supplementation, or – shock horror – just eating a good diet.

I was recommended to try a reverse osmosis water filter. For around £225 this unit has revolutionised my water drinking habits. First, gone are the heavy bottles of water; second, gone is the hassle of remembering to bring in unopened bottles from the car;

and, third, now there are fewer plastic bottles clogging up the environment. By the way, the plastic always was a bit of an issue with me, not just from an environmental point of view. Some schools of thought believe that substances in the plastic bottles leach into the water over time, creating another potential pollutant. There are some ardent bottled water drinkers who advocate drinking only water stored in glass. They have campaigns on the go aiming to rid us of plastic bottles altogether. If I weren't imperfect I'd get seriously involved.

The reverse osmosis water filter from Dryden Aqua (www.drydenaqua.co.uk) is the one I found to be most cost-effective. The filtration bit is meant to last for a couple of years, depending on how much you use, and it comes with a little monitor so that you can check the water yourself. Replacements are around £50 – well worth it compared with what I'd been spending on the bottled variety every year. The other huge difference it's made is to my kettle. I used to need to clean it out every few weeks with vinegar and replace it every two years, but, since I had the under-sink reverse osmosis filter fitted, I've seen no staining or scaling and the water boils quickly and tastes better.

One word of warning, though, if you go for the same one I use. The very helpful girl at Dryden Aqua told me that 'anyone' can install the reverse osmosis unit under a suitably sized sink. She said she did hers herself and she's not at all a DIY expert or even 'handy'. Check that one out! My advice is to budget for a couple of hours from a plumber, too. Darling Husband is pretty good around the house but this one flummoxed him and ended up costing us £50 to call in a plumber to complete the job. But, now it's done, we all love it round at our place. I drink copious amounts of this stuff, which tastes great, and if I need to take a small bottle out I just fill it up from my own tap.

It's also worth contacting your local water company to find out the mineral content and fluoridation content of your water supply.

If you're still going to buy bottled water, though, you might like to know that my favourites are the French ones. Evian, Volvic and Perrier. S Pellegrino, the Italian one, is also nice. Try to keep them in the fridge, though, not the car, and buy glass bottles wherever possible.

Ingrid

Ingrid, 48. Partner to Chris. Two children, 6 and 7. Never worked harder in my life for no money than now – home educating.

Bright and early
A mug of hot water and lemon.

Typical brekkie
Muesli recipe:
- 2 cups oats
- 1 cup oats dry toasted
- 1 cup each of chopped almonds, desiccated coconut, chopped apricots, raisins

Muesli, gluten-free:
- 1 cup each of millet flakes, brown rice flakes, dry toasted buckwheat flakes, chopped hazelnuts, sunflower seeds, chopped apricots, raisins

Porridge:
- Cook with rice milk and you have a dairy-free porridge that doesn't need sweetening.

Lunch
Yellow rice:
- 1 mug dry brown rice
- ½ teaspoon turmeric (and most people won't know it began as brown)
- Add organic veg, seeds and grains

Dinner
Buckwheat pancakes:
- 4 oz Buckwheat flour
- pinch salt
- 1 egg
- ½ pt milk
- 2 oz melted butter
  Add egg to flour and salt. Add milk bit at a time and then add melted butter. Leave to stand for at least 1 hour before using.
Oils: use olive oil for cooking and instead of butter (e.g. in mashed spud) wherever you can. Have sunflower and sesame oils for salads etc. For example, in a stir fry: cook in olive oil, and drizzle with sesame oil just before serving.
Veg wedges: cut veg (potato, sweet potato, beetroot, swede, butternut squash, parsnip) into chunks, toss in hot oil in a pan with lid until coated and then put on baking trays in oven. Try mixed herbs in the oil for the potatoes, cinnamon for sweet potato, ginger for swede.

Chicken stock:
- Put all bones with skin and fat removed in pan with close-fitting lid
- Add whole onion, carrot and celery stick, bay leaf and other herbs.
- Cover with water.
- Simmer for 2 hours.
- Remove all bones, picking off any bits of meat, and bay leaf.
- Smoothie up the rest, including bits of meat.
- Use as it is for simple soup, or as base for more complicated soup, or to cook grains in.

Drinks – water – bottled or tap?
In the morning I fill my big jug with still bottled water, I need to finish this by the end of the day to know I've had enough.

Favourite superfoods I couldn't live without
Fresh organic fruit and veg.
Savoury seeds: 1 part each of pumpkin, sunflower, hemp, linseed and sesame – dry-toasted, removed from heat and mixed with tamari sauce (mixed half and half with water) – for sprinkling at the table on rice or other grains, or on salad, as the protein element of your meal.
Rice and other grains: 2 parts brown rice to 1 part other grain (amaranth, quinoa, millet, wild rice) increases nutritional value without challenging the palate too much. White rice with red quinoa looks lovely as well.
Veg wedges: See under 'Dinner'.
Ground almonds: Add to mashed potato or soups for extra nutrition and thickening.

Vitamins and minerals
Vitamin C, echinacea.

Favourite treatments
Whole-body massage, not in a beauty salon, preferably in a darkened room with candles, nice aromatherapy oils, no talking or music.

For exercise
Walking fast in the countryside and dancing, fast – my style!

For relaxation
Take showers and sing!

Save my skin
Wash with water, no soap. Organic, Soil Association-certified face cream, no essential oils, no perfumes.

Sunscreen
Prefer to cover up but if I need sunscreen it must be chemical-free.

Favourite beauty products
Foot creams and butters.

Haircare
Organic shampoo, no scent. No hairdryers.

Cleaning and laundry products
Vinegar and water for windows and glass, Ecover products, beeswax and turpentine. Ecover liquid for wash. Bicarbonate of soda to soak nappies and menstrual pads.

Recycling and composting tips
Bucket under the sink for compost. Offer your compost to neighbours if you haven't any more room. Most stuff is collected; cardboard and plastic we take to the recycling centre. Buy big - reduce packaging waste.

Pets
We treat our cat homoeopathically and give no vaccinations.

Babycare
Nappy rash: 100gm pure aloe vera gel, very well mixed with 1 drop each of chamomile and lavender, kept in lidded jar in fridge.

For the kids
Lots of fruit and veg every day, as little sugar, dairy and wheat as possible, lots of fresh air and laughter. Don't use shampoo or soap on the children for as many years as possible - just use water. [See the chapter 'Natural Cures for Common Ailments' for more of Ingrid's tips for children.]

Top parenting tips
Be open. Says it all.

To achieve balance in my life...
Meditate, walk in nature or go to the sea.

To revitalise my soul I go to...
Shower and massage body butter or cream with essential oils into feet.

The one thing I couldn't live without
Water.

Guilty secrets and imperfections
If there is chocolate in the house I must finish it all! When I go out I enjoy a couple of glasses of white wine or champagne and a couple of cigarettes.

If I had a magic wand, I would...
... meditate twice a day and make love more often.

Natural Cures for Common Ailments

This book is not meant to be a medical directory or even an alternative 'cure-all'. I'm no doctor or expert but I can tell you what I find helpful when I'm feeling under the weather.

I'm sorry to get all cosmic on you again (just when you thought I might simply be passing on the instant cure for a hangover) but I must mention the philosophy that suggests we each create our own disease. There is a school of thought that believes we choose (albeit subconsciously) any ailments or illnesses that we 'catch', or at any rate we allow the environment to be in place for the 'bug' to take hold. 'Tosh and rubbish!' my sceptical friends will be shouting out at this point. 'I got that stinking cold because I sat two seats away from a guy in the theatre who was sneezing for Britain.' Well, that may be true but it's highly likely the person who sat the other side of him did not develop any symptoms.

Of course it depends on our immune systems. If we're run down, we are far more likely to be affected by more viruses. But where does the 'choice' come in? Remember when you were a child and going through a difficult time at school? You tried telling your parents you didn't want to go but that fell on deaf ears. Then one day you had a tummy ache and a tempera-ture. You made a big deal of this and, lo and behold, no getting dressed and rushing out into the cold morning. Instead, you were installed in front of daytime TV with a mug of Lucozade and your favourite biscuits. 'This is the life,' you thought. It's not to say that you may not genuinely have had a slight stomach ache, but it's a fair bet that it would have disappeared sharpish had it been your birthday party that day.

As adults we have to be a little more responsible but sometimes we go the other way and become so conscientious that we don't actually listen to what our bodies may be telling us. Maybe we do need a rest or a change of diet and, of course, our emotions are intrinsically linked with our health.

Louise Hay is a writer and metaphysical counsellor who cured herself after being diagnosed with terminal cancer. In her book, *You can Heal Your Life* (Eden Grove Editions), her philosophy is simple:

We are each 100 per cent responsible for all our experiences. Every thought is creating our future. The point of power is in the present moment. When we really love ourselves, everything in our life works. We create every so-called illness in our body. We must release the past and forgive everyone.

To suggest that there is a mental cause for physical disease can sound woolly and esoteric, I know, but over the years I've always kept one toe in this world, asking, whenever I get ill, what did I actually do to allow that particular malaise to manifest itself? Often the answer is as clear as daylight and it's even easier to see it in others. Take, for example, my friend, who was going through a difficult situation in her marriage. She found out that her husband was having an affair. Meanwhile, she was trying to cope with two children, one of them a teenager with drug problems. She developed a terrible pain in her upper back and shoulders. There seemed to be no reason and no amount of osteopathy could help. In *You can Heal Your Life*, Louise Hay says the mental cause of upper-back problems is likely to be 'feeling lack of emotional support, feeling unloved, holding back love'. Louise offers affirmations that can be said as an antidote to disabling emotions and beliefs. Of course, it's too simplistic to use only this one thing but I've found it very useful to check out what might really be going on when I'm under the weather.

In an illness as serious as cancer, for example, there is data to suggest that there exists a 'cancer personality', a common denominator in the type of person who could be more likely to develop the disease. Certainly, the state of mind or personality of a sufferer plays a big part in their own chances of defeating the disease, as was shown by Brandon Bays, who describes her experience in her book *The Journey*. There are workshops held across the UK run by practitioners who have trained with Louise Hay. (See www.aplacefortheheart.co.uk.)

Apart from the affirmations, what else can we do to alleviate the symptoms of common ailments? It goes without saying that I am totally against using conventional medication unless you are really convinced there is no alternative. In my opinion it merely suppresses the symptoms and, over time, compromises the immune system by subjecting it to an onslaught of chemicals.

Health professionals would have you think that all over-the-counter medicines are totally safe, but as recently as 2004, a friend of mine in the States came across a list of drugs that were being recalled urgently. Each contained phenylpropanolamine, which had been linked to increased haemorrhagic stroke (bleeding in the brain). The recalled products included common, household name, store cupboard 'staples' such as cough and cold medicines, expectorants and powders, preparations for sinus and nasal congestion, even some children's chewable tablets. The next time you want to take some of these over-the-counter drugs or pop a headache pill, just check out (a) the list of ingredients and (b) the possible side effects of consuming them (that is, if you've got a spare half hour to read it). Fortunately, there are alternatives.

Colds, sore throats, coughs

I'm convinced I get more than my fair share of these, even when I'm eating really well and getting the right amount of exercise and relaxation (a time in my distant memory!). I still seem to come down with a cold or a sore throat, occasionally completely losing my voice, which is not ideal for a radio presenter. (Louise Hay would have a field day with that one.)

When I feel a cold coming on, I take vitamin C, usually the crystals – sodium ascorbate – at least 1,000mg, twice a day. I really believe vitamin C taken at the onset of any infection helps and, if you do overdo it and take too much for your body to process, you may just have mild diarrhoea, though it hasn't happened to me so far. Biocare make a tiny bottle of Micellised Vitasorb C. Basically, these are high-strength Vitamin C drops, which are an excellent way of getting it into your system without the addition of too many gelling and other agents (see www.biocare.co.uk). If you can drink freshly squeezed orange juice, too, fantastic (though for some people it is too acidic and can cause skin problems). And try adding lemon and a slice of fresh ginger. You can also get a full range of vitamins from www.vitserve.com.

I usually take one garlic capsule and a zinc tablet, too, for a few days and drink copious amounts of honey, lemon and ginger. I make up a big pan full with one or two chopped lemons, a big chunk of fresh ginger and hot water. I boil it, then simmer for ten minutes or so and sip with one teaspoon of, preferably, manuka honey added once it's cool. Ginger, by the way, is a wonderful spice to have in stock. In Southeast Asia and India, it is still considered to be an essential ingredient of the daily diet as a protection against disease and an aid to digestion.

Commercial Epsom salts are great for adding to bathwater, particularly if you feel you're coming down with a cold. Have a hot (not too hot!) bath, put in a large cupful of salts and a couple of drops of essential oil, wrap up warm and go to bed. You should wake up feeling quite different. A huge three-pound bag of Epsom salts used to be very cheap to buy but unfortunately it's become trendy and now you often pay quite a bit for a tiny box.

Tea tree oil is never far from my side when I've got a virus or an infection lurking. I put a few drops on a tissue and breathe in the aroma and leave a few drops on my pillow at night or in a bowl on the radiator or oil burner. For a sore throat, or when I feel I'm losing my voice, I put one drop in a glass of water, shake it around and then gargle. It's brilliantly antiseptic.

Coughs can be a devil to treat and I don't believe any of the commercial brands available in the chemists actually work, even if you're prepared to put up with the chemicals and their side effects. There are some alternatives, though. Ainsworths Pharmacy have a great Bryonia Tincture that has lemon juice, bryonia, purified water and alcohol. It's OK for children over two years and tastes pleasant. The homoeopaths there are always happy to discuss the symptoms and recommend the appropriate remedy for the problem. (See www.ainsworths.com or www.helios.co.uk.)

Even cheaper is my homemade cough syrup. I steep 1oz of thyme leaf in 1 cup of boiling water, cover it and leave it to cool, then strain and mix with ¾ tablespoon of honey. You can take a teaspoon whenever you need it and it will keep in a glass jar in the fridge. The children love it. A friend swears by a mix of honey and onion, or onion and brown sugar. Both onion and honey are anti-inflammatory and anti-microbial, but, so far, I haven't been able to persuade my kids to go near the stuff.

Steam works a treat on any respiratory problems. For young children, fill the bath and get the whole room steamed up but, for yourself, boil a kettle of water, add a few drops of tea tree oil or, better still, crush a couple of eucalyptus leaves. Position your face about 10 inches from the hot water (being careful not to scald yourself) and drape a towel over your head to keep in the steam. It not only works as a brilliant decongestant but you'll get a great facial in the process. My kids usually shout, 'Oh, look, Mummy's boiling her head again!'

In the examples of Imperfectly Natural People there are several more ideas for health tips. For example, Ingrid has some great ideas that she uses for her children.

- **Bronchitis** – 1 clove garlic finely chopped in manuka honey twice a day, taken off the spoon and swallowed quickly or on bread.

  Drape a blanket over chairs and sit underneath, breathing in steam from bowl of boiling water stood in larger bowl three times a day.
- **High temperature** – lime flower tea with manuka.
- **Cough and sore throat** – warm drink made with carrageen seaweed and chamomile tea. Simmer carrageen in big pan (1 tbs to 1 pint water) for 20 minutes. Take off heat, add chamomile. Strain after 10 minutes. Add honey and keep warm in flask – extraordinarily soothing on the throat.

  Bump up the vitamin C and echinacea.

  Organic essential oils – 3/4 drops in a burner, or 1 drop on clothing near face, or under blanket (see above).
- **Agitated and feeling tender at night maybe also with headache, stuffed nose, little cough** – lavender and chamomile.
- **Bad respiratory problems** – pine.
- **Even worse** – eucalyptus.
- **For the throat** – sage.
- **For the chest** – thyme.

Thanks, Ingrid.

Teresa from Imperfectly Natural Parents, one of the Yahoo! discussion groups I'm a member of, has some more suggestions for colds, coughs and breathing problems.

- Wet towels draped over the radiator.
- Eucalyptus and lavender oils to help breathing and aid relaxation.
- Raise head.
- Stay hydrated.
- Cut out any dairy or wheat in the diet.
- Get a vaporiser.
- Unless you're a veggie – chicken soup.

  Boil about a pint of water with juice of at least 4 lemons, chucking a bit of zest and the lemon halves in, too, some cloves, some ginger and at least 4 cloves of crushed garlic. Let it simmer a bit, then strain off the 'juice', add some honey and drink it hot.

Thanks, Teresa.

For headaches, steaming is good, too, and Tiger Balm applied sparingly on the temples will help. Also, drink lots of water – it's amazing the number of people with chronic headaches who are 'cured' when they start drinking two litres a day.

Hay Fever

A miserable affliction, I know, and I'm lucky that I don't get it year after year like some of my friends, but in recent years I've had a few symptoms, enough to show me how debilitating it must be. If you are a sufferer, try a couple of things before you hit the antihistamines. First, the local-honey theory. This works on the premise that we're often intolerant to certain pollens which may be grown locally. Get hold of some locally grown honey and eat it as you normally would, before the hay fever season starts, preferably in February/March. Hopefully, if it's grown within a few miles of where you live, it will correspond to the pollens you're allergic to and you'll be desensitised when it all kicks off.

Once you've got the symptoms, try coating the inside of the nostrils with olive oil or apricot kernel oil, which will protect the sensitive mucus membranes from the flying particles. A friend of mine puts Vaseline up his nose for protection and it works for him.

Cystitis and thrush

This is one I know about because it often flares up in pregnancy and is utterly horrible if you get a bad attack. Don't even think about prescription drugs: they can increase the pain and discomfort and even cause it. Cranberries are the best natural remedy for cystitis, although often women think it's OK to buy a bag of sweetened ones and munch their way through them in the name of health. You should try to get unsweetened cranberry juice and drink 16fl oz a day in addition to at least 2 litres of water. The more water you drink to dilute the urine, the less painful it will be. Cranberry supplements in capsule form taken with meals are good, too.

Lemon barley water will neutralise the acid but, again, avoid the sweetened version and make your own if you can.

Avoid dairy, wheat and sugar for a day or two if possible and boost your intake of vitamin C. Eat lots of apricots, green peppers, broccoli and citrus fruit.

Obviously, avoid any chemical irritants such as soap and bubble bath (you wouldn't use them, anyway, would you?) but it's OK to use a few drops of essential oil in the bath. Bergamot is meant to be good for thrush and vaginal itching. Sandalwood oil is also very useful for the urinary system and lavender and chamomile oils may also help. Tea tree oil can also be inserted into the vaginal area, but be careful to use only one drop in about a teaspoon of virgin olive oil (otherwise it will sting like hell).

Take probiotic supplements as long as you're not having antibiotics (if you are, take probiotics afterwards), and you can use a regular probiotic capsule as a pessary, too – it's far less messy than the over-the-counter pessaries! (I've also heard of inserting a clove of garlic but must confess I haven't tried that one in case it doesn't make its way out again!) Ideally, we'd be able to eat enough live yoghurt not to need probiotics but that's unrealistic, so take a good supplement of acidophilus in powder or capsule form – but note that most need to be kept in the fridge.

Digestive upsets

Let's face it, we all have times when we get food poisoning, a really nasty stomach bug or a self-inflicted dodgy bottom, usually from the excesses of rich food and drink. The best way to deal with them is just to let nature take its course. I definitely would avoid any medication that suppresses the problem. After all your body is trying to rid itself of toxins and poisons, so let it do its work.

It's interesting to observe animals when they're ill. They usually retire quietly and consume nothing at all. A self-imposed fast will work wonders and allow your digestive system a rest. When you begin to feel better and hungry again, drink plenty of filtered water and allow yourself the blandest of foods, plain cooked rice, ripe pears and loads of water. Introduce other foods slowly to allow the detoxification of your system to continue.

If it's just a mild digestive upset you won't go wrong with peppermint tea or, if you can get it, peppermint essence. As I've already mentioned, ginger is also good for digestive problems. You can chew on a piece of fresh ginger, make a ginger tea, even have a ginger biscuit as long as the problem won't be compounded by an intake of wheat and sugar.

First aid

I'm not going to start a section on this here, as I'll be looking at the Bach Rescue Remedy, arnica and calendula in other sections. Suffice to say that, as I write this, only half an hour ago I was taking a roasting tray out of the oven and managed to burn my hand. The pain was excruciating, as I'm sure you've experienced, and nothing gives relief like neat lavender oil. It's not instant but, trust me, it works – just a drop or two directly on the burn. Also, friends who are more into gardening than I will tell you that the aloe vera plant is amazing. You just slice open the leaf and put the sap directly on any skin irritations or burns.

Sleep

Sleep is something I don't get much of. I was a 'can't exist without my ten hours a night' kind of gal till I had children. Then you quickly learn that one can survive on far less, though I wouldn't recommend going below six hours.

If you are an insomniac, no amount of suggesting you relax and have a milky drink will have any effect. However, if the problem is just that you occasionally feel your mind is too active, I have a couple of suggestions that are so simple you'll either be using them already, or wonder why I'm bothering to write them down because they're so daft. First, if you have a TV or computer in your bedroom, remove them. It's not only the electromagnetic frequencies that are the problem (see 'Electromagnetic frequencies' in the chapter 'Get on the Right Wavelength') but I believe the bedroom should be for sleep and sex – and sleep and sex alone! If you fill your mind with a horror movie or even the news late at night, it's obvious that it will be harder to relax into counting sheep.

The best little exercise I learned was to clear my mind of all the worries and thoughts of the day. Writing it all down is good, 'journalling', as the self-help books call it, but

I am often too lazy to find a pen. So I visualise a big sack and I 'see' myself putting all my worries in there at night: the intricate schedule for the next day, the fears, the lot. Each time another thought or fear pops up I slip it into the bag. Then I imagine hanging the sack at the foot of the bed so that the sensible and rational part of my subconscious brain knows I'm not trying to kid myself that it's simple to erase all worries – they will be there ready and waiting after a night's rest.

Sometimes I use a relaxation tape, slightly imperfect, I know, as it goes against my rules of minimal electrical equipment. Make sure you like the voice of the person reading the meditation or it will really grate on you. You may find a type of music that is sleep-inducing for you. Much as I adore their music, I can put on any Cocteau Twins album and I'm asleep in ten minutes, especially one album called *Victorialand* – the ultimate relaxation CD.

If you want to try sleep-inducing foods, then obviously avoid cheese, coffee and wine and go for bananas and warm drinks. Chamomile tea is relaxing, if not exactly soporific, and, if you can bear it, green tea works. We all know of its antioxidant properties but it also contains a natural relaxant, L-theanine. The herbal remedies valerian and passiflora can also help with insomnia.

Also, I know it sounds obvious, but we should sleep in darkness. Our bodies are designed to sleep when it's dark and wake far earlier than most of us actually do, when it's light. Unless we live in very remote areas, often we don't experience true darkness because there are always street lights or intermittent lights from neighbouring houses or passing cars. Even with eyes closed, light will interfere with the brain's natural sleep patterns. We probably aren't going to change our lifestyles but at least we can turn off that bedside lamp and draw the curtains.

Even if a child is frightened of falling asleep in the dark, rather than leave the light on, use something that gives just a tiny amount of light – a plug-in night light, for instance – or leave the landing light on and the bedroom door ajar. You can gradually reduce the wattage of the bulb in their lamp too from 60 to 40, then 20, every few days, ending up with a 5w fridge bulb. After a few weeks, turn it off and they'll be fine with the darkness. Also try the wonderful 'Stars' a blend for sweet dreams from www.speciallittle people.co.uk.

When it comes to waking up, ditch that horrible cockerel alarm clock you had when you were a student and invest in a 'natural alarm clock'. I love the Sunray. The light slowly builds up over a period of about twenty minutes so that you are awakened gently by a nice sunrise effect. In case that doesn't rouse you, a gentle peeping sound continues till you wake up. (See www.wholisticresearch.com.)

Anxiety, depression and SAD

Of course, serious mental health problems can't be classed as a common ailment and must be treated professionally, but so many people suffer from mild depression and anxiety, which can include anything from PMS or a miserable case of the winter blues to a minor case of postnatal depression. There are a few well-documented mood-boosting natural remedies, but it's worth checking with a practitioner and, if you are taking prescribed medication, always check before supplementing it with complementary remedies of any kind.

For starters, it seems too simple, but talking is usually the best treatment. Find a sympathetic ear, whether it be a friend or a counsellor (see 'Soul Searching') and talk to them. If you choose a friend, be careful not to lay so much on them that they want to avoid you. Sometimes it's easier to talk to someone with no personal ties.

If you're suffering from seasonal affective disorder (SAD), you may have thought about a light therapy box, but if you're just feeling 'down' you may think this route is not for you. Think again! We need our daylight as a fish needs water and, if it's a dull winter's day or we're working long hours under horrible fluorescent lighting, a dose of full-spectrum light works wonders. (See 'See the light!' in 'Get on the Right Wavelength'.) It goes without saying that exercise is a mood, booster too: even just a twenty minute brisk walk in the fresh air can change your perspective on everything.

> One kind word can warm three winter months
>
> JAPANESE PROVERB

Look at your intake of essential fatty acids (see the section 'Essential fatty acids and dietary supplements' in 'Let Food Be Your Medicine' above). Fish oils are very effective at easing and treating depression, especially where it has a hormonal origin. Nutritionally, supplements of vitamin B6 should be helpful, preferably as part of the B complex. Buy foods that are rich in B vitamins and eat them in as unprocessed a form as you can. Get yourself a good multivitamin/mineral supplement, too, but bear in mind that the benefits of vitamin therapy may take time to kick in. Consider also Vitex agnus castus and raspberry leaf tea, which will help to balance hormones. Aromatherapy, too, may help, as essential oils can be very mood-enhancing. Get a friend to recommend a really good aromatherapist and make sure they know how you're feeling so that they can mix the perfect balance of oils.

You should also consider seeing a homoeopath. Homoeopathic treatment can offer a healing system that will deal with pretty much every complaint. Another complementary therapy is reflexology, which can be profoundly helpful in balancing the thyroid gland function, frequently out of kilter after childbirth, which can contribute to postnatal depression.

St John's Wort is often recommended for depression, although it can have contraindications with other medication (notably in the case of tissue rejection after a transplant), and it may not be suitable for breastfeeding mums. This may well be due to its hypericin content.

Bach flower remedies may also help. The correct remedy is hard to suggest off the cuff, but looking at www.bachcentre.com and browsing the different remedies to see what sounds closest to your present state of mind may help. (See 'Flower remedies' on page 151.)

You can get some great tips for a whole range of ailments from *What Really Works* by Susan Clark. She offers simple explanations of alternative treatments and remedies as well as an A–Z guide of complaints and suggested treatments. If you have children, you should buy *What Really Works for Kids* by the same author. Be prepared to be scared, though. She reveals what's in most of the processed foods that our children can't seem to get enough of.

Homoeopathy

You'll find that, throughout this book, I refer to homoeopathic remedies for use in certain cases. It's another one of those huge issues that are very difficult to skim over in just a page or two, but I'll tell you my thoughts and you can research the rest.

There have been TV documentaries on homoeopathy. One recently set out to prove that it doesn't work. As a rule, scientists don't accept it, but I feel entirely different. OK, if your arm is broken, a pillule won't repair it, but, then, neither will allopathic medicine. It has to be reset in the correct position first, but you can speed up the knitting of the bone with homoeopathy. There are undoubtedly an increasing number of people, not just your 'lentilburger-eating' types, who use homoeopathy, including for instance certain members of the royal family.

How does it work? The theory, now more than 200 years old, is that 'like cures like' and it is one whose basic principle even Hippocrates acknowledged. Samuel Hahnemann, a German pharmacist and the founder of homoeopathy, formulated his theory in 1796, and realised that certain substances, if administered to a person, can cause similar symptoms to known diseases. If these substances (which can include toxic poisons such as arsenic, snake venom and deadly nightshade) are administered in an infinitely dilute dose when someone is producing that same set of symptoms, they have the effect of triggering a response in the body that helps it cure the symptoms of the disease, without side effects.

One of the problems, as with so many complementary therapies and treatments, is the skill and integrity of the practitioner. For the first consultation, most homoeopaths will spend about an hour and half with the patient, filling in forms and asking all manner of questions, even how often you break wind! I know it may not seem relevant when you've gone in with a nasty cough but it's not because they're voyeuristic: it's to get an overall picture. It is a 'holistic' approach.

The homoeopath then tries to determine the right remedy to treat the whole person rather than just the individual symptoms. It can be hard to get it right and I must admit I've had a few sessions with homoeopaths where I've felt they just haven't quite cracked the right remedy. I took my son, Buddy, to see one when he was four and had what I thought was whooping cough. It wasn't an infection, so, even if I'd been that way inclined, antibiotics wouldn't have helped.

The homoeopath asked lots of questions, observed him playing and chatting and coughing, and finally gave me a remedy. She asked me to phone in 24 hours to see if he was any better, but he wasn't. She gave him a different remedy and we

tried again. No change. He had eight different remedies and nothing alleviated the symptoms of coughing and vomiting, even slightly. After the ninth remedy, something did happen. He came out in an allergic rash on his face, so it did something but didn't cure the cough. It's important, therefore, to find a homoeopath who works for you.

When Sonny (my eldest) had a similar problem at five, I used another homoeopath, Mary Taylor. Mary has an added string to her bow in that she is also a psychological astrologer, so practises 'astrological homoeopathy'. What's your star sign got to do with it? I hear you ask. Well, lots, according to Mary. She asks you for the date, time and place of birth, goes off and prepares a birth chart, and then asks all the usual homoeopathic questions (yes, I think we still got the farting one!). She is then able much more clearly to diagnose the picture of what's going on by linking it with what's happening for you astrologically. I soon realised that I may have found the right practitioner. This was someone who was dedicated to gaining a complete understanding of the 'whole person' before any treatment was administered.

While we're on this subject, no, I don't bother reading the horoscopes in the newspaper columns, since each sign and its prediction seems entirely interchangeable to me; but I do believe that a proper birth chart, deciphered by a fully trained astrologer, will definitely show results. DH once had to arrange to see a barrister within a three-month period. His lawyer had warned him that he would need to be available at that barrister's request, however inconvenient. DH had his birth chart done around that time and was given a very auspicious date for 'anything legal'. He rang his lawyer and said 'Listen, I know it's a long shot but I need that meeting on June 22nd.' The lawyer just laughed and said, 'We fit in with the barrister, not the other way round!' We waited and the next day a totally nonplussed lawyer called and said, 'You won't believe it but the only day the barrister can accommodate us is June 22nd!' It went well and the legal matter was concluded satisfactorily.

Anyway, Mary did Sonny's chart and mine, and advised me how to help him. It's rarely as simple as needing to give different food, drink or medicine, as there are almost always emotional issues involved. She also sent a constitutional remedy (the major remedy characteristic to him), which I gave him only once. The change was almost immediate and the recovery miraculous.

Here's what Mary has to say:

> Your biography is your biology.
>
> The biochemistry of the body is a product of awareness.
>
> Wherever thought goes, a chemical goes with it.
>
> Healing is not primarily a physical process but a mental one.
>
> Mind can go deep enough to change the very patterns that design the body.
>
> Every thought/experience has been stored as a memory in the cellular system. Love, for example, an attribute of mind, will find a chemical pathway that the brain can follow and talk to the body. At the very moment that you think 'I am happy', a chemical messenger will translate it into the emotion (which has no solid existence in the material world), into a bit of matter that will inform every cell (of which there are millions) in your body. Literally every cell will have been informed that you are happy and react accordingly… you can see how important your thoughts are… you are what you think…
>
> An in-depth knowledge of the subtle energy system which sends information to our endocrine system (our hormones) puts an astrologer in the unique position of understanding the dynamics which are occurring at any given time for an individual. Working with the planetary energy patterns enables the astrologer to facilitate the life development of her client in a

positive way. It truly is a holistic tool, the chart is a map of the psyche, it is truly a sacred ancient art and science.

Candace Pert is a neuroscientist who has proposed that the mind is not just in the brain – it is also in the body. She suggests that the body is the unconscious part of the mind. Molecules that she believes to be the 'bio-chemical correlate of emotion' can be found in your brain, your stomach, your muscles, your glands and all your major organs. This knowledge can empower us to understand ourselves, our feelings and the connection between our minds and bodies.

Perception and awareness play a vital part in health and longevity (back to 'as you think, so you are'!)

So, to the way that I work with a chart… firstly, identify the various dynamics of the natal chart… this gives me the patterns that the individual has from birth e.g. parental influences, communication etc.… then secondly, identify strengths and weaknesses manifesting in the present day. A programme of treatment is then decided offering various ways of releasing, facilitating and empowering the person. Various treatments offered are homoeopathy, massage (various types) and body energy work…'

MARY TAYLOR

Homoeopathic consultations are not cheap. You can pay anything from £30 to £80 for an initial consultation, but there are some colleges that will offer reduced rates for supervised consultations with students.

Many people of course simply 'self-prescribe' and there is lots of help available. It's a good idea to get a few of the most common remedies to keep in the cupboard.

Arnica is an absolute must, brilliant for shocks, bruising, injuries and jet lag. You'll see it referred to quite a bit in this book. I persuaded a 75-year-old neighbour to take Arnica 200 for a day before he went into hospital for major surgery. He took more for a few a days after the operation and when he went back to see the surgeon, he was asked what he'd taken, because the surgeon had never seen postoperative bruising heal so quickly in an elderly person.

Always keep arnica cream on hand, too, for bruises where there is no open cut.

Belladonna is good for fevers and inflammations and for the onset of an infection.

Chamomilla is excellent for teething babies, colic and pain. It really helps to calm and relax them (as does chamomile tea of course).

Calendula accelerates wound healing and counters infection and, if calendula tincture or cream can be applied directly to a wound, it will help to heal it without scarring. Try Hypercal cream, which is the homoeopathic version of Savlon, available from Boots the Chemists, Holland and Barrett and many other retailers.

Nux vomica – yes, just as it sounds – helps with hangovers, indigestion and vomiting usually due to excess of alcohol or rich food. It's also good for colds, nervousness and irritability.

Those are just a few of the ones I use most often. I found I was running to the health-food store to buy them all the time, so eventually treated myself to a 'kit' of 42 remedies from Ainsworths Homoeopathic Pharmacy. It comes in a handy travel-size box and includes a brilliant little book *The Remedy Prescriber*, which gives an introduction to homoeopathy, tells you how to prescribe and which doses to use, and lists all manner of common ailments and personality 'traits' to help you choose the right remedy.

There are different potencies ranging from 3x to LM. However, those sold in chemists' shops are usually the 6x and 30x. Basically, the lower the number, the nearer it is to the material product and the less the dilution.

The great thing is that these remedies are safe for all ages. If you've chosen the wrong remedy it just won't work, so, as long as you follow the instructions and stop taking it, you'll do no harm.

Also, I don't have any pets but lots of my friends do and use homoeopathy regularly. The guide tells you what symptoms to look out for in animals and to prescribe for them (I'm sure you'll have lots of dogs being given remedies to alleviate their terror on Guy Fawkes night!) Ainsworths also supply remedies to more than 5,000 farms in Britain and have the royal warrants of Appointment to HM the Queen and HRH the Prince of Wales as suppliers of their homoeopathic remedies. (See www.ainsworths.com; 020 7935 5330.)

Another excellent supplier who also offer a 'kit' is Helios Pharmacy (www.helios.co.uk; 01892 537254). There are also travel first aid kits available. You'll also find various recommendations throughout this book for products by Weleda. They do a full range of homoeopathic remedies and plant medicines plus of course skincare products and toothpaste. (See www.weleda.co.uk.) To find a registered homoeopath in your area, try the Society of Homeopaths (www.homeopathy-soh.org).

Miranda Castro is a leading writer on the subject. Try to get her *Complete Guide to Homeopathy*. It's a really comprehensive A–Z of ailments and suggested remedies, both internal and external. *The Family Guide to Homeopathy* by Dr Andrew Lockie (Hamish Hamilton) is also brilliant.

If you want to go more deeply into the philosophy behind the process of disease and its cure by homoeopathy, you can't do better than read Colin Griffith's *Companion to Homeopathy* (Watkins Books).

Herbs

It's thought that the rainforest contains a cure for every disease ever known and any disease yet to be encountered. Plants with medicinal properties have been around for centuries and the modern pharmaceutical industry makes great use of them, mostly in combination with chemical ingredients. But there are plenty of pure variations available to treat a host of ailments, usually in dried form.

If you're looking for books on the subject of herbs and herbal remedies, it's hard to beat one of the originals – *Culpeper's Complete Herbal* (Foulsham), Nicholas Culpeper's world famous herbal guide to radiant health. Culpepper was a famous astrologer and physician who lived in the early seventeenth century. He left a legacy of a vast collection of herbal remedies that, because of their healing properties, are as invaluable today as they were during his lifetime.

From time to time, most of us use herbs and plants as remedies without even considering it. For example, the last time you had the misfortune to sting yourself on a nettle you may have instinctively reached out for a dock leaf to rub on it; for a toothache you may have reached for a drop of clove oil; and the last time your breath ponged you may have chewed on a sprig of parsley.

As with so many of my experiences, I got into herbal supplements during pregnancy. Most pregnant women have heard of drinking raspberry leaf tea in the last trimester to try to help speed up labour, but I was also recommended to take a drink made of various Ayurvedic herbs. My birth guru, Gowri Motha (see 'Pregnancy and Birth – It's Not a Disease!' for more details) gave me this bag of what looked like sawdust or floor sweepings. It's called Baladi Choorman and the main ingredient is the herb bala, which helps to regulate the hormones of pregnancy, soften the cervix and pelvic tissues, control blood sugars and regulate blood pressure. Gowri told me to take a teaspoon (two by the third trimester) mixed with a cup of rice milk every evening after my meal. Well, I was on the phone to her after the first evening saying, 'I can't get this down. It's like trying to drink curry powder and the consistency makes me gag and it tastes terrible.' 'None of my other pregnant ladies have complained so much,' she said. 'Try it in yoghurt.'

I tried it mixed in with soya yoghurt and it was bearable. Still 'chewy' but I forced myself to take it. That scenario went on for two pregnancies. Last time, on my fourth pregnancy, I'd recommended my friend Mary to Gowri's gentle birth method and I was bemoaning the nightly agony of the herbal drink to her. 'Do you take it with yoghurt?' I asked. 'No,' she said, 'I just boil it up in the rice milk and strain it and it tastes OK.' Strain it? No one had mentioned that to me – or, at any rate, my pregnant brain hadn't computed. I'd been 'chewing' the raw herbs. Gowri howled with laughter when I told her and said, 'Well, you probably got extra roughage.'

At one time, we'd have needed to go foraging in fields and hedgerows to make up our own remedies. It's all much easier for us now because there are companies that sell dried herbs, tinctures, herbal teas and 'medicines'. Most good health-food shops stock a range of Bioforce products and, they produce an excellent *Quick Herbal Guide*. (See www.bioforce.co.uk.)

Here are some that I keep in my herbal medicine cabinet:

▨ hypericum – antiviral action, especially appropriate for the nervous system;

▨ echinacea – take internally as tincture and externally as cream; antiviral and a boost to the immune system;

▨ gingko biloba, for poor circulation – improves blood supply to extremities;

▨ ginger – warming blood tonic that boosts circulation;

▨ vinca minor – increases tone of blood vessels; and

▨ feverfew, for headaches – can protect against migraine headaches if taken daily.

It's helpful to keep a quick-reference guide alongside a couple of herbal remedies in your bathroom cabinet but be aware that certain herbs do have contraindications. It's best to check with your doctor if you're taking any prescribed medicines and, despite my anecdote about my pregnancy herbs, remember I was under supervision. On no account take herbs without advice if you are pregnant. Plants and herbs are powerful. They are the basis of all our modern medication. Treat them with respect and don't exceed the recommended dose.

There are also a few good mail order suppliers:

Hambleden Herbs supply a range of more than 130 organic herbal products, including teas, tinctures, infusions and culinary herbs and spices. (See www.hambledenherbs.co.uk.)

Halzephron Herb Farm in Cornwall have a huge range of medicinal herbs and foods and spices, including organic herb and spice dips. They have a shop in St Ives, which carries the whole range, and a full mail order catalogue. They also produce a helpful free guide to which herbal medicines could help you, *The Natural Alternative* by Deborah Fowler, available from www.halzherb.com.

Granary Herbs (01622 737314) supply tinctures and creams made from fresh organic home-grown herbs.

Neal's Yard Remedies are a good source, of course. See their website at www.nealsyardremedies.com.

G Baldwin & Co sell a huge range of herbs for teas, tinctures and flower remedies. (See www.baldwins.co.uk; 0207 703 5550.)

For more information on **Gowri Motha's** herbal recommendations in pregnancy, look up www.gentlebirthmethod.com.

Flower remedies

You'll see a few references throughout this book to the Bach Rescue Remedy. If you buy only one thing, make it a bottle of Rescue Remedy and keep it in your bag. You'll be amazed how grateful you are the next time you trip up, get anxious, panicky or stressed out, perhaps when flying or on a long journey. It can even be used on animals. For example, if you sense that your pet is fearful on Guy Fawkes Night, give him a drop or add it to his water.

I was once a witness to a near-disaster situation involving a woman in a van who had crashed through some railings near to a railway line in front of my very eyes. She came to a dazed halt with her front wheels hanging over the precipice of the railway embankment. The next stop would have been the railway line! My husband (then boyfriend) quickly coaxed her out of the seat of her van into our haphazardly parked car, whereupon I immediately administered the Bach flower remedies. Almost straightaway, I began to see some light in her eyes. Then came the realisation of what had just happened! Nothing that drastic has happened since, but the Rescue Remedy has always softened the upset of the grazed knees, bonked heads and plain, tearful tantrums that are part of our everyday family life. (By the way, the next time I drove past the railway bridge, the flimsy fence had been replaced with a concrete one.)

> The art of healing comes from nature and not from the physician. Therefore, the physician must start from nature with an open mind.
>
> PARACELSUS

Flower remedies, like homoeopathy, are one of those treatments that, as yet, have had no scientific evidence to support their effectiveness, yet so many holistic practitioners swear by their use. The essences are said to capture the 'life force' of various flowers, so it is a kind of leap of faith, but one that, if you are tuned into it, may work for you. And, let's face it, if we waited around for scientific proof for things like this, the contents of this book would be very small indeed! All I can say is they have worked for me. I've tailored various concoctions to suit the needs of different situations for myself and my kids. I've found them useful after mild traumas and seen positive results in the treatment of subtle mood problems, especially with the children - and of course children don't mind taking them, because they taste fine.

Rescue Remedy is now widely used. It's a blend of five of the 38 flower remedies identi-fied by Dr Edward Bach, an eminent doctor who gave up his thriving practice to follow his intuition and wander the fields and woods in search of flowers. Bach doesn't have the total market now, though, and there are loads available, including bush flower rem-edies from Australia. Often, they come with a booklet or detailed list of which emotional states they can be used for.

A very intuitive friend of mine teaches special needs children (see 'Imperfectly Natural People': Felicity). She sits individually with each child and shows them a range of flower essences and they look at the pictures and names of the sometimes quite obscure flow-ers and plants and choose four or five that appeal to them. She then refers to her com-prehensive guide and works out the significance of the flower essences they've chosen. Invariably, she is amazed by their accuracy in picking out exactly what they seem to need at the time. For example, a child whose mother has just had a new baby often picks a flower that responds to jealousy and feeling 'usurped'. She's seen so many examples like this that she really believes that all of us, but particularly children, have the intuition that enables us to recognise exactly what we need, perhaps on a subconscious level. When the essences are chosen, she makes them up into a tincture and the children take a few drops under their tongue morning and night. The changes in their behaviour and emotions are usually apparent within a week or so.

Flower remedies are available in most good health shops and Rescue Remedy and cream is sold in Boots the Chemist. For more information on Bach remedies, see www.bachcentre.com, see also Indigo Essences for children www.indigoessences.com.

Felicity

Felicity Evans, 59, special needs teacher and founder of NatureKids – Health and Education Together (www.naturekids.co.uk). One son, Jestyn.

Lots of family illness, including diabetes, hormone problems and hyperactivity have made me realise I must work very hard to maintain good health.

Bright and early
Fifteen minutes to two hours of quiet contemplation – my time for insights and answers. Glass of water. Body brushing. Sit by full-spectrum light box.

Typical brekkie
Try to follow my blood group diet (A) aiming to eat two-thirds alkaline foods to one-third acid-forming foods. Favourite macrobiotic breakfast – miso soup, grains, beans and salad.

Lunch
Tofu burger, vegetables, rice seeds, or homemade soup, rice cakes and nut spread.

Dinner
Soup, salad, or fish with millet, quinoa, buckwheat or rice.

Drinks – water – bottled or tap?
Mainly Pi-mag water or bottled. Herb teas – two a day.

Favourite superfoods I couldn't live without
Green veg. Seaweed.

Vitamins and minerals
MSM Max. True Food Supernutrition Plus.
Bio-acidophilus. Colloidal gold and silver.

When I'm under the weather
I have regular radionics. Bush flower remedies, healing/Reiki.

Favourite treatments
La Stone treatment, Reiki.

For exercise
Pilates, Biodanza, walking, swimming when possible.

For relaxation
Retreats, camping.

Save my skin
Green People: REN: live aloe vera plant, Rich's MSM Lotion.

Sunscreen
Green People.

Haircare
Lamas Botanicals.

Cleaning products
Ecover, Bio D Clear Spring, Bambule hygiene spray, pine oil diluted in boiled water.

Recycling and composting tips
Door-to-door collection.

Gardening naturally
Liquid seaweed.

Pets
Avoid antibiotics and chemical treatments. Real food, healing, bush flower remedies.

I'd also like to recommend…
We create our lives by what we say and do.
Allow everyone to express their anger, sadness and fears without 'dumping' on anyone else.

To achieve balance in my life…
Fresh air, exercise. A job that is a way of life.
Meals without any allergens.

To revitalise my soul I go to…
The sea, watch dolphins. See a child blossoming with joy.

The one thing I couldn't live without
Rice and water.

Guilty secrets and imperfections
Intolerance.

If I had a magic wand, I would…
… find more time to relax, meditate, exercise and have fun.

Tea tree oil – nature's own antiseptic

Throughout this book I've often mentioned tea tree oil. I've been aware of it since having my first aromatherapy session and slowly it's becoming less of a well kept secret. It smells great, is antibacterial and antiseptic and really does seem to have amazing properties, which can cure a multitude of ills.

Experts have traced the oil of the tea tree back to its roots in Aboriginal Australia. Apparently, it was used during World War Two and is now widely used for first aid applications, easing symptoms of a cold and sore throat, for blending with other essential oils, making toiletries, treating pets, freshening the air and even cleaning many household accessories and furnishings.

The versatility and effectiveness of tea tree oil is amazing. I would never have believed that an essential oil could lend itself so successfully to so many different applications. Nothing but nature could have created such valuable, broad-spectrum substances, and that is the beauty of tea tree oil – it is totally natural.

The best recommendation I can give you is to go and buy yourself a couple of bottles. Get good quality essential oil (not a blend). It tends to vary in price from around £2.99 to £4.99 and nearly all health shops will stock it.

When you've done that, order a copy of the fantastic *Those Amazing Tea Tree Oils* by Karen MacKenzie. It's a book based on *The Tea Tree Oil Encyclopaedia*, which was originally published in 1995 but is now out of print. It's an updated version that's presented as a unique website where the book can be downloaded and used offline or you can order a printed copy.

The book includes: an A–Z of first aid applications and chapters on how to use the product all around the home; how to use it safely in veterinary applications; how to make your own creams, lotions and toiletries; a look at the history of the tea trees; and much, much more. There are also links to guide you into researching tea tree oil for yourself. Karen says,

> We are just beginning to wake-up to the fact that the synthetic chemical cocktails we encounter during the course of a lifetime are systematically weakening and even changing our individual body's natural functions. Hairsprays, cosmetics, deodorants, polishes, detergents, perfumes, aftershave, first aid treatments, medicines, air fresheners to name but a few. It is undeniable that our immune systems are beginning to suffer. Where will it all end?

Germs, bacteria and other parasites are evolving to beat their chemical killers, the superbugs, including MRSA (Golden staph), thrive. Mystery illnesses are on the increase. Do we then try to make stronger chemicals?… you bet we do! Are we not forgetting one simple, fundamental fact? Bacterium is a basic, one-celled form of life and these chemicals are harmful to all life – including our own! When we use harsh chemical cocktails against pathogens we can also unbalance and destroy our own vital body cells too.

I am not denying that synthetic medicine was, and is, a great gift, but it is the indiscriminate use, in addition to all other synthetic pesticides, fungicides and food additives, that is causing so many problems to people and to the environment. Over sixty years ago society started to turn its back on nature and the chemical industry took centre stage. We seemed to forget that we were part of nature and, to turn against it, we would be turning against ourselves. It is only now that we are beginning to pay the price. Now, wouldn't it be marvellous if we could find a safe, non-toxic, non-irritant substance that replaced many of the strong chemicals in our cupboards? Well, we have!

Here is a product that is made by nature for nature; a completely natural, topical, clinically proven, anti-bacterial and anti-fungal substance. It has anti-inflammatory, immune system strengthening, pain killing and wound healing qualities too. It also exhibits anti-viral, expectorant and balsamic characteristics. All this and it can be used as a powerful antiseptic, parasiticide and insecticide and, it can be kind to our skin cells (subject to a patch test).

I still find it ironic that if man had made such synthetic substances and had spent millions of pounds on their development programme, they would have been hailed as the wonders of the century. Everyone would have known about them, and everyone would be utilising their many properties. However, because tea tree oils are created by nature they are viewed with suspicion and indifference.

KAREN MACKENZIE

I'm with Karen. Tea tree oil is a must-have around our house. It has a multitude of uses. For starters, whenever anyone has a cold or blocked nose, we apply it liberally. I put a couple of drops on our pillows, even a drop on the baby's sleepsuit. It's the new Vick's VapoRub that your mum probably put on your chest as a child. It helps people to breathe easily. Even better, put a few drops in a vaporiser or in a bowl of hot water on the radiator – as long as it's out of the reach of children, obviously.

Sore throats will respond brilliantly to gargling with tea tree oil diluted with water. We almost always use it in the bath and, if you're not so fussed about the smell, you'll find it mixes well with lavender (one drop to three or four of lavender), or you can put a drop on a flannel or sponge and use it in the shower. It's fantastic on spots, too. Just dab a bit of neat tea tree oil on those zits and away they go.

Remember disinfectant? Well it takes its place beautifully. If you check out the sections on cleaning products and air fresheners in 'Get Your House in Order' you'll see I use tea tree oil to clean surfaces, mop floors and freshen the air by diluting it in a plant spray. God forbid that a pet or a child should vomit on your carpet, but, if it happens, tea tree oil is your answer.

When it comes to laundry, I put a couple of drops in the washing machine rinse compartment if I want a really fresh smell and, if you use cloth nappies or sanitary protection or need to soak any heavily soiled items, it's perfect. Just put a couple of drops in a bucket with the soiled linens till you're ready to wash them and – voilà – no smells (no chemicals, either). It's good for pest control, too: the ants don't seem too keen on it and, if you apply it to your susceptible areas, you may also help ward off mosquito bites.

To order Karen MacKenzie's book, call 0871 784 3007 (national rate). The retail price is £9.95 and the postage and packing costs £1.75. The website is www.teatreebook.com.

Lynda

Lynda, 40, married to Alex. Three children Ellen, 9, and twins Robert and Andrew 7, all home-educated.

Bright and early
At 7.30a.m.–ish, warm drink of lemon and honey with a pinch of turmeric.

Typical brekkie
Smoothie made of pumpkin and sunflower seeds, tofu and blueberries and papaya, pineapple or mango, blended together with rice milk. I also add a probiotic, hemp oil, linseeds and wheatgrass powder. It keeps me going till lunchtime. If I make juice, it's carrot with celery, beetroot and ginger for a quick vitamin boost.

Lunch
I make a huge batch of veg soup twice a week. I eat it with rice or corn cakes and salad.

Dinner
Always start from scratch using organic ingredients and tofu etc.

Drinks – water – bottled or tap?
Under-sink water filter so we drink and cook with filtered water. Before that we bought copious amounts of bottled water so we now spend less and have fewer plastic bottles to recycle.

Favourite superfoods I couldn't live without
My mother died in her early twenties when I was very young, so I now avoid dairy as much as possible and eat more soya products, including tofu.

Vitamins and minerals
Probiotics, vitamin C and we use homeopathic remedies as needed. For the kids, Kindervital and Eye Q Fish Oil (citrus) daily.

Save my skin
I skin-brush all over before taking a warm shower followed by a shorter, colder one. It has solved my dry-skin problem and my cellulite! I use Neal's Yard Mother's Massage Oil because I love the smell, but I avoid any unnatural chemicals on my skin. I use Weleda Citrus Deodorant.

Feminine care
I use washable pads - Many Moons Menstrual Pads (from Green Woman). Once used, you just soak in cold water and then bung in with the laundry.

Sunscreen
I'm very fair skinned - I cover up.

Cleaning products
We use Ecover products for cleaning and laundry. They're great.

Recycling and composting tips
We recycle cardboard and plastic by choice. We fill two green bins over a couple of weeks and then take them to the recycling centre. Paper, tin and glass are collected by the council as well as garden waste. We have a compost heap (well, worm heap), which I find difficult to dig.

All our veg, fruit peelings go in it but I'm not sure it gets 'hot' enough. We stopped adding citrus peel, as it takes ages to rot. Last year, everywhere I used the compost, we had cherry plants growing.

Gardening naturally
We love the 'wild' look, so our garden is self-seeding perennials. Those that sort themselves out are foxgloves, yellow iris, hollyhocks, lady's mantle, evening primrose, etc. I avoid anything tender that isn't slug-proof. We never use chemicals and we encourage dandelions because the rabbits and guinea pigs love them!

For the kids
A balanced diet, even though they are all fond of pizza, fish fingers and sausages. We always try homeopathic remedies and I try to let an illness 'take its course' rather than use conventional medicines. I would never give anything other than belladonna 200 for high temperatures, as I believe they are part of the body's natural defences. I try to support rather than suppress this natural process.

Top parenting tips
I like Steve Biddolph's advice in *The Secret of Happy Children*. He says that the three simple responsibilities you have as a parent, in order of importance, are:
■ take care of yourself;
■ take care of your partnership; and
■ take care of your children.
We're much more loving, patient and enthusiastic as parents when we're happy and fulfilled.

I'd also like to recommend...
... *The Family Guide to Homeopathy* by Dr Andrew Lockie (Hamish Hamilton).

To revitalise my soul I go to...
... Monkton Wyld Court in Dorset and collect fossils on the beach. [See the chapter 'Beat a Retreat'.]

Guilty secrets and imperfections
Not getting up early enough or going to bed early enough. I often start the day feeling I'm already 'behind' and the not-quite-catching-up remains with me all day.

If I had a magic wand, I would...
... make space to still my mind and gather my thoughts more often; make a conscious effort to just be 'in the moment' instead of rushing on to the next thing.

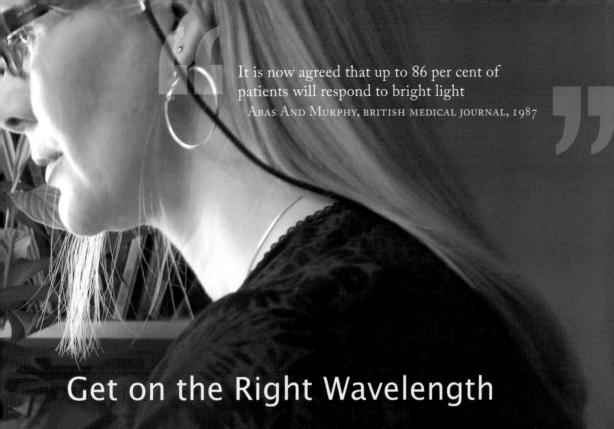

> It is now agreed that up to 86 per cent of patients will respond to bright light
>
> ABAS AND MURPHY, BRITISH MEDICAL JOURNAL, 1987

Get on the Right Wavelength

See the light!

Winter blues? You may not be working nights or needing to get up at ungodly hours, but are there times, particularly in winter, when you feel really down for no other reason than the nights are drawing in?

Sunlight is essential to good health and wellbeing. Lack of it can induce a form of depression, known as SAD (seasonal affective disorder). What's that? Well, it is an acute form of winter lethargy or tiredness, hence the winter blues, and with it - boom! - everything suffers: work, play and, to add insult to injury, you can put on weight.

Exposure to the 'right kind' of light will alleviate or even cure SAD. You know that feeling you get standing at a window, surveying a sunny scene with the warmth shining through onto your face? Well, with that in mind let me tell you about the wonder of full-spectrum light boxes.

One of the first radio jobs I got was on Richard Branson's brand-spanking-new Virgin Radio. As a budding presenter, I never turned anything down and four months of the graveyard shift through winter seemed just lovely. I also worked on my day of rest, do-

The night shift was gruelling. Yes, there are many people who do turn their days upside down but there's no doubt it's not ideal for the old body clock. We're designed to retire early and rise early and I was crawling into bed at about 7.15 a.m., just as it was getting light in winter. I would sleep fitfully, trying not to be woken up by doorbells ringing, workmen cursing and the courier trying to deliver a package for a neighbour at 11 a.m. I'd get up at around 3.30 p.m., only to find it was practically dark. So I'd had, well, zero daylight. When I found that this regime was going to continue into my day off, too, leaving me cooped up in a windowless TV studio, I was seriously worried. I've also always been prone to catching colds and sore throats and, when you're doing live radio and TV shows, illness is just not an option.

I met a wonderful nutritionist, Eileen Fletcher, at that time. I chatted to her about how I could best stay well on that heavy schedule. We talked about diet, the vitamins and the minerals. I said I'd carry on with regular aromatherapy sessions and swim at least weekly. She suggested vitamin C, zinc and also garlic capsules to help ward off colds, and then we discussed light therapy. Back then not so many of us knew about SAD and I was pretty sure I wasn't actually suffering from it but Eileen said that if you are not getting enough daylight, you are far more likely to suffer from depression. She told me about light boxes and I was all ears. It all seemed to make great sense. Airline stewards who change time zones use them, as do as-

tronauts! I asked Eileen, 'If I could do only one thing to help myself get through, what would it be?' Her answer? Get a light box.

So get one I did, and switched it on when I got up midafternoon. You don't need to sit and stare at it: just have it on a few feet from where you're milling about. I sat with it on for around half an hour while I ate food, made phone calls, watched TV, worked on the computer. The difference in how I felt was incredible. I swear I could actually feel the light giving me a buzz. I've had that same light box now for nearly ten years and it's still going strong, though the bulbs do weaken eventually. I still use it when I get up for an early radio show or if I'm working late afternoons in the winter.

I've recommended light boxes to so many people and always have good feedback. After I mentioned them on Steve Wright's show one day, a guy emailed me and said his wife had suffered mild depression for years, usually in winter, and was it worth a try? He bought one for her and the next week he contacted me again to say it had made a tremendous difference. She was feeling really bright and had dumped her drugs.

Why is light so important? There is a physiological basis for SAD, involving the nervous and endocrine centres in the brain and the glands in our bodies that control our moods. The amount of light falling on the retina of the eye influences these centres, which, in turn, affect the pineal gland, modifying the amount of the hormone melatonin, which it secretes. Melatonin is involved in our mood and emotional balance and, through this connection, sunlight can make us feel good and an absence of it can make us feel awful. In the States you can buy melatonin tablets in any pharmacy but they aren't licensed here in the UK.

So why won't just a regular standard lamp or work light give us the same boost? They don't have to be full-spectrum lights but they are many times brighter than the average light bulb. Light intensity is measured in lux, the Latin word for light (you may some-times see the plural given as 'luces'). On a summer's day we may have up to sixteen hours of daylight at 100,000 lux, but an eight hour winter's day will give less than 5,000 lux. Indoor lighting can be as low as 100 lux. It's best to choose a light designed to give out at least 24,500 lux in order to rectify symptoms of SAD. The amount of time you'll need to use it will depend on the type of light it is. A recent survey found that most people suffering from SAD felt considerably better after using the light box for just seven days for only twenty minutes a day. With some of the smaller lights it's suggested that you sit about an arm's length away, but, if you need to sit further away, you could just have it on for more time.

I used mine in the afternoon but, to get the full benefit, use it when you get up in the morning. There are a huge range of lights available now and it can be confusing know-ing which one to buy. So get on the Internet and do some research. You can now get full-spectrum light bulbs, alarm clocks and portable lights. If you can afford it, buy a couple in different sizes – then you get to use them in different rooms.

I do mention this in the section on sleep above, but you really must try a 'natural' alarm clock. The Bodyclock Sunray is a simple digital model with a thirty minute 'sunrise' that wakes you gently. If you're not awake by then, a very soft 'peeping' sound will rouse you.

There are lots of websites now that stock light therapy products. The best range I've found is on www.wholisticresearch.com and www.sad.uk.com Theres also the excellent Portable 'Litebook' www.litebook.com.

Electromagnetic frequencies

I once had a 'geopathic stress expert' visit my house who advised me to turn off all my electrical equipment at night, not just to save on the electricity bills but to save my health. She told me to get rid of any electrical equipment in my bedroom and that it's particularly harmful to sleep with your head next to a clock radio or a television. Let's face it bedrooms are for sleep and sex, so why not be minimalist!

Unfortunately, we live surrounded by electromagnetic frequencies (EMFs) from all manner of sources that are polluting our environment, from electricity pylons to electric shavers. It's a huge subject that I can't go into at great length here, but check out any of the extensive research done by Roger Coghill and get hold of a copy of his book *Electropollution*. Short of wrapping ourselves in a lead duffel coat or a Faraday cage (a very sophisticated EMF screening system), is there anything we can do to minimise the harmful effects?

Well, for starters, limit the number of electrical gadgets you own and use and, at the very least, turn them off when you're not using them.

One of the most relaxing holidays I've ever had was a Christmas spent with a friend in Wales. She lives in a remote cottage with no TVs, radios or computers, but we were planning to cook our Christmas dinner in her electric oven and the microwave. There was a huge storm. In the style of a Hollywood movie, we peered outside our shelter and, at the same moment, saw a wooden electricity pylon come crashing down, wires flailing and sparking in the gale. Everything went dark. It was 7.30 p.m. on Christmas Eve, so we didn't hold much hope for a visit from the electricity board. We settled down to a lovely candlelit evening and played games by the open fire. On Christmas Day, we just got on with it. We borrowed a tiny camping stove to cook a few bits of veg, threw jacket potatoes and chestnuts onto the fire and had the best time. After those two days, I really felt I had given my whole body a rest. It was probably the first time I'd been away for a whole day from anything vaguely electrical. Most of the time we're not even aware of electrical pollution or the low-level buzz that's going on all around us.

My expert advised me to get into the habit of turning off electrical appliances *at the wall* when you're not using them or, better still, install a device to cut off the current at the mains when the circuits aren't in use. There is lots more information about this in the fantastic book *Creating Sacred Space* with Feng Shui by Karen Kingston. The main defence against this hidden enemy is just to be aware. There are a few other little tricks as well to protect ourselves against harmful radiation and the effects of electromagnetic frequencies.

Pulsors

Dr George Yao developed pulsors in the early 1960s. They are said to provide protection from negative environmental energy and also correct any polarity reversals to make you stronger and better able to function in any environment.

The technical information says,

> Pulsors are a solid-state composite of purified microcrystals that resonate with the subtle energy vibrations that affect our sense of wellbeing. Pulsors can be placed around the body in a pocket, on a pendant or around the room. They can also harmonise the energy in electrical equipment and be placed near wiring, telephones, computers and water pipes.

A nutritionist advised me to wear a pulsor about fifteen years ago, particularly in the environment of the radio studio, which is absolutely jam-packed with electrical equipment. I bought a Toroid Pulsor, a little doughnut-shaped, 5cm-diameter bunch of crys-

tal inside a blue plastic casing. I stuck a cord through it and still wear it around my neck or carry it in my pocket if I'm wearing a low-cut top (they aren't particularly attractive). I have definitely noticed a difference in my energy levels when I've forgotten to wear it.

You can now get pulsor sets, credit-card-sized pulsors to use on a TV or computer and acu-pulsors, strong pulsors on a chain to stimulate acupressure points.

They're very expensive at around £100–500, but will last you forever. (See www.wholistic research.com.)

Magnets and silica crystals as therapy

It's strange, isn't it, the way we are so sceptical about things that work? It's as if we want miracles but are too afraid to allow them to happen. In the course of writing this book I've obviously remembered the many therapies and products that I've used and sworn by for years, but I've also come across some new ones, whether by accident or design.

Yet again it was a Radio 2 listener who pointed me in the direction of the Ecoflow products. She'd heard me talking about my fears over mobile phone usage. *The Observer* had reported that 89 per cent of eleven- and twelve-year-olds owned a mobile phone, as did 58 per cent of nine- and ten-year-olds. The show's presenter Steve Wright had also been commenting on a new report stating that landlines could become obsolete and everyone would soon be on mobiles. She heard me say I was horrified by the idea because the health risks are not known and she wrote to tell me about the Biophone – a tiny little silica crystal and metal device that sticks to your phone to combat the harmful effects of mobile phones by using the principle of bio-resonance feedback.

She sent me a brochure that explains how Ecoflow products have helped thousands of people and how I too could become a distributor with the Ecoflow business opportunity. Well, it kind of turned me off. Every week in the Sunday papers there are ads telling me I could be rich if I join this or that selling scheme and become a millionaire with no outlay. If those ads sound too good to be true, they usually are. To be fair, Ecoflow weren't promising untold riches and they are confident enough in their devices to offer 90 day money back guarantees but I had no intention of becoming an Ecoflow distributor or trying their products, so I thanked her for her information and duly binned the catalogue. I couldn't help but think about the implications of using the mobile phone, though, and when my curiosity got the better of me I looked into it further.

The Biophone was invented by one Professor S. Danev, who hails from Bulgaria. It's designed to combat the harmful effects of mobile phones and was on field test for eighteen months, with outstanding results, before its commercial release in the early 2000s.

It's difficult, though, to prove that these things really do have an effect. The sceptic in me thought that maybe I'd be shelling out cash for a little bit of metal that did nothing, but I got hold of a copy of an interview with a scientist, Bjorn Overbye, who proved the effectiveness of the Biophone. He explained that, after becoming convinced that Biophone users were reporting major improvements since fitting the device to their phones, he needed to find out why. Since he could measure no change in the phone before or after it was fitted with the device he realised something was happening to the users, and decided to test them using electromagnetic measurements. As he said, 'Conventional medicine tries to explain everything using chemistry and morphology. Life is more than that. It is primarily an energy thing. Creation is about energy and life is a special type called life energy or vital energy.'

He continues to explain in scientific terms how the body is affected by the radiation emitted by mobile phones and how the Biophone, which he too had at first dismissed as just another little gadget, actually prevents body reaction to radiation for up to ten minutes. It's worth checking out www.radiationresearch.org for more technical research, but Bjorn Overbye ends the interview by saying, 'I therefore conclude that adding Biophone to a mobile phone or body diminishes the ill effects of radiation by rectifying the spin-inversion caused by the harmful radiation. Biophone helps the body protect itself where evolution cannot.'

It's strange, though, how some things are meant to be. I was in my favourite place, St Ives, a few months later, holed up at the Garrack Hotel to write a few chapters of this book, when I decided to take a walk down by the harbour. I stumbled across a shop front filled with notices claiming relief from pain. I wondered whether it was a Chinese herbalist's. The sign said, 'Are you in pain? Come in and have a free sample treatment.' Six months of nighttime breastfeeding had given me the most tremendous crick in my neck. It had been going on for a couple of weeks, so now was my chance, and in I went.

They were selling Ecoflow products and such was their belief in their wares that they were offering a free sample treatment to show how effective this magnotherapy really is.

Phil Watson and Kathy Coleman run Changing Lives in St Ives, Cornwall. They are independent distributors of Ecoflow, which is a company that started in Cornwall. The advertising blurb promises 'innovative health, lifestyle and environmental products'. I quickly realised it was the same company the listener had emailed me about, so I asked for more information. I tried the treatment Phil offered and for twenty to thirty minutes I sat there covered in bizarre magnets, rather like weights, around my arms and legs and felt, well, odd, with a tingling sensation here, a cold patch there and a pulsing in another area.

Phil seemed to know exactly what each sensation meant and moved the magnets around to alleviate the symptoms. Bizarre as it sounds, this was the first time I'd ever tried magnotherapy and I was amazed by its effects. After the treatment I felt more relaxed and warmer, and the crick in my neck had gone. Phil could see I was dehydrated, though, and urged me to drink lots of their 'ionised' water.

Of course, you can't be popping in for a free treatment every day so what were they actually selling? Well the Bioflow is a strong body magnet that uses a unique Central Reverse Polarity magnetic system (which is what makes it different from others). There are various styles available and the magnets are worn in the form of either a wristband or a bracelet. There's a range of designs and the idea is that they help the body to maintain a balanced pH and, according to the blurb, 'good conductivity to the cells due to the blood passing through the magnetic field being subjected to the CRP magnetic pulsing effect'.

If you think about it, it's widely known that hospitals use electrically generated pulsed magnetic fields and the medical profession accepts that this can relieve pain. Bioflow was designed to mimic this prohibitively expensive equipment with its unique 'CRP' or central reverse–polarity system.

Kathy and Phil certainly don't look like your average charlatans or New Age healers, but they'd decided to become distributors for the products because of the miraculous results Kathy had achieved in alleviating her own serious health issues. Here's Kathy's story:

> I was born with spondylitis, a form of arthritis that affects the spine. It was genetic, my relatives had similar problems, and I had been in pain since my early teens. In my early twenties I developed rheumatoid arthritis. I also had dermatitis, quite severe PMS and circulatory problems as well as high blood pressure. My partner Phil heard about the Bioflow and wore one for a couple of months. He was convinced he felt better and nagged me to try it. I was totally sceptical because of the severity of my problems but, in the end, I tried a bracelet just to prove him wrong. After three weeks at my regular check-up they were surprised to find that my blood pressure was normal. It then took about three months and I noticed a huge difference in my health generally. I have now been pain-free and drug-free for three years. I really believe the Bioflow magnetic wristband helped my body to fix itself. After knowing my and my family's history, my doctor cannot believe how well I am.

The Arthritis Research Campaign has also funded a trial on patients with osteoarthritis of the hip and knee. This used Bioflow CRP magnets and was carried out by a group of mid-Devon doctors for the Peninsula Medical School. I know Ecoflow are delighted with the results of this report, which was published in the *British Medical Journal*. To quote them, '... wonderful news... it confirms what we at Ecoflow have known for years – our unique Bioflow magnets really do work!'

I was convinced. My neck pain had gone, so, 'Sold – one Bioflow magnetic bracelet.' They cost between £30 and £125 depending on your choice of wristband or bracelet.

We then got on to the very scary discussion about mobile phones and their effects on us. I told her I'd read some of the research done on the Biophone and Kathy produced a little radiation tester – the kind that checks for leaks in microwave ovens. She asked me to dial her number on my mobile phone and, as it was dialling (and before her telephone even rang), she held the tester over my phone. The needle shot into the red danger zone. Now, if that was your microwave oven leaking those levels of radiation, you'd be throwing it away. How scary, then, is it that we carry these phones around with us in our handbags and pockets? I remembered my husband complaining of aches in his right thigh for months on end, which miraculously vanished when he lost his mobile phone! He had always kept his phone in his right-hand trouser pocket.

But we're imperfectly natural, aren't we? And, much as I'd love to be able to dump my mobile, it's just not going to happen. So what do we do? Stick a Biophone on it. Convinced again! 'Sold – one Biophone around £30.'

You may wonder why mobile phone manufacturers don't build these into phones. Well, I suspect that, if they did, they would have to concede that there could be an issue with mobile phones in the first place, but that's another problem. (Remember smoking-related cancer and the tobacco industry?)

So, what about other electromagnetic frequencies and their effects on us? We're all aware that this fabulous modern electronic world we live in is full of electropollution, which could damage our health and weaken our immune systems. Everything including computers, microwave ovens and electricity pylons, not to mention mobile phone masts, combine to assault us a on daily basis. Ecoflow's Bioguard also uses the principle of bioresonance feedback, which acts on every cell of our body to help protect us against the dangers. Totally convinced? Sold! Bioguard is available as a lapel pin or pendant for approximately £75. See also www.sheerprevention.co.uk. For location of mobile phone masts, check out www.sitefinder.radio.gov.uk.

I spent a small fortune that day, all in the name of research, but I haven't looked back. I've recommended the Bioflow to a neighbour who has had a minor stroke and her recovery was amazing, and to an aunt who has suffered from chronic arthritis for many years. She's as sceptical as they come but try borrowing her bracelet for a day. Not on your life!

What's interesting about Bioflow products is that there is also a range especially designed for use on animals and amazing results have been achieved. It is estimated that there are currently over 2,000,000 satisfied customers. As Kathy says, 'Success with animals destroys the common misconception that it's all in the mind.' When a dog limps in, has a magnotherapy treatment and runs out, you know something has worked, as animals don't have the choice of scepticism or judgement on the placebo effect. If you see an improvement, it's real.

I realise there are probably many other brands of magnetic products that also work well, but I can only recommend what's worked for me. I really believe this company is onto a winner. I haven't tried all their products but they have some very interesting ones, including nutritional powders and magnetic technology for the home, easy-to-fit units that treat your water supply magnetically and a device that will cut down your heating bills.

If you can get down to St Ives, have a treatment with Kathy and Phil Watson and let me know if it helped. There are many other distributers who use bioflow products as part of other treatments such as nutritional testing.too See my forum at www.imperfectlynatural.com.

Ecoflow will be happy to let you know how to contact Phil and Kathy and others local to you. The company has independent distributors in eleven European countries and in Australia. You can locate one in your area by contacting Ecoflow directly. Check out www.ecoflow.plc.uk or call 01752 841144.

June

June, 40, married to Scott, with four daughters aged 11, 8, 4 and one born 4 December 2004.

Our daughters are home-educated in a child-led style. We don't follow any curriculum but help the children learn about whatever interests them.

Bright and early
I'm a fly-by-the-seat-of-my-thong kinda gal in the mornings. I do only what I have to! At the moment, breastfeeding my youngest comes above any beauty routine, so washing my face, brushing my teeth and hair is about it!

Typical brekkie
Tend to not bother, although I know I should.

Lunch
Usually something left over from the night before, or sandwiches. I'm a great believer in eating the leftovers! In the summer we'll often have salad from the garden for lunch. Yum! It's so much nicer fresh and warmed by the sun (not refrigerated)!

Dinner
Hmm, could be a wide variety of things! I do try to make things from scratch if I have the time but it's not always possible. I also try to buy organic, too, but the expense stops me being able to buy it all that way. We're vegetarian, and also eat a few vegan dishes, but do still use milk, eggs, cheese, etc. We rarely have a takeaway - the standard just isn't the same as fresh, home-cooked food.

Drinks - water - bottled or tap?
Bottled water, but cheap bottled. I'm sure it's full of bacteria, as we keep reading, but then bacteria aren't all bad. At least it doesn't taste of chlorine like my tap water does sometimes!

Favourite superfoods I couldn't live without
Lentils. When you think you have nothing in the cupboard, there's always something you can make with lentils!

Vitamins and minerals
Flax oil, vitamin C, vitamin E, zinc and pro-biotics. Plus Spatone iron supplement when I remember it, useful when you're pregnant or breastfeeding, And it doesn't constipate you like iron tablets do!

When I'm under the weather
I resort to childhood/comfort food. Creamy mashed potato with veggie sausages, peas and gravy. Oh, and lots of vitamin C!

Favourite treatments
None, I never seem to get time to have any done. I really fancy having a reflexology session, though. Right now I'd settle for a very long soak in the bath without the baby wanting me to get out. No bubbles, though, because that stuff is nasty for your skin and health.

For exercise
Ooh... [looks embarrassed]. I've got a membership to the local gym, but...

For relaxation
Cruising around the Internet, watching TV, craft stuff with or without the kids.

Save my skin
Virgin organic coconut oil.

Sunscreen
Ugh, none preferably! It's skin cancer in a bottle in my opinion. Instead we cover up, use the shade and stay out of the midday sun.

Favourite beauty products
I try to avoid things that are sold as 'beauty products' for the most part. Most of them are full of parabens, formaldehyde and other such nasties.

Haircare
This is where I fall down on avoiding the nasties - shampoo, conditioner and de-frizzer every time. And I also dye it!

Feminine care

I use a Mooncup and washable pantyliners. I did use a Keeper for a while but found I'm sensitive to latex, so changed over to the Mooncup. I can't recommend it enough – it's excellent! I also use the Ladycare magnet and it really helps with any menstrual pain.

Cleaning and laundry products

Now you're talking! I don't like shop-bought sprays and cleaning fluids, I leave them to my husband (who loves them). I use hot water and lavender essential oil to wash down work surfaces, bicarb and vinegar for the sinks, or lemon juice if it needs to be whitened a bit. I do use Ecover toilet cleaner, mind you. Washing: homemade laundry gloop! I also use borax if the wash needs a bit of a boost, and sometimes one of the oxygen-based laundry boosters. Sunlight is also a good bleacher!

Recycling and composting tips

Our local authority does a kerbside collection for organic waste, glass, plastic bottles, cans, paper and light cardboard, so we put all of this out. I also have a composter which I fill to make compost for the garden. Clothing, toys, books, furniture, etc. is offered around to family and friends, and then taken to a charity shop if no one else wants it. The children's clothing is passed down from one to the other and to cousins, so it's usually rags before we get rid of it. We also buy a lot of our clothing on eBay, therefore recycling other people's unwanted goods for our own use.

Gardening naturally

We don't use pesticides and I use only organic seeds. Every summer I grow tomatoes, cucumbers, courgettes, peas, beans, radishes and whatever else takes my fancy from the seed company. If we have an aphid problem the girls will collect ladybirds and set them to work!

Pets

We currently have two cats, Butch and Quincy, who we got from the Cat Protection League a couple of years ago. We also have 25 baby stick insects - hmm!

Babycare

Washable nappies, and fleece wipes and flannels for nappy changing instead of horrible shop-bought wet-wipes that burn their skin! Lots of lovely breast milk, no paracetamol solutions, and we use homeopathic remedies.

For the kids

I pretty much give them free rein with food, within parameters. I serve reasonably healthy food. They can eat it or not – I won't make them clear their plates. If they crave something I try to give them it, unless it's sweets etc. Our bodies know when we need something - we just have to listen to them. I do buy them multivits but they're not keen so rarely take them. It's far better for them to get the vitamins and minerals direct from the food, anyhow.

If they have a cold etc. I'll make them a drink with unwaxed lemons and honey. I'll always try a natural remedy before reaching for a pharmaceutical one. For earaches we use olive oil that's had garlic steeped in it; it works a treat. We also use homeopathic remedies.

Top parenting tips

Listen to your children. Just because they're smaller than you, it doesn't mean that you always know better. Don't reach for the paracetamol all the time. We have fevers and pain for a reason. If you believe in them, they can do it, whatever it is.

I'd also like to recommend...

... home education, of course! (See www.education-otherwise.org.)

To revitalise my soul I go to...

... Neopets - virtual pets on the Internet (laugh out loud!).

The one thing I couldn't live without

My lovely iMac and broadband.

Guilty secrets and imperfections

Using Mr Mash instead of making real mashed potato - despite all the other organic, healthy food!

If I had a magic wand, I would...

... spend more time on myself, and get to bed earlier.

" Man is ill because he is never still

PARACELSUS "

Touch Therapies

As you might have guessed, I'm seriously into these. The power of touch is amazing. Have you ever seen how elderly people respond when touched or cuddled by children, or pets for that matter? Most people have heard of a scheme a few years back in which a charity took friendly dogs into care homes for elderly people to stroke. I believe we can actually boost our immune systems when we are stroked and touched. It can help with our response to pain and increase our feelings of wellbeing.

Most of us don't think of treating ourselves to a therapeutic touch session. We just expect our bodies to do their thing day in day out and feel greatly miffed when we develop a pain or pull a muscle. In truth, if we all had regular treatments as a preventive measure, we would probably have far fewer aches and pains and we'd certainly have an increased sense of wellbeing.

All the many forms and styles of touch therapies have different things to offer for different people. You have to find what works for you. Try them all, mix them up or just choose your favourite. I'd had only aromatherapy until my first pregnancy. Suddenly, when your body starts to take on a (new) life of its own, you often feel you need to be more aware of any potential weaknesses and problems. Added to this, of course, pregnancy and labour can be so gruelling that you want to prepare yourself as much as possible. In my case, I wanted to alleviate the aches and pains of pregnancy and, to a certain extent, have as natural a labour as possible. So, for me, these treatments were invaluable. That's why I bang on so much about their use in pregnancy, but of course they are wonderful at any time. Don't wait until you're racked with pain. Book a course now. There are too many to mention so I've just listed my favourites.

Bowen technique

In 1999, I was one of those women who were due to have a millennium baby (and, no, it was not planned that way!). I was seven months gone and taking my daily stroll through Regent's Park to co-host *Steve Wright in the Afternoon* on Radio 2. Up until this point I'd been 'blooming marvellous' but, for the first time in my life (without revealing my age, save to say the hospital records showed 'primagravida'), I was racked by excruciating back pain. It hurt like hell and I could barely walk, let alone lift anything. It felt as if I were dragging around a huge ball and chain but, because I'm the trouper I am, the show had to go on. So I made it to the lunch break. The show was all prepared. Steve Wright was happy and straightaway I was on the phone to helpful midwives and friends. They all informed me cheerily that back pain was common in pregnancy and 'not to worry, it will probably go after the birth'. I didn't particularly care for two more months of mild agony, so I decided to throw money at it. Aromatherapy relaxed me but there was no real pain relief and osteopathy was a bit more heavy duty, to say the least, but that didn't work, either.

I turned to my wonderful natural birth 'guru', Gowri Motha, who recommended I see a lady called Fiona Meekes, a Bowen practitioner. She'd been having good results with pregnant women. I was willing to try anything, so off I hobbled to meet her. She was an unlikely-looking 'healer'. Not your regular, floaty, New Age, hippychick type smelling faintly of patchouli, but displaying the more regular, calmly confident style of a former NHS director of nursing. I'd never heard of the Bowen technique but Fiona explained it a little as she went along.

'Bowen is not a miracle,' she told me, 'but it is amazing! It was devised by an Australian, Tom Bowen, working alongside osteopaths, before developing the treatment on animals.' (At this point, my shoulders tensed a little.) She went on, 'Physios, osteopaths and doctors are now training as Bowen practitioners, but it's not actually officially recognised.' She had a track record in successfully treating lower-back pain, RSI (repetitive strain injury), migraine, hay fever, arthritis, MS and worse. 'Sometimes one treatment is all that's needed,' she told me. Chequebook in hand, I firmly decided that I was all hers.

I lay down, fully clothed, and Fiona gently stimulated and 'rolled' muscles, which in turn (I'm told) stimulated a nervous response in my brain saying, 'Listen, brain, there's a problem here, please sort it.' With a Bowen treatment it's your body that actually takes on the information and starts to take action. It's painless and I could hardly even feel it. After a few little 'moves', though, she quietly left the room. This is the point where you may suspect there's a charlatan at work but it's all for a good reason. Apparently, it allows the body's energies solo space in which to heal.

Twenty minutes later and she had finished, leaving me alone again to 'cook', as she called it. I had to pace around the room and drink lots of water, continually, every hour, which is interesting when you're eight months pregnant because you pee for England every few minutes anyway! But would Bowen have persuaded my body to heal its own muscular problems? Well, I had limped in to see her as if carrying the weight of the world on my lumber region, but after the session I leaped up the steps from the basement treatment room like the recipient of a veritable miracle from the New Testament!

A few months on, I was back on air, waxing lyrical. Now, some of you who listen to me on the radio may know that my fellow broadcasters, Steve Wright and Tim Smith, have me down as a bit cosmic and New Age, anyway, so, after much cackling and impressions of Jim Bowen, Tim bet me 50 pence that the treatment wouldn't work on his tennis elbow. He had tried everything and was now taking drugs for it, even considering an operation. After one session, sweet relief; after two, cured. Ever the cynic, he was totally converted. He never paid me the 50 pence, though!

Many listeners called me after that little plug on air, including a guy whose elderly mother heard me talking about the 'bone lady'. This 82-year-old woman, who could barely walk after a nasty fall, had one treatment and is now another satisfied and totally amazed customer. I've since had great reports from a friend who has been cured of early-onset arthritis, and a neighbour who was told he'd never walk again but is now driving, walking and back on the golf course.

So does it work for everyone? Fiona says it's not always a total cure but, in her experience, it almost always alleviates symptoms. I'm convinced that it is an amazing treatment, though I would guess it depends on the quality of the practitioner. It's important that they know how to treat the whole body. Our bodies are amazing, and, as Hippocrates said, 'The body has the innate ability to heal itself, provided it's given the opportunity to do so.'

Bowen worked for me. It's honestly like a miracle, but get a recommendation if you can. A treatment usually costs around £45 but the beauty is that you rarely need many treatments.

For further information, look at www.the bowentechnique.com. Fiona Meekes can be contacted on 0208 876 3010.

Aromatherapy

This was the first 'hands-on' treatment I ever had and it was bliss. I now have regular aromatherapy massages and use essential oils on a daily basis (see the chapter 'Save Your Skin').

It's probably the most popular treatment because it's usually affordable, there are loads of excellent therapists and its benefits are felt instantly. Try to avoid experiencing your first aromatherapy session at a health club or beauty salon unless you've been recommended to the practitioner. Of course I'm not writing them all off. It's just that, although 'aesthetic aromatherapy' is very relaxing and may help with skin troubles, it's not a patch on holistic aromatherapy, which uses the healing properties of essential oils and the wonderful aroma not only to relax and destress you but also actually to treat lots of different ailments, including physical and emotional problems.

For those of you who decide just to use essential oils at home, there is a wide range available. Always buy pure essential oils and then learn how to dilute them with a carrier oil. Never use them neat on the skin (with the exception of tea tree oil and lavender to dab on spots) and treat oils with care, since they are potent and can be dangerous in the wrong hands. Be aware that certain oils have contraindications for certain conditions. For example, there are many oils that must be avoided in pregnancy, including lavender, and, similarly, you may need to avoid some oils if you have high blood pressure. So, if you're at all unsure, try to see a practitioner first. In any case, read up on it. There are some great books around.

The best oils are from www.essentiallyoils.com.

To find a qualified aromatherapist, contact The Federation of Holistic Therapists www.fht.org.uk.

See also www.aromatherapycouncil.co.uk.

Cranio-sacral massage

I hadn't come across this until I was in labour and my birth guru gave me cranio-sacral massage throughout. It's basically very gentle manipulation, usually focusing on the skull. It aims to normalise the natural rhythms of the body to encourage wellbeing. You barely feel a thing while you just lie back and allow the weight of your head to 'hang' in the hands of the therapist. The touch is very gentle and it's a lovely feeling. After a while you feel a sort of floating sensation. During labour I was away with the fairies for what seemed like an hour and, when she'd finished, I was concerned that contractions had slowed down. 'No, you were contracting every three minutes,' the midwife said. Wow – some pain relief!

Cranio-sacral or cranial osteopathy is also brilliant for newborn babies, helping to heal birth trauma and to put back tiny little nerves and muscles that have shifted during the birth process. I know of one therapist who had a woman bring a fourteen-month-old baby to see him. This poor boy was red and screaming, sleeping very erratically and not eating well. Doctors could find no medical reason for his obvious discomfort. The cranial osteopath gently manipulated his skull and was convinced that he'd managed to shift a tiny trapped nerve that would have been pressing on the baby's brain. He had probably had a raging headache since his very difficult and lengthy birth but did not yet have the where-withal to communicate this fact. The relief was instant: the child relaxed, stopped crying and even managed a smile. At his check-up appointment one month later his mother reported that it was like having a different child. Even newborn babies usually respond really well to this massage, which can also involve little movements on their tummy, and it usually has a beneficial effect on colic and sleep problems.

For adults, it's excellent for neck and shoulder aches and pains, migraines and problems with circulation. The practitioner uses very gentle manipulation to help circulate the blood and balance the lymphatic system.

As always, find a good practitioner – try the Cranio-Sacral Therapy Association (www.craniosacral.co.uk) or check out the College of Cranio-Sacral Therapy: 9 St George Mews, Primrose Hill, London NW1 8XE (020 7483 0120).

Reiki

This is another therapy that has become very popular. It's a form of Japanese spiritual healing, during which the practitioner acts as a channel for healing. It's claimed that the energies used are on a higher 'vibration' than, say, aromatherapy or cranial osteopathy and this opens it up to criticism by sceptics. It usually involves no actual contact and the therapist will place their hands over the patient's body in certain set positions. If it does involve touch, this is very light.

Sometimes, you don't really feel very much but subtle healing should be happening. Often, one can feel deeply relaxed and even fall asleep during or after a session. Yes, you've guessed it, I had it during my labour because my Reiki treatments were combined with cranio-sacral massage and guided visualisation. It's hard to interpret the effectiveness on its own but I do know of many friends who believe it's incredibly effective for alleviating headaches and symptoms of stress. See www.ukreiki alliance.co.uk for further information.

Reflexology

Yes, it's the fiddling-with-feet treatment. Apparently, the foot reflects the body of a seated person with the toes relating to the head and the heel corresponding to the bottom. The instep area is like a map of the internal organs. For some reason, this absolutely brilliant diagnostic and therapeutic practice often manages to get a bad press. It may be because it's often offered at health spas and beauty salons and sometimes the masseurs are doing nothing more than that – massaging the feet. Actually, reflexology can hurt. The reflexologist stimulates certain points on the foot using his or her thumbs and, as with the Bowen technique, it is thought that this triggers the body to heal itself. When your energy (*chi*) is not flowing correctly and there is a blockage, you may feel a sharp stabbing pain. It's bearable (usually), so don't worry. If the practitioner really knows their stuff, they'll be able to diagnose conditions and potential problems from the points in the feet that correspond to different organs in the body.

Like acupuncture, reflexology has been used in China and India for thousands of years and the philosophy is that the life force, or what is known as *prana* in Indian practice, circulates in a rhythmic way around the body. If the energy is disrupted by injury, signals are transmitted down energy channels within the body to the feet. A trained therapist can then feel the affected areas by identifying points that feel like grains of sand under the skin. Hence it can be an excellent diagnostic tool as well as actually dispersing the 'blockages' and cleansing the area. I suppose that when we were all running around over uneven ground without shoes, it was nature's way of keeping us healthy by doing its own type of reflexology.

In the hands of a fully qualified prenatal practitioner, reflexology is very safe in pregnancy. It's best to wait until twelve weeks, but, after that, regular treatments are one of the best indicators of your internal health. Dr Gowri Motha uses reflexology as one of the main tools in her gentle birth programme. She also uses it when a woman has reached forty weeks to actually initiate contractions and labour. With my very long second labour, contractions had all but stopped when Gowri kick-started it again by stimulating certain reflex areas.

For general use, it can alleviate anxiety, stress, skin disorders and some injuries.

Try to get a personal recommendation and check out the Association of Reflexologists, 27 Old Gloucester Street, London WC1N 3XX, 01823 351010 (www.reflexology.org).

Creative healing

This is a treatment that is not widely known about in the UK but is used and taught by Dr Gowri Motha. It was apparently developed in England in 1874 by Joseph Stevenson, but he emigrated to America and continued to work as a therapist and teacher there.

It is widely known and practised in the States and that's where Dr Motha trained before she invited some of its main practitioners to England to teach it. Gowri now uses it extensively in her gentle birth method and teaches creative healing courses across the UK. (See www.gentlebirthmethod.com.)

To conclude, I've gained benefits from all of these treatments, although Bowen for me was the big revelation, even for serious muscular problems. So try them out if you can. If you just don't have the cash or you can't steal the time, get your partner or friend to give you a good rub down. It's all touch therapy!

Sue

Sue, 49, and feeling it! Married for 13 years, daughter Robyn, 7 going on 17! Reflexologist, aromatherapist, homoeopath in training.

Bright and early
On weekdays up at 6 a.m. to pack lunch bag for school. Take dog out, feed the fish in the pond. Large glass of mixed pineapple and orange juice to perk me up. Quick bowl of cereal, then off to get daughter up at 7.15. Weekends – crawl back under covers and wonder why night passed me by so quickly!

Typical brekkie
Juice (can't start without it), cereal and toast with lemon marmalade. Large mug of tea. Croissants in place of toast when feeling in the mood for celebrating. Always with organic butter.

Lunch
Being up early, feel very peckish by lunchtime. Something with pasta goes down a treat, or salad sandwich. Prefer hot food – gives me more energy and I find it more appetising.

Dinner
Usually something that doesn't take too much imagination or time. Maybe fish or chicken, and a pizza treat with a bottle of wine on Saturdays.

Drinks – water – bottled or tap?
Mostly water for me, sometimes wine for DH (darling husband!). If wine, always low-alcohol. Get tiddly otherwise! Sometimes organic squash or refresher. Always reverse osmosis filtered water. Don't drink coffee, always organic tea, not usually herb, mostly black, sometimes rooibosch.

Favourite superfoods I couldn't live without
My homemade cottage pie and my roast chicken dinners. Cheesy mashed potatoes, DH's chilli con carne.

Vitamins and minerals
Good quality multivit/mineral (always use Biocare) and Omega 3 supplement. Don't like oily fish except salmon, so necessary for me.

When I'm under the weather
A nice cuppa! And an occasional homemade chocolate chip muffin, I'm afraid.

Favourite treatments
I do them for others but never get them!

For exercise
Mostly walking, sometimes swimming. Never enough – does running up and down stairs count?

For relaxation
What's that? A good book. Dancing – ballroom and Latin American. Music from sixties and seventies. Chess. Good conversation.

Save my skin
Good old plain water. Haven't used skincare products for years. Chemicals make you look older. A healthy inside shows on the outside. Clean living too.

Sunscreen
Don't touch with a fifty foot bargepole. Too many carcinogenic chemicals. Could this be the reason for the explosion in the cases of skin cancer?

Haircare
Basic – shampoo every couple of days, occasional condition. Don't use colorants – haven't for many years now. I'm lucky – have few grey hairs at present. Always use essential oils of lavender, rosemary, sweet thyme in daughter's bath to 'dissuade' nits! She's never had them yet, either.

Feminine care
Always use pads - should use washable but have enough to do, so, regrettably am polluting the planet. Never use tampons. Have never got on with them and I don't like the way they work.

Menstruation tips - come back next time as a man! Menopause - can't wait! After ten years of nightmare periods it is going to be sooooooo liberating to leave periods behind me. I see it as a new chapter - hopefully one of wisdom and knowledge and quietness of mind and spirit.

Cleaning and laundry products
Vinegar. Bicarb of soda. Lemon juice. Borax if I could get it! Hydrogen peroxide if all else fails. And microfibre cloths, a brilliant invention. As for washing, working on that. Use salt to remove blood stains. Use Oxyclean for other stain removal. Use vinegar in final rinse. Still use Persil for wash. Haven't found anything better that gets the clothes clean.

Recycling and composting tips
We recycle paper, cardboard, glass, tins, plastic and chuck what we can in the composter. We've been composting for three years and have only needed to empty the bin once. Don't know how so much rubbish can produce so little compost! Use lime in the composter to deter flies. Looking for ways to deter wasps in summer. We have a 'dog loo' in the garden. That recycles dog poo! Saves adding to household rubbish.

Gardening naturally
Use any washing water on the garden. Use washing-up water on roses to deter aphids. Am going to try using essential oils on roses to try to eradicate blackspot. Will advise on efficacy in due course!

Babycare
Natural - first, last and always. Plain water for cleaning nappy area, cloth nappies (although I only found out their virtues after I'd used disposables - not proud of that). Only homoeopathy or aromatherapy for ailments. No oils, lotions, creams. No sun creams. Definitely no vaccinations or Calpol.

For the kids
Homoeopathy, aromatherapy, reflexology. Good children's multivit, Omega 3. Organic food wherever possible - especially dairy, bread and chicken.

Top parenting tips
Love them and show it - talk about everything. Breastfeed and co-sleep. Be proud of it! Don't vaccinate and don't medicate - educate yourself properly.

To revitalise my soul I go to...
... usually the sea - but definitely near running water.

The one thing I couldn't live without
My daughter.

Guilty secrets and imperfections
Secret!

If I had a magic wand, I would...
... eat less, exercise more - get a better figure. Lose weight. Love myself more. Stop beating myself up and expecting myself to be a perfect parent. A perfect parent doesn't exist. We just do the best we can with what we have available at the time - and it's usually good enough. Stop worrying about what has been and what might happen tomorrow. Enjoy this moment - that's why we call it the 'present'.

When friends enter a home, they sense its personality and character, the family's style of living – these elements make a house come alive with a sense of identity, a sense of energy, enthusiasm and warmth, declaring, 'This is who we are, this is how we live.

RALPH LAUREN

natural
home

Time to dust again
Time to caress my house,
To stroke all its surfaces
I want to think of it as a kind of lovemaking
… the chance to appreciate by touch
what I live with and cherish

GUNILLA NORRIS

Get Your House in Order

Cleaning and products

Cleaning is that horrendous, time-consuming, essential job that I hate – but I love the results. The smell of the cleaning products was the worst thing about having to clean my first flat. That stuff would give me a headache and bring me out in rash. OK, the thought of having to move my backside may have contributed but I now know what all this chemical muck does not only to our very fragile environment but also our very fragile health.

What our lovely global chemical conglomerates don't want us to know is that it's entirely possible to clean things 'naturally'. That doesn't just mean eco-friendly products, though they are fantastic for the most part, but things that are dead cheap, natural and easily available. Once you change your philosophical approach, it's so easy to do.

I've stayed many times at the fantastic place in Cornwall, Making Waves Vegan Guesthouse, which I've already mentioned, where the owners are so dedicated to the 'philosophy' that it's an inspiration! Boy, are they keen. This six-bedroom B&B is 'green' throughout. It's not just the cleaning: we're talking energy-efficient fridge freezers, low-water-consuming washing machines and dishwashers, organic paint on walls, furniture made from reclaimed wood (some of it driftwood), flooring made from seagrass or coir matting and even floorboards made from jute laid with adhesives and varnishes manufactured without the use of chemicals. They use organic unbleached cotton for bed linen and furnishings and rugs made from hemp or cotton coloured with vegetable dyes. I could go on but, believe me, being there is like a fresh sunny breeze for your senses. (See the chapter 'Beat a Retreat' and 'Imperfectly Natural People': Simon.)

At home, we become so attuned to the whiffs and ambience of background chemicals in our everyday surroundings that we just don't notice them any more but, rest assured, they're still there, still seeping their way into your body and doing their work.

There is a school of thought that regards the gradual depletion of our immune systems over the past fifty years as an effect of the long-term infiltration of multiple manmade substances in our everyday environments. Did you know that, when you buy a new carpet, the chemicals used in the production process are still present and detectable fifteen years later? Have you ever had your house damp-proofed or protected against woodworm? Think about that one. The companies who deal in woodworm prevention can offer 10-15-year guarantees to kill bugs in your house with one treatment. That means highly toxic chemicals are present and active in your living environment for as long as you are likely to stay there. (I have more to say on this in 'Healthy House – Your Home Loves You'.) The companies would argue that the toxins are within acceptable levels and therefore not harmful, but what's your opinion? I've certainly never seen the operatives work without breathing protection!

What am I coming to? Well, this is all part of the philosophy that the owner of the Making Waves Vegan Guesthouse is so passionate about. It is to be aware of the constant back-ground infiltration and cumulative effect of these domestic (and industrial) substances in our everyday lives and to ring in the changes. Come on, if one guy can clean and maintain a small hotel, I'm sure we gals and guys can manage it at home.

The totally naturalistic approach at Making Waves is something to aspire to, but I am of course imperfect and I must confess I've made my best progress on the cleaning bit. I was a tad worried when I threw away my aerosols and cream cleaners. Would my toilet ever be clean again? The answer was *Yes!* To achieve it, you'll need to stock up on:

- white vinegar (distilled if you can get it);
- bicarbonate of soda;
- soda crystals;
- borax (ask at a good independent chemist and they may order it in for you);
- commercial Epsom salts;
- household salt;
- lemons; and
- tea tree oil (see 'Tea tree oil' under 'Natural Cures for Common Ailments' above) and, if you like the smell, lavender oil.

You can clean just about everything with that lot!

Whenever possible of course just use a cloth and water. The best I've found are E-Cloths. Simply wet the microfibre cloth and 98 per cent of dirt and bacteria will be wiped away. They're machine-washable, too. If you've got any terry or cotton nappies you no longer need they make great cleaning cloths and will last for years. See www.e-cloth.com.

Experiment with different items for the best results. Often, I use a mix of water, distilled vinegar and a couple of drops of lavender oil and use the microfibre cloth, as it will clean surfaces, the loo, the bath or whatever. For a really stained loo I buy cheap cola and chuck it down, leaving it overnight if possible – and it works a treat. Denture tablets are more expensive but will really make it sparkle.

There are hundreds of 'recipes' but my fave is probably my ultra-cheap bathroom cleaner. I use a half litre bottle (a reclaimed washing-up liquid bottle) and fill with:

1½ cups bicarbonate of soda mixed with 1 cup filtered or distilled water
2 tablespoons white vinegar or lemon juice
½ drop of essential oil

If I'm feeling imperfect I add half a cup of liquid soap too. It works a treat!

Bicarbonate of soda

We refer to it as plain old 'bicarb', but, in technical terms it's 'sodium bicarbonate' or 'sodium hydrogen carbonate', a white crystalline or granular powder, commonly known as bicarbonate of soda or baking soda. It is soluble in water and very slightly soluble in alcohol. It gives off carbon dioxide gas when heated above about 50°C, a property made use of in baking powder, of which it is a component. It is also decomposed by most acids. The acid is neutralised and carbon dioxide is given off. The major use of sodium bicarbonate is in foods such as baked goods. It is used in effervescent salts and is sometimes used medically to correct excess stomach acidity. The important thing is that it's environmentally friendly and cheap.

I came across a great little leaflet many years ago called '200 fabulous frugal uses for Baking Soda'. As I understand it, bicarbonate of soda is much the same thing but it's sold in bigger quantities. There's a wealth of uses for it apart from aiding digestion and here are just a few. Once you start using it, you'll start to discover your own uses.

- Add bicarb to hot soapy dishwater. It will cut grease and speed removal of sticky foods on dishes and utensils.
- After washing, soak your dishcloth in bicarb and water, swish out the sink and wring out the cloth; everything will be odour-free.
- Use as a nonabrasive cleaner for stainless steel sinks.
- Mix with borax (two tablespoons of each) and make your own dishwasher detergent (add a drop of lemon oil or fresh lemon if you want extra freshness).
- Clean baby bottles with bicarb. Actually, nothing cleans plastic as well as bicarb, so make a paste and use with a sponge to scour plastic bowls. It won't scratch the surface.

- Fill vacuum flasks and teapots with a tablespoon of bicarb and water, let it stand and then rinse thoroughly. It will stop teapots and coffee pots from staining and you can also remove tea stains from mugs by rubbing on a paste of bicarb and water.

Here are some ideas to soak up smells (see also 'Air fresheners' below).

- Keep an open box of bicarb in your fridge to avoid odours, bin it and start afresh every three months or so.
- Sprinkle bicarb in the bottom of your kitchen bin before you insert a fresh bin liner.
- Sprinkle bicarb inside smelly shoes (oh, come on it can't just be me!) after wearing them and shake out excess powder the next morning, it will significantly reduce the whiff.
- Remove the smell of smoke from clothes by soaking in bicarb before washing.

Bicarb is also useful when it comes to washing clothes. See 'Those Washday Blues' for more on that. Meanwhile, there are, amazingly, even more uses for this wonder product. For instance, to clean jewellery, rub a paste of bicarb onto the piece, rinse off and buff dry.

Clean your oven with a paste of bicarb and elbow grease or, to clean really dirty ovens, add distilled vinegar. Wash appliance exteriors with a mix of ¼ cup bicarb, ½ cup clear vinegar, 1 cup household ammonia and 1 gallon hot water.

You can clean your windows with bicarb, and you can also wipe down your Venetian blinds with the stuff. Just about any surfaces can be cleaned with bicarb, even wood-work, and it can remove crayon marks from washable walls and linoleum floors.

Remove wine or grease stains from a carpet by sprinkling the bicarb on immediately, dabbing a little up, then leaving till the wine has been absorbed before vacuuming up any residue. Also, you can sprinkle bicarb over carpets every few weeks and leave it for a while, overnight if possible, before vacuuming the next day.

There are hundreds more uses, but you get the idea. This wonderful, versatile little gem is available from good chemists. Get as big a box as you can for economy's sake.

Soda crystals

Soda crystals are similar to bicarb but courser and with a granular texture, and definitely not for internal use! Use soda crystals weekly to flush out drains. Dissolve some crystals in hot water and flush down to neutralise odours and get rid of blockages. You can also clean worktops, floors and greasy cookers and pans with soda crystals and water and, like bicarb, they work well as a solution mixed with white vinegar to clean teapots and chopping boards. Try www. soda-crystals.co.uk to buy it in bulk.

Borax is a great old-fashioned 'powder' perfect for mixing with bicarb and excellent for laundry, (not to be ingested though!) You can usually get it in good chemists. Boots now stock it too.

It's always worth having plenty of household salt to mix with bicarb for many cleaning uses. Also, some recipes call for household ammonia. Just keep it out of reach of the kids!

Lemons and other natural solutions

No one ever dares throw away a lemon in my house. Even when it's wizened and long past its juicing days, it can be used for cleaning. Just a quick squirt will leave your sink or loo sparkling, and don't forget to slice off a bit of the rind and put that in the cutlery tray of the dishwasher for sparkly crockery but remember to remove it when you unstack, though, or else it will be oh so soggy.

Nowadays, it's easy to find ecologically friendly products made from natural substances that are biodegradable. Ecover is a well-known make of washing-up liquid, laundry liquid, lavatory cleaner, floor cleaner, fabric conditioner and other products. (See www.ecover.com) A great

new company is 'Natural Clean' founded by mothers Krysta and Felicia who wanted to avoid using toxic products around their children. Their product list includes a limescale remover, an orange degreaser and a lemon multi-purpose cleaner. See www. naturalclean.co.uk.

There are lots of websites that will help if you want to get really adventurous and make up your own cleaning preparations. Check out www.thenewhomemaker.com, which is an American site, so some of the products talked about there are not very easy to find here in the UK; but the principles are much the same.

If you have allergies it's even more important to clean without chemicals, and there are also many ways to help reduce allergens. My life changed when I finally found the right vacuum cleaner! For me it's the Miele Solution Hepa 700. Depending on whether you like uprights or cylinders and have lots of stairs to clean, choosing a vacuum is a very individual thing, but I would recommend you look for one with a HEPA filter, they do need to be changed approximately every year but they're worth it. You'll find lots of helpful tips at www.allergymatters.com. There is a list of all recognised allergies and an extensive list of suggestions as to what could help. Through the site you can buy allergy-proof bedding, dehumidifiers, air purifiers and pet allergy products. They also sell steam cleaners, even my cheap one, which I got via mail order from an ad in a Sunday paper, but it's been fine. Steam cleaners are wonderful for shifting stubborn dirt from surfaces, furnishings and even carpets, but don't forget that, once you've loosened the dirt, the wet mess still has to be mopped up!

Dishwasher powder

Once you stop using too many chemicals around the home you'll really notice the terrible chlorine-type smell that seems to come from some of the commercial dishwasher tablets and liquid detergents. It's easy and cheap to make your own dishwasher powder and as long as you're scrupulous about scraping all the food off the dishes first and rinsing them it's just as effective as the shop bought ones and oh so much kinder to the environment.

There are a few variations but try getting a large plastic container with a lid, mixing 2 cups of borax and 2 cups of baking soda with half a cup of salt and half of citric acid (which you can get in chemists) and giving it all a shake up. You can add a squeeze of lemon as you put it in the machine.

Personally, I find it hard to beat Ecover dishwasher tablets but if I run out I find you can just liberally sprinkle bicarbonate of soda across all the stacked crockery and add a bit of lemon rind to the cutlery tray - works a treat!

There's an excellent website www.ukparents.co.uk where you'll find some great 'recipes' for cheap eco-friendly household cleaning, general purpose cleaning 'solutions', oven cleaners, kettle descalers and a great recipe called 'gloop, no-more-detergent'. Just click on 'Forum info' and then 'Families on a budget'. You'll notice most of the recipes call for the same general ingredients – bicarbonate of soda, washing crystals, vinegar, essential oils, and salt. If you've got most of these you won't go far wrong. I'll make eco-warriors of you yet!

Burn, baby, burn

If like me you love open fires but hate buying coal and logs, check out eco-friendly fuel. There is a company selling recycled fire logs made from sawdust waste that has been processed into high energy fuel. The logs produce more heat than coal, create very little salt, are clean to handle and kind to the environment. The raw material comes from sustainably managed forests. They also make barbecue wood chips, natural pine firelighters and briquettes scented with cinnamon. (See www.ebc-ecofuel.co.uk.)

Why do we love certain houses, and why do they seem to love us? It is the warmth of our individual hearts reflected in our surroundings.

T H Robsjohn-Gibbings

Air fresheners

SHOCK, HORROR! IS YOUR AIR FRESHENER MAKING YOU ILL? That's the headline that greeted me one morning over my three minute organic egg and soldiers. The article below it concluded that people who used air fresheners (and furniture polish) were more likely to complain of headaches, nausea and stomach pains than those who didn't. Also, it could exacerbate symptoms of asthma.

Now, one scientist's fact is another's fiction, I know but, as with everything I'm talking to you about in this book, you have to absorb all the information you can (preferably information from people who don't have a vested interest), then trust your instincts. This study reckoned that women and children, perhaps because they spend more time in the home environment, were particularly affected. (Thanks, guys – rather obvious, you'd have thought). The research added that, generally, people were taking more and more days off sick from minor complaints. Now this is a fairly general observation, I know, and it relates to a whole host of issues concerning twenty-first-century life, but I believe that the alleged 'toxins' in everyday products, and products you may have been taking for granted for years, play a fairly major part. The more we zoom in on each little topic, as this article did, the more I believe we can address the problem.

The chemicals contained in some of these products are known as VOCs (volatile organic compounds). They're low-level toxins that have been linked to a wide range of diseases and skin irritations. Also deodorants, it was suggested, were to blame for the rise in ill health – and not just the aerosol kind. (See 'Save Your Skin' for alternatives to aerosol deodorants.) It won't surprise you to know I wholeheartedly believe all of that. You've only got to take a fleeting glance at the cocktail of chemicals in any aerosol can to know that it's going to be bad news.

So what are the alternatives? Well, air fresheners only mask a smell rather than attacking its source. So treat that first. Bicarbonate of soda is amazing for absorbing odours, as we saw earlier. Have you ever noticed that many of that 'shaky/powdery' types of freshener contain vast quantities of bicarb, anyway, and cost several times the raw bicarb cost? Why not cut out the middleman? Put some in a bowl and leave it next to smelly areas. Buy a big box. Don't bother with the tiny supermarket containers that are designed for cooking.

Plants are also wonderful for detoxing the home, absorbing vapours and releasing oxygen back into the atmosphere, thereby enhancing the air quality in your room. Remember those trailing spider plants we all had in the seventies that were very popular in student bedsits because they need zero care and attention? Research by NASA apparently found that just one spider plant can reduce dangerous levels of toxins in a room by over 90 per cent in 24 hours. They are also supposed to absorb the radiation from computers. Rubber plants are thought to be effective as well and, of course they're low-maintenance; they'll also survive with just a little bit of love and a wipe-down.

So, what if you want to introduce a nice fresh smell? There are a few ways. We all know the old trick of brewing fresh coffee and baking bread when we're trying to sell the house, but lemons are also a fabulous, if rather expensive, way to get rid of any lingering odours. If you can get hold of them cheaply, simmer four lemons cut into quarters on the hob for around 45 mins. Now there's a smell to give you a real kick. Also, as we saw earlier, you can pop lemon rind into the cutlery tray of the dishwasher. If lemons weren't any good, why would all the conglomerates proudly emblazon words like 'lemony fresh' over a whole host of their products?

If you want to whiz around with a spray (I know, there is something quite therapeutic about squirting something!), there's a very simple, very cheap alternative to chemical aerosols. Buy yourself a couple of plant spray bottles, at around £1.50 from any garden centre or bargain shop. Fill one with cold water and add two or three drops of essential oil. The choice is yours, depending on the smell you like, but I usually keep one on the go that just contains tea tree oil, since it is a pretty effective room deodoriser as well as a wonderful, natural, mild antiseptic.

For another quick room deodoriser, soak a flannel or a cotton nappy in warm water, add a few drops of tea tree oil and place it over a radiator (do not put it over or even near a naked flame). Or fine-mist the area with an atomiser filled with 250ml hot water five drops tea tree oil and five drops lavender oil. Shake it well before use.

Stand a bowl of steaming water in your room (safely out of reach of children, of course!), and add 5-10 drops of tea tree oil, or use an aromatherapy lamp/candle. An electric diffuser is the safest - again, placed out of the reach of the kids.

Add a few drops of tea tree oil and lavender oil to potpourri basket and place it on the floor under the radiator. For more on the wonders of this substance, see the section on 'Tea tree oil' under 'Natural Cures for Common Ailments' above.

A lot of these products that I've been banging on about are so (to use advertising speak) incredibly 'multiuse'. Dear Mother Nature has supplied us with so many little things that treat and deal with our everyday shenanigans and we are all in danger of forgetting about them. So pass this information on to your kids and hope they pass it to their kids! I believe that our dear old, well-intentioned scientific community will research for generations (chemical corporations reaping vast incomes in the interim) to eventually arrive back at the 'old wives' tale'. (Aren't maggots making a comeback? Seriously, and it's not the topic of this book, I know, but there is ongoing research about the amazing ability of maggots to clear infections and wounds where all else has failed. Remember, scientific innovations can become mainstream in a generation, whereas 'nature's own' can boast the benefit of hundreds of years of being tried and tested.)

Back on topic, I keep another plant spray on the go that has lavender oil and maybe a drop of geranium to lift my spirits. Other great ones are lemon oil and citronella, which both help scare off the wasps and mosquitoes in summer. Also, tea tree or eucalyptus with niaouli is excellent if anyone in the family is coming down with a cold or flu.

I have a quick spray around once a day after cleaning or whenever a particular area needs it. Obviously, the water needs changing every few days. Even water with essential oils will start to whiff a little if left too long, as my husband so delicately pointed out when I forgot and used a bottle of lavender and water that had been kicking around for a couple of weeks – It smelled like a gents' urinal (well, only he would know!).

The spray will cost you in the region of £2 for the bottles and the oils at around £4 each and will last you ages.

If you do want to throw money at it and prefer a professional bottle on your shelf, you won't go wrong with the fabulous room sprays from Spiezia Organics. Using essential oils, they make an office spritz and a real 'zingy' bathroom one. Their range is 100 per cent organic too, (www.spieziaorganics.com). Theres also some excellent natural sprays and cleaning liquids fragranced with essential oils from www.homescents.co.uk.

Those Washday Blues

Now here's a man after my own heart! Richard Pashley, an English scientist living in Australia, has found a way of cleaning clothes without using detergent! He found that, if you remove tiny air particles from water, dirt disperses in the water as fine droplets. It's a process known as 'degassing'. It acts more like a solvent, readily mixing with oil and grease, thereby lifting the most stubborn stains from your clothes. Wow! This could be a bright new future!

Imagine washing machines, dishwashers and the like, all cleaning beautifully without the need for any soap at all. Well, good luck, Richard – let's hope the chemical giants don't have you tied to a rocket ship and blasted into outer space. In the meantime, detergents are with us for a while yet.

I've never liked using conventional detergents for laundry. I've tried using the nonbiological liquid rather than powder, but still find my skin feels dry and flaky. Also, if you care about the effect on the environment, here's a fantastic 'green' alternative that is very cost-effective and has no smells – and works.

Balls

Yes, I'm talking balls, supercharged laundry balls, one of today's best-kept secrets! I'm astounded that more people don't know how brilliant these little wonders are. (I suspect the manufacturers don't have the marketing budgets that big detergent companies have.) Basically, they're little balls that are placed in the washing machine instead of regular detergent. They contain pellets, which produce ionised oxygen, activating the water molecules naturally, allowing them to penetrate deep into the clothing fibres to lift away the grime. They are totally environmentally friendly, unperfumed, nontoxic and very gentle to fabrics. Also, they are hypoallergenic and particularly suitable for babies and children, though you may have to remove the really stubborn stains from garments first. They also help to soften the water, so there is no need for fabric softener and, amazingly, they last for around a thousand washes, so they work out considerably cheaper than conventional detergents and are 'kinder' to the average washing machine. I'm a big fan and have been using them for about five years, and I don't stink (do I?). They can also be used for clothes that need hand-washing and often come with an eco-friendly stain remover.

Remember, if you actually want a slight fragrance 'à la fabric softener', add one or two drops of lavender oil in the fabric softener compartment.

You can get the Aquaball, which costs around £15 for a pair, by going to www. aquaball.com or www.healthyhouse.co.uk. There is also Eco-Ball, which sells for approximately £29.99 for a set of three plus stain remover and refill pellets (www. ecozone.co.uk).

The Sensitive Skincare Company now also offers natural washing balls. See 'Save Your Skin' above for details.

Nuts

We're talking soapnuts. I must confess I don't use these as often as I use the eco-balls, mainly because I'm lazy or rushed off my feet. However you look at it, I can't talk about 100 per cent natural detergents without mentioning soapnuts. Their proper name is – wait for it – 'sapindus mukorross!' and they've been used to wash clothes and linens in India and Nepal forever.

They're NOT actually nuts. They are a berry. They are not part of the nut family and won't cause any nut allergy (and they're a renewable resource).

They grow as a cluster of berries, each containing a small, black seed. The outer bit of the berry, the fruit, is tough and leathery and full of saponin that acts like soap when it comes into contact with water. At one time you used to have to crack the seeds with a mini-hammer – the kids loved it but I felt as though I needed the engine running to head for Casualty, but the good news now is that several companies sell soapnut shells that already come in a little muslin bag (see directory). The seed is useless for anything except growing a new tree so pre-cracked shells get you more cleaning power for your money!

For an average load of washing you need seven or eight half-shells added to the drum with the clothes. Put them in an old sock or a muslin bag. As with the eco-balls, they help to retain the colour and brightness of fabrics and there's no need for softener.

You can also make an infusion by boiling the nuts, and the amazing thing is that it's said to make a fantastic shampoo that leaves your hair really soft and silky and protects against head lice. It can also be used as a general cleaner for kitchens and bathrooms, and even to clean the car. I think I've just re-convinced myself, actually! Soapnuts are 100 per cent natural, so great for anyone with allergies, and totally environmentally friendly. They are also very economical at around £3 for 100g (they reckon 1kg will do at least 100 washes). You can buy them from www.ethicstrading.com, www.soapods.com or the wonderfully named www.inasoapnutshell.com.

Happy washing!

If you want to add just a bit of brightness to your white wash, bicarbonate of soda will do the trick, as we saw earlier, as will old-fashioned borax and a couple of tablespoons of white vinegar in the rinse cycle. (See 'Bicarbonate of soda' under 'Get Your House in Order'.)

If balls or nuts are just not for you, make sure you use an eco-friendly laundry detergent. Ecover's Integrated non bio powder is excellent as is their fabric softener. It's way kinder to the environment than that gloopy stuff! Ecover also make 'laundry bleach', which really does whiten your whites.

It goes without saying, of course, that, if you get an opportunity, wait for a nice day and hang your whites outside to dry. If they're yellowed or stained, squirt them with bit of lemon juice. It mixes beautifully with the sunshine and they come up like new.

I told you I was imperfect! We've talked about eco-friendly washing powder, laundry balls, vinegar, borax and bicarbonate of soda, but here's a product that as yet I haven't found a totally natural, old-fashioned and cheap alternative for.

I came across this when I first started using washable nappies – shamefully, not till my third baby was born. I quickly realised that I wouldn't always have the luxury of being able to do an exclusively white wash, so there were times when the whole lot had to go in together – hence red dye from boy's T-shirt turns white nappy pale pink. We had to warn our three-month old boy not to go up to the Arsenal football ground in that!

It was actually the local 'nappy lady' working for an environmental group who told me about this little wonder item. She said, 'Oh, I always mix coloured items with white. I just use a colour catcher.' Now I'd seen 'dream catchers' in New Age shops but somehow, I thought, unless she is destined for a higher life as a washer woman, she couldn't mean that. So off I went to the supermarket and bought Glo

Care – 'the sheet that catches and holds colour runs'. In the box there are twenty sheets of what look like blotting paper. You simply pop one at the back of the drum of the washing machine and wash as normal. When you unload the washing you find a now dirty funny-coloured bit of old blotting paper and throw it away. Incredibly, the makers claim that 'each Colour Catcher sheet is bio-degradable and NOT harmful to the environment', so I'm still doing my bit. It's amazing how it works. The sheet acts like a magnet catching all those traces of dye that usually go into the washing water and discolour the clothes.

If you use one every time, they work out quite expensive (they're around 15 pence per sheet), but I've saved many a small boy's shirt from being 'tie-dye pink', so I think they've paid for themselves. I'm sure there are other brands on the market and, if you know of a homemade version of the same thing, let me know. Check them out at www.colourcatcher.co.uk.

When it comes to aiming for an eco-friendly wash day, it must be said that most of us don't fare well. Of course we should use a short wash cycle or economy programme and, to save money if you use a washing machine and tumble dryer most days, you'd do well to get your electricity priced on Economy 7 or your supplier's equivalent because these appliances simply guzzle units of electricity, particularly tumble dryers. We've all been sold a bit of a pipe dream when it comes to these expensive items. Yes, they've got reverse action and we can get the clothes completely dry, but at what cost to our pockets and our clothes? It's well documented that the majority of fabrics will last longer if they're not tumbled around in extreme heat and you'll have noticed that, if you put T-shirts and tops in there after a few times, the fabric starts to 'bobble'.

Of course most of us aren't going to get rid of our tumble dryers completely, but here's another little tip that you probably won't read anywhere else. I predict this little plug will do great things for the second-hand furniture shops or junk emporiums across the UK. If you regularly need to dry off your laundry quickly, get yourself an old-fashioned spin-dryer. Yes, the top-loading drum type that you will remember your mum had. In fact, if you go and ask your mum, aunt or grandma now she'll say, 'Oh, yes, my old spin-dryer was wonderful. I really don't know why I got rid of it.' Well they got rid of it because washing machines offered high spin speeds and we were told tumble dryers were better, but there is a world of difference.

I came to realise this when I had a run of guests staying at my house one winter. I needed to wash and dry four or five sets of bedding and towels in a few hours and I didn't have the luxury of hanging anything outside. I saw a Creda Debonair spin-dryer looking all sad and sorry in the corner of a local antique/junk store and thought that at £20 it was worth a try. I did my usual short wash and fast spin and then loaded as much as I could get into the drum of the spin-dryer. Some have a front outlet so you have to stick a pan under it to catch the water. Mine has a pump with a pipe that you hang into the sink or drain. I pressed down the top and watched it vibrate (no gags about desperate housewives, please!). To be honest, I wasn't expecting anything to happen, as the laundry had already been on a 1,400 spin cycle in my washing machine as usual, but, sure enough, first a trickle and then a torrent of water came gushing out for about two minutes. I gingerly opened up the drum and, lo!, almost completely dry laundry. To get that dry in my tumble dryer would have taken over an hour.

You'll find most of them have a 4kg load and 2,800rpm spin speed. As with so many things in the States, they're ahead of us or still behind, depending on how you look at it, so they're still widely available there. In the UK you can buy them in most electrical stores, but I couldn't find anywhere that had them in stock. There's no call for them, I was told, so they have to order them in. Well, if you're anything like me, once you've made up your mind, you want the item now!

Let's see if we can start a revival in old-fashioned appliances. My mum says no way is she going back to her old mangle, though.

Dump the Junk – Space Clearing for Mortals

My dear wise friend Janice, at great expense, once commissioned a consultation with a renowned feng shui master. He came, he looked, he studied, he contemplated. He looked at the direction of the house, the river backing onto the garden, the tall trees at one side and the sloping driveway. Hand on chin, he was deep in thought for what seemed like, well, quite a long time. Janice and the master sat and, after a cup of green tea and a hobnob, he clasped his hands and quietly delivered his conclusion. 'You move,' he said.

Now for a strict feng shui assessment, he may well have been right but, needless to say, Janice wasn't about to move house, having moved in only three months earlier. What am I getting at here? Well, I'm not about to slag off feng shui. I actually think it's conceptually wonderful, but, if you think about it, you can bring it all down to lovely old common sense. Maybe not the mathematical/astrological bit, but that's the bit I wouldn't get too bogged down with anyway. Remember, feng shui was created in ancient China in an environment not too similar to twenty-first century Western life. So let's take the good bits that relate to us and our way of life!

'Feng Shui is so passé, darling,' I actually heard a woman say in London the other day. She's right to a certain extent. We did all become obsessed with it and what it could do for us in a 'go-getting' eighties sort of way. We all took the advice about placing the mirror on this wall, moving the fish tank over there, and shifting the rubbish bin out of the wealth corner – but did we do the really important bit – the bit that any consultant would, no doubt, have identified as being the most important? That is clearing out the clutter. It's now more fashionable to talk 'space clearing', which means literally clearing space. It's a good rule of thumb. You just have to be rid of the old for the new to come in.

Most of us live surrounded by an astounding array of, well, stuff we don't use or need. It takes over our lives, we can't find anything when we need it and we feel our energy dip every time we open the cupboard or look behind the cloakroom door. There's a great rule here: if you haven't used it in six months and it's not beautiful to look at, bin it!

I'd come across a fantastic book by Karen Kingston called *Creating Sacred Space with Feng Shui*. If you're looking for any book on the subject, this is the one to get. It's beautifully and simply written and totally inspirational. Karen herself is a space-clearing and feng shui expert and simply the best I've come across at putting this in an understandable way that connects with me. The book gives you excellent instructions on how to space-clear your own home. I couldn't get Karen to give me a consultation (she lives in Bali, I think) but I knew I wanted someone like her, someone who could speak my language (in the metaphorical sense).

I first heard of Dinka Cinnamon (great name, eh?) when we moved into our new home. The house had been lived in by a variety of people for over two hundred years and I could only imagine held a ragbag of possibly tattered lives. I'd learned from Karen's book that buildings retain energies and soak up patterns and emotions from people who have lived there. I needed to clear out the old energies to refresh the place and bring in the new. When I first chatted with Dinka I knew that this would be her first priority. We had the luxury of a week or so 'turnaround' to move, so, while the new place was still empty, I asked her to come and sort us out. It was interesting as I waited for her in that empty, cold house that was to become our home. I could feel the sadness and the fear in the walls. A builder popped in to survey some work. 'Spooky old place, isn't it?', he said. 'Don't worry, love. It'll be all right when you've got your bits around you'.

Dinka arrived with her little box of tricks, slowly walked around the whole house to work out the *bagua* (the directions and what each area corresponds to) and then she set to work. She set up a kind of altar right in the centre of the house, lit some candles and began her journey from room to room. To be honest, I'm not sure what she did. I went out for a walk and from the top of the street I could hear the sound of tribal drumming and chanting. A neighbour stopped me in the street. 'What do you think is going on in there?' she asked. I shrugged. 'Sounds a bit odd,' she said. Little did she know she was facing one of her new 'odd' neighbours. But I'll tell you what: when I went back in, it was like entering a different space. She'd opened all the windows to let in fresh air and it *felt* different. Dinka had 'clapped out' the corners (as she calls it) and cleared the energies of the centuries of previous dwellers. She'd also used dowsing rods and found a couple of lines of geopathic stress, one running directly over where we were about to place our beds, which was bad news from the start!

After she'd cleared the energies, she looked at the specifics of the layout of the rooms. This semidetached house was a conversion, and the *bagua* literally had a bit missing. What would once have been the centre of the house had been divided, so we had a long narrow corridor leading from the back door to the stairs, which meant that, effectively, the whole of one side of the house was missing in terms of the complete *bagua*. Dinka said this missing bit corresponded to our fortune corner, so it was very important to boost this area. She suggested we represent greenery and tall trees in that area to boost fortune. Now we love contemporary art but I'd never thought of putting up pictures of trees. We found some, though, and some inspirational posters of Muir Woods in California, which we'd visited, and we put a whole range of them along the wall. It was amazing how good they looked! We can never be sure if it was down to the pictures but our fortunes were good in that house.

Dinka made suggestions as to where we should place certain items of furniture and decorative pieces, and she also asked us what we wanted to achieve and what was going on in our lives. At the time my husband needed more work. He is a TV composer and work had seemed to dry up. Dinka pointed out the area in the house that corresponded to our 'helpful friends and contacts' corner. She suggested we boost this by putting items or pictures that represent our work there, such as a telephone and a picture of a TV or something that DH could identify with his work.

There was no phone point there but we did have a great contemporary art piece – a picture of a telephone. I went off to work and an hour later got a phone call from Simon. 'You'll never guess what,' he said. 'You got a new commission!' I said. 'Looks like it. I had to down tools while I was putting up the picture to answer the phone and it was not one, but two commissions!' Incredible!

> " Out of clutter find simplicity. From discord find harmony. In the middle of difficulty lies opportunity.
>
> ALBERT EINSTEIN "

Does it work for everything in such a literal and pictorial way? Some years later when we needed childcare, I called Dinka and asked what to do. She said, 'Go to your "helpful friends" corner and put something there that represents what you need.' I said, 'Well, I've got a little framed picture of Mary Poppins.' (Don't even *ask* why.) 'Perfect,' she replied. Julie Andrews didn't come flying over my rooftops but I did place an ad in the sweet shop. I had just one phone call, from the perfect mother's help, who stayed with us for five years!

'You're just lucky,' friends have said to me, but I don't think so. The techniques haven't always worked for me, either, but I think that, when something is meant to be, if you are really specific about what it is you want, and you put your intentions there, you attract towards you what it is that you need (that is, as long as it's for the greater good).

Dinka Cinnamon is available for consultations and her website is www.fengshui 4you.co.uk (see also 'Imperfectly Natural People': Dinka). If you don't want a consultation, just get Karen Kingston's book. I can't recommend it enough.

Of course there's much you can do when it comes to space clearing. At its most basic, it's just the new version of the old spring clean.

Don't do it yourself

205 DUMP THE JUNK

Trinny and Susannah would have a field day round at my place. I'm a hoarder when it comes to clothes. I'll do my best to look a million dollars but in a £6.99 kind of way. True to my cheapskate ideals, I'll get all my designer gear from discount outlets and Oxfam. 'It's because she's from the North – always likes a bargain,' my husband says fondly whenever I'm wearing a nice bit of 'charity shop chic'. Consequently, I've got loads of clothes, many of them mistakes, some just worn out and some just don't fit me or suit me any more.

Although I knew it would help me to get my wardrobe (or, to be precise, three wardrobes plus drawers) in order, I just never could seem to get round to it. Whenever I tried to attack the pile, the phone would go, the kids would kick off, or I'd find a lovely old polka-dot thing that I'd forgotten about and nostalgia would halt me in my tracks. Then I'd be on the phone for 45 minutes with the friend who was with me when I bought it! We've all been there, haven't we, trying to clear out the attic and then coming across a box of old photos? And that's it: nothing gets done.

In the end, I had to throw money at it. Naomi Saunders is an author and also a 'clutter doctor'. She is a woman who has talents I do not. She is the most incredible organiser, cleaner and clutter clearer you can ever imagine. She markets her business as being 'helping hands' to do whatever needs doing', whether it is clearing out your attic, packing your boxes as you prepare to move house, sorting out all your old photographs, dealing with stuff after a bereavement. A sort of 'stuff genius', she came in and whipped through my clothes, my makeup and my toiletries (which were in a frightful state) in no time.

I was embarrassed at first. This was a stranger going through my dirty washing but she put my mind at rest and I realised that, rather like a doctor, she'd seen it all before. She brought all her own equipment, sorted, chucked and helped me decide on the 'not sures'. She cleaned and organised the room and then left with a mountain of bin bags full of clothes for the charity shop (she absolutely refused to tell me which charity shop – just in case!).

Shell-shocked I was, but my life has been changed since. It was expensive, at around £20 an hour, but for around £100 I saved a fortune and my sanity. Naomi unearthed clothes that I'd bought and never worn and items and accessories I hadn't realised would go together to transform certain outfits. What a star! For the first time in years I could actually see what was in my wardrobe and on my dressing table. Somehow, I'd created more options than I had before. I can't say that a year on it still looks quite that way, but now I try hard to clear out ruthlessly and often and, once I get started, I find it both cathartic and energising. Karen Kingston suggests starting with just one drawer.

It's amazing how, once you've cleared, you get a newfound energy and want to continue till the whole room is done.

The main point here is to get rid of stuff and, if you don't want to pay an expert such as Naomi, get someone to do it for you. There are lots of companies like this across the UK and, if your funds dictate that you really must do it yourself, then try to team up with a friend whose life also needs a declutter. Let her loose in your wardrobe, basement or whatever and let her sort the piles. Someone else's perspective is fantastic and they won't get sidetracked by the old photos or be tempted to hold onto that dress that's two sizes too small just because you wore it on your first date. It's painful, but a sort of nice pain, and, boy, do you feel good afterwards!

Here are Naomi's top tips for de-cluttering -

- Clear one area at a time
- Stay focused on the end result - reclaiming your space
- Don't dither - if in doubt , chuck it out
- Ask yoursef if all this stuff makes you feel good
- Put on your favourite music
- Make separate piles (cherish, charity, chuck)
- Do remember, you will always enjoy space more than stuff
- Fill your life, not your home.

Naomi's book is *Simplify your life - Downsize and De-stress* Naomi Saunders Sheldon Press. www.clearlyorganised.co.uk. Rosi Flood also offers a complete styling service, clearing your clutter and revamping your wardrobe. She also offers personal shopping. Email info@rosiflood.co.uk.

If it's not just storerooms and wardrobes full of old stuff but your daily life that is cluttered, if you can't even get a new packet of sugar out of the cupboard without a mountain of teabag boxes falling on you or can't find a comb in your handbag for the tangled-up bunch of receipts, lipsticks and loose change, then you need flying lessons! A wonderful website that's full of fantastic tips is to be found at www.flylady.net. Here's where you'll find a myriad of house-cleaning and organising tips. This hilarious American woman shares her daily routines and injects great humour into it all. As she says, 'If you're living in CHAOS (Can't Have Anyone Over Syndrome), it's time to do something about it.' You can sign up to receive daily tips and suggestions and, if the whole idea still seems overwhelming, start with what she calls 'flying lessons', the 'fly lady's' very own suggestions for clearing clutter in a few easy steps. See also Organized Home at www.organizedhome.com.

A great way to recycle your unwanted items is to join www.freecycle.org.

Have nothing in your home that you do not know
to be useful and believe to be beautiful

WILLIAM MORRIS

Dinka

Dinka Cinnamon, 39, married with two children, Max, 4, and Abigail, 8. Living in north London. Feng shui consultant (www.fengshui4you.co.uk).

Bright and early
Alarm goes off at 6.30 a.m. Waking up the kids, getting ready, rushed breakfast, have to leave the house at 730 a.m.

Typical brekkie
Normally eat after dropping the kids off. Cup of black organic Earl Grey, no sugar. Rye crackers with apricot jam (love it!) or porridge or yoghurt.

Lunch
Sometimes skip lunch (I know it's bad!). Smoked salmon/tuna salad/salad.

Dinner
Fish or chicken/salad (my husband makes the best salad dressing in the world)/rice.

Drinks - water - bottled or tap?
Water (we have reverse osmosis system in the house), green tea, no caffeine, glass of organic red wine for dinner.

Favourite superfoods I couldn't live without
Dark chocolate (ha-ha-ha!)

Wild horses wouldn't get me to eat...
... fast food from burger bars, meat.

Vitamins and minerals
Blue-green algae.

When I'm under the weather
Royal jelly capsules.

Favourite treatments
Massage

For exercise
Go to gym (did every day before going skiing!), otherwise don't do enough.

For relaxation
Try to meditate regularly (TM); if that does not work, go shopping.

Save my skin
Dr Hauschka products - I swear by them.

Sunscreen
Gosh! I need about factor 100 - Jason's.

Favourite beauty products
Stilla eye shadow.

Haircare
Mop products.

Cleaning and laundry products
Ecover products.

Recycling and composting tips
Fortunately, Haringey council has given us new boxes and will now take almost everything for recycling.

Gardening naturally
Use only natural/organic stuff.

Pets
We tried our cat on organic foods and he had diarrhoea! Now only the cheapest food works with him.

For the kids
They like 'animal' vitamins and eating organic. We start the day with fresh juice that we make. Never had Calpol!

Top parenting tips
I wish I had any! I think eating meals together is great bonding!

To achieve balance in my life
I have problems with that one at the moment!

To revitalise my soul I go to...
We went skiing recently – did wonders for me.

The one thing I couldn't live without
Green & Black's chocolate.

Guilty secrets and imperfections
What a long list this could be!

If I had a magic wand, I would...
... eat less/drink less/do more exercise/have more fun with my children/shout less at my husband.

Healthy House – Your Home Loves You

I'm certainly not your average DIY type (though I have been credited with the occasional builder's bum when I wear those terrible hipster jeans!), so this is a tricky subject for me to write about. However, this stuff is so important that I have to tell you what I've discovered.

Your home is your second skin. I've been banging on about cleaning products, skincare, the food that you consume, all manner of stuff that, on a daily basis, can affect your wellbeing, adversely or otherwise. But have you ever thought of the other products that surround you all the time: your walls, your carpets, the paint on your ceiling? Had any woodworm treatment or damp-proofing work lately?

You probably spend more than half your life at home, so isn't it good to know the history of just what's gone on and what may still be going on in your home? Just check when DH (Darling Husband) or your local Mr Odd Job arrives home with the latest can of anti-fungus-kill-rot plaster treatment in pastel pink for the bathroom redecoration and ask yourself a few questions about what it contains. Probably no one will know the answer.

Woodworm and damp treatments are a big bone of contention with me. I recently acquired an 1820s house. After years of living in a modern property, I wanted to trade my 'white' house for a 'brown' one. The first issue was the damp, so what's the first thing you do? Phone the damp company. And there's the lesson I mentioned earlier: never get advice from someone who has a vested interest. Apparently, I was going to need 'tanking/chemical injections/dry walling/ floor membranes' – the works. It might as well have all been in Klingon to me. In short, it meant a layout of about £5,000 – and who would supply and install all of this? Why, my very same friendly damp-proofing company! Now this is not a very girly subject, so I got on the Net, seeking enlightenment as well as friendly advice from organisations such as the Society for the Protection of Ancient Buildings, or SPAB (www.spab.org.uk).

Old houses need to breathe. New ones are different: they were made to keep moisture out. But the older ones work best by living in harmony with the elements, rather like people. Most houses built up to the 1940s have been working perfectly happily keeping us dry and warm without the intervention of modern treatments, perhaps containing potentially carcinogenic chemicals that will remain in your home environment for as long as you are there.

All a damp company is concerned about is the absence of moisture, not the possible adverse effects of such drastic intervention on your house or on you.

How did I fix the damp problems? I put a fan in the bathroom; I had a wall replastered with lime plaster (a porous plaster that absorbs moisture and releases it evenly); I put little vents in the chimney breasts, since a lot of damp is the result of blocking up natural sources of ventilation; I cleared out the gutters, which can get blocked and cause damp problems; I repointed a small bit of brickwork with lime mortar (this lime business has almost become a religion – ask the people at SPAB); and, lastly, I created a good balance of heating and ventilation in the house. The saving? Well, aside from the prevention of any damage to my lungs if my walls had been injected with substances that the damp company's contractors would go to great lengths to avoid inhaling themselves, about £4,000.

I became fascinated with this whole issue of looking after buildings – especially old ones. Houses built before the thirties had the benefit of several centuries of tried and tested construction methods. Believe me, by the beginning of the twentieth century they certainly knew how to build them. Concrete, meanwhile, was not invented until the 1920s, and we're still paying the price. There is a whole group of professionals in the UK who see the damp-proofers, wood-rot specialists, double-glazing companies and concrete merchants as the 'enemy'. They are firmly against these companies who claim to improve the quality of our housing infrastructure by leading homeowners away from cheap, simple, holistic building maintenance solutions into expensive, complicated and potentially damaging ones – damaging not only to the buildings but also our health.

If you live in an old house, here's a tip for you. A modern fix for an old house is usually bad news. Always look for the simple solution and here's a little anecdote to reinforce that. A friend had damp on an outside wall. The damp-proofing company advised the whole works, including chemicals and a new damp-proof course. The quote for the job was £6,000. A SPAB member came to give a second opinion. He saw that the ground level against the wall was slightly too high (above the damp-proof course), so the gardener dug away a small trench (about six inches deep) against the affected wall, effectively lowering the level at which the soil touched the brickwork. Problem solved. The cost? Thirty quid (gardeners aren't cheap round her way!).

Here's another tip. In an old house when hubby wants to get a wall repointed (that's filling in the cement gaps in between the brickwork), check that it's suitable for 'lime' repointing. Most builders will want to use cement, but lime will allow the joins to breathe and release moisture instead of sealing it inside your wall and possibly creating more penetrating damp.

If you have a woodworm inspection, the chances are you'll be advised to go for a chemical treatment. Now you may have a few boreholes in some bits of old wood, but these may have been dormant for a hundred years. Tape sheets of paper over areas of boreholes and leave for a few weeks. If your bugs are active you will see new holes in the paper. If not, they're probably long gone. Too simple, eh? It certainly is for a company that wants to sell you – and inject – large quantities of very strong poisons into all your wood-work. And these are poisons that will re-main active (and you will be breathing) for the next twenty years, according to their guarantees. One problem is that mortgage companies require a woodworm treatment 'certificate'. That's one problem I don't have a solution for.

There's some great advice on how to care for old buildings in Richard Oxley's *Survey and Repair of Traditional Buildings* (Don-head), and Janet Collings' book *Old House Care and Repair* (Donhead). And SPAB are a fantastic organisation always willing to give advice.

I've dwelled a bit here on damp and woodworm, but there's a whole holistic approach to looking after your home, old or new. Organic and eco-friendly paints and natural floor finishings are available, again reducing the toxins in your rooms. Find them at www.ecospaints.com and www.auro.co.uk.

At www.greenbuildingstore.co.uk (01484 854898), you'll find eco-friendly paints and wood finishes and the 'Ecoplus sys-tem' high-performance timber doors and windows (environmentally friendly mate-rials). There's also a rainwater drainage system that's a solid-steel alternative to PVC guttering and ultra-efficient WCs. Similar products can also be found at www.ecomerchant.co.uk.

If you want to look into installing a 'so-lar system', you can now get 100 per cent solar electric pumps that join on to your existing pipes (www.solartwin.com). For advance solar collectors, boilers and heat pumps for heating and hot water, try www.greensystemsuk.com.

When it comes to energy efficiency I must confess another imperfection. I live in a draughty old house that costs a fortune to heat. I also love my open fires and don't want to seal them up. But I do at least make sure I get environmentally friendly wood, fuels and firelighters, as they're easier to light than regular logs and kinder to the environment. (See www.ebc-ecofuel.co.uk.)

For very special organic candles without any carcinogens being released into the air, try www.naturalmagicuk.com. Organic aromatherapy candles are around £30 each. It's much cheaper to buy pure bees-wax candles and put a couple of drops of aromatherapy oil in the candle holder or on the actual candle if it's large enough.

There are so many other little things we can do to conserve energy too. We are all aware that by turning our thermostat down by just one degree we could save in the region of £30 a year. Switching the

TV off altogether instead of leaving it on standby overnight can save the quids over time, too. Many of us are already on to energy-saving light bulbs, which seem expensive at first but result in a huge saving in the long run.

Saving water

Turning off the tap, having fewer baths and reducing the water we use in the garden is obvious stuff, but an enormous amount of water is flushed down the loo every day. There are now water-saving toilets available. See the green pages of the *Ecologist* for stockists. But, if you're not about to buy a new loo and you want to spend just a few quid, get a Hippo. These are ingenious little things. The Hippo is made from durable heavy-gauge polyethylene, which opens up, origami style, into an open-ended box shape when installed. It sits happily in the water underneath the large cistern float. When the toilet is flushed, the water confined within the Hippo is the volume saved. The Hippo also has a small hole that acts like a relief valve, allowing slow circulation of water to prevent stagnation and evaporation. They work better on older toilets, where the volume of water lost is greater, anyway, but they're not bad at a saving of approximately three litres of water per flush. Of course, they'll save you money too if your water is metered.

The good thing is that they're simple to install: you just pop it in the cistern. They're great value, too, at about £7 for a pack of three. (See www.hippo-the-watersaver. co.uk.) For general water-saving ideas go to www.environment-agency.gov.uk.

Carpets

Beware of some of those professional treatments that make your carpets like new. They can continue to release solvents into your room for a long time, and you could be living in your very own solvent-abuse den! Better still, get rid of the carpets altogether, have hard flooring and rugs, preferably made from sisal or jute.

Sadly for me, it's not an option to lose the lounge carpet, but I make sure I use a vacuum cleaner with a HEPA filter (see page 191) and scrub away at the stains with bicarbonate of soda and a few drops of lavender oil. Steam cleaners are excellent for carpets, too. There are now 'scary detergent free' professional carpet cleaning services available. www.Direct-cleaners.com.

EMFs

A couple of years ago, I took the kids to an amazing holistic homoeopath named Grace Hall. Using a very powerful diagnostic machine (similar to those used in Vega testing for allergies), Grace could detect unusually high electromagnetic frequency (EMF) levels in my youngest. We found, after a report from our friendly feng shui consultant, I hasten to add, that there were high EMF levels in the wall of his bedroom right next to where he slept!

There was a bottleneck of electrical cables embedded in the wall. We moved his bed away from the wall and, one month later, his EMF levels were back to normal. Everyone's home has electricity but this shows how hidden things in your house can create a potential problem.

In a few years, I may have my little castle as clean and safe as I can get it but, in the meantime, I am going to be extra aware of everything to do with my home surroundings. It's outside that we normally feel vulnerable and home is traditionally our safe environment – but let's not get complacent. It's worth being aware of lurking dangers around us all the time. After all, we spend most of our lives at home. Think of your home as you do your body! Your home really will love you, but only if you love and nurture it in return.

Plants

For years, I had my student bedsit festooned with spider plants and rubber plants. I can't admit to talking to them or even watering them very often, but, amazingly, they survived. Years later it surprised me to read that these hardy plants, along with many other types, are incredibly beneficial.

Many of us now have an office in our home. Often we have several computers, a television and various bits of electronic equipment, and it's worrying to learn about their negative effects on us in a confined space.

Let's look at computers first. I've found using a good quality anti-glare filter helps a lot but, when sitting close to a VDU, you are being bombarded by lots of different emissions. Among the practical things you can do are give your eyes a break as often as possible and try to restrict your time to no more than four hours a day. You should also sit as far as possible from your monitor or TV. Another tip is to switch to a laptop with an LCD (liquid crystal display screen), a big improvement on the conventional cathode ray tube on most monitors because they emit lower EMFs. (That said, don't work with a laptop actually on your lap.) You don't *have* to have a laptop to use an LCD screen, however. They're still fairly expensive compared with conventional monitors, but you can buy LCD flat-screen monitors, which also have the advantage of taking up less room on your desk. You should also keep all your electronic equipment turned off when not in use.

Best of all, a really aesthetic and therapeutic way to neutralise the harmful effects of VDUs and electrical appliances generally is to have plants, lots of them. That old spiky cactus your aunt gave you years ago can work well. I read that the New York Stock Exchange introduced lots of *Cereus peruvianus* cacti for just that purpose. Other plants that compensate and are beneficial in small areas are peace lilies, dwarf banana plants and peperomias.

Plants are amazing: they increase the oxygen content, improve humidity and negative ionisation and generally lift the energy of a space. In her excellent book *Creating Sacred Space with Feng Shui*, Karen Kingston talks more about this subject and recommends the rather alarming quota of one plant per piece of equipment placed as near to the computer or TV as possible. Yes, I know you may feel you will have to wear khaki shorts to wade through the jungle that is your office but, believe me, you'll feel better. This is because, through photosynthesis, plants will supply a room with fresh oxygen during the day.

Throughout this book, I've written at length about how we are at risk from the chemicals and pollutants found in our homes. Not just in the commercial cleaning and freshening products we buy but also those used in the manufacture of carpets, fabrics, paints and wallpaper and even composition wood furniture. The good news, though, is that plants really do purify.

Research funded by NASA found that the common Spider Plant was very effective at removing formaldehyde (a common household pollutant) from the air. Other plants effective in removing formaldehyde, benzene and carbon monoxide are bamboo palm, Chinese evergreen and Mother-in-law's Tongue. As a guide, it's reckoned that one pot plant approximately 30 centimetres high can clean the air of a small 3-by-3.5-metre room. (See also the chapter 'Dump the Junk – Space Clearing for Mortals', and www. theecologist.org.)

Green Living

You will remember that in the 2005 general election the 'green issue' was thrown into focus. Prime Minister Tony Blair said of climate change, 'It's the most important issue that we face.' The *Independent* newspaper carried a front page of 'green factoids', including some staggering statistics on waste. For instance, 434,000,000 tons of waste is produced in Britain each year, enough to fill the Albert Hall every two hours; 22 million tons of rubbish from British homes is sent to landfill sites every year; 17 per cent of household waste was recycled in 2004, yet the target is 35 per cent by 2015.

I've already admitted in the Introduction that, when it comes to green issues, I'm a very late developer and still only on the 'lime' side rather than a nice dark olive. But these facts really started me thinking about my own personal rubbish mountain.

Some 30-40 per cent of the fresh produce we buy is thrown away every year. Isn't that barking mad! A report in the *Ecologist* says that, whereas one-third of the average dustbin is filled with materials that could be composted, only 2 per cent of the UK's waste is actually composted.

We like our fruit to look beautiful and our vegetables to be fresh but, if we're done with it, we should use it in the garden, not stick it in the bin alongside the plastics and the packaging to clog up the landfill sites.

We sometimes feel that, because our rubbish collection is free, or at least the cost is included in our council tax bills, then it doesn't matter how much waste we produce. But imagine if, as has been mooted, a law is passed that enables councils to charge per bag of rubbish. Then we might all think again. In the US, where rubbish collection is charged differently, it's thought that, if the majority of people there recycled and composted, they could collectively save £60 million pounds in rubbish collection fees.

I've needed a steep learning curve on all of this. This has been a major imperfection of mine for a long time, but just receiving the first of the information from my Imperfectly Natural People made me realise that masses of folk with gardens do this now, and there's no excuse for me not to do so as well. I realised that I do buy a huge amount of fresh produce and, yes, I do chuck it away, so at least I could start composting. I set about learning the basics and, of course, ended up wondering why I hadn't done it years ago.

Here's the deal in case you're still thinking about it. The 'idiot's guide' to composting.

All you need to get started is a compost bin and a bucket. Choose a big bucket that you don't use any more, preferably with a lid. Every time you prepare a meal, put the uncooked food scraps in the bin. This is the only bit to get your head around really. You can add the following to your bucket: fruit and vegetable pieces, skins, peelings, cores, egg shells, teabags, coffee grounds, old flowers and dead plants, cardboard, paper towels, egg boxes, hair (yours or your pets'), nail clippings, spices and herbs, matches, stale bread, milk, mouldy cheese, vacuum cleaner dust bags, pencil shavings, woollen socks and other raw, biodegradable stuff.

You must *not* add to your compost bucket any cooked food, or meat and fish, either raw or uncooked, coal, cat litter, disposable nappies or glossy magazines. Most people keep their composter in the back garden. If you don't have a garden, you could always look for a community composting scheme in your area (see www.communitycompost.org).

There are a few types of composter, but you should check before you buy one because some local councils offer compost bins to residents at reduced prices.

Open-air bin

Buy a wooden or plastic compost bin or build one by cutting the bottom off a plastic dustbin. Bury it a few inches into the soil. Alternatively, you can use wire fencing to create a cylinder or stack a few old tyres on top of one another and cover the top with a piece of wood.

Closed-air composters

These retain the heat better than open ones and, as a result, speed up the process. You can buy them and they are usually made from recycled plastic.

Rotating composter

This is one that does just that: it turns the whole bin, rather than your having to turn the contents with a fork. You put the contents of your bucket in through a hatch in the side.

Worm composter

This will produce the best compost and it's really 'worm farming'. Basically, you keep worms and feed them. They eat the rotting matter, including paper and cardboard, and their droppings, worm casts, make the compost very rich. The kids of course love worms and if you want an eco-friendly 'gadget' you can buy the innovative Can-O-Worms. It's a tiered system that allows you to see the worms, and it makes both solid compost and liquid feed. (See www.wigglywigglers.co.uk.)

So that's it. I started with the basic compost bin from the local DIY shop and got going immediately. We all love stirring the compost round with a big stick to aerate it and, if it gets too dry, just add water; if it's too wet add cardboard. Lo and behold, proper compost for my garden and potted plants that costs nothing. A standard composter will produce the equivalent of six or seven Gro-bags a year. I can hardly believe that, until a year before I wrote this, I had been slogging to the garden centre to pay large amounts of money and dragging home huge bags of the stuff.

Recycling

Just do it! It seems so simple and now I'm finally doing it too. Local councils are now much better at providing recycling bins, separate containers and door-to-door collection services. If you don't have one in your area, nag them and find out why not. Obviously, take your larger items to the refuse tip. It's become the new Sunday morning activity, hasn't it? Many refuse tips now have the full range of facilities to enable you to separate green, brown and clear glass bottles, cardboard, paper, garden waste and, of course, non-recyclable waste (hopefully, by the time it's separated out, there'll be much less of that).

> " Be the change you want to see in the world
>
> MAHATMA GANDHI "

Once you start reducing your waste, it makes you think differently, too. I now take a basket or big jute bags if I'm out grocery shopping to reduce the number of nightmare plastic bags. They're a veritable hazard of this century. In the UK alone we use 150 million plastic bags a week and they can take 500 years to decay in landfill. I ask for paper bags wherever possible, though they are a dying breed, and I refill glass bottles if I'm taking drinks out with me. Don't even start me up on plastic bottles or polystyrene cups! Around 6 billion a year are thrown away in the UK. Take your own mug!

You can get 100 per cent unbleached cotton shopping bags with side panels for support, along with a whole host of information from the Women's Environmental Network (www.wen.org.uk).

Water

I'm almost old enough to remember the ads in the 1970s: 'Save water – bath with a friend.' We're used to the concept of bathing with a friend and of saving water now but often we think just in terms of having more showers instead and not hosing down the lawn unless it's really scorching hot. But what about the little things? When you last cleaned your teeth, did you leave the tap running? Statistics show that this wastes up to 26,000 litres of water per family every year. We're always being encouraged to spend a bit longer cleaning our teeth (concentrate on the gums, remember!) – at least three minutes – so it's bonkers not to turn off the tap until you're ready to rinse.

When it comes to flushing the loo, there are now water-saving devices for toilets (we met the Hippo under 'Saving water' in the last chapter; see page 213.)

You'll be doing all of this already, I know, but, just in case you want to remind yourself why, two great books are *Composting For All* and *Reduce, Re-use, Recycle, An Easy Household Guide*, both by Nicky Scott (Green Books).

And for some generally excellent eco-tips, get *Saving the Planet Without Costing the Earth* by Donnachadh McCarthy or *Save Cash and save the Planet* by Andrea Smith and Nicola Baird.

Also, check out my Imperfectly Natural People elsewhere in this book, since several have some excellent tips for recycling, composting and natural gardening.

Josie

Josie Frater, over 30, singer/songwriter. Married to Steve, musician /teacher, mum to Rosie, 6.

Typical brekkie
Cereal and fruit plus porridge – or chocolate croissants!

Lunch
Veggie sandwich, fruit, healthy cereal bar.

Dinner
Veggie stir fry, chilli, pasta salad.

Drinks – water – bottled or tap?
Filtered or bottled water and Sauvignon Blanc.

Favourite superfoods I couldn't live without
Sunflower seeds, almonds, apples.

Vitamins and minerals
Multivitamin, evening primrose, Omega 3, herbal tinctures and remedies prescribed for me by Jan De Vries.

When I'm under the weather
Port and brandy, echinacea, hot water and lemon juice, tea tree oil in a vaporiser.

Favourite treatments
Bowen (it cured my frozen shoulder), aromatherapy.

For exercise
Yoga, running about with my daughter.

For relaxation
Yoga, gardening, walking.

Save my skin
Weleda cleanser. Moisturiser – pure coconut oil. B4 Oil (Sensitive Skincare Co.).

Sunscreen
None, I always cover up.

Favourite beauty products
Aveda or any new 'natural' products.

Haircare
Faith in Nature shampoo. Neal's Yard range.

Cleaning and laundry products
Ecover. Ecover washing liquid.

Recycling and composting tips
Throw all your old woollen jumpers in the compost bin; you can add egg-shells, newspapers (not too much, though!).

Gardening naturally
Salt for slugs, or eggshells. Washing-up water complete with bubbles on aphids.

For the kids
Water, fruit, seeds.

Top parenting tips
Make a game of trying one new food every week. Include your child in the cooking process.
Accept that a little bit of 'rubbish' now and then is OK.

I'd also like to recommend…
… lots of laughs, have a good sense of humour.

To achieve balance in my life
Lots of swaps with other parents for a few hours.

To revitalise my soul I go to…
… my garden.

The one thing I couldn't live without
Music, laughter, lavender oil – oh, that's three!

Guilty secrets and imperfections
Coffee and wine. I get overstressed. I resort to fish fingers sometimes.

If I had a magic wand, I would…
… employ a chef.

Beat a Retreat

Girls, tell your fella that you're leaving! No, I'm not really advocating the break-up of your marital (or otherwise) bliss, but I want to renew, refresh and invigorate it!

In July 2005, you may have read in the newspapers that experts say increasing numbers of women are suffering from a condition known as 'hurried woman syndrome'. It's caused by chronic stress from the demands of juggling work with a hectic family life. Sound like you?

I've certainly had an attack of it in the past but, as I write this, I'm sitting on the porch of a wonderful holistic B&B in Cornwall scribbling as fast as I can, no children, husband, work calls, domestic shenanigans – just me with a cup of organic Earl Grey and the low sun over the Cornish coast. It took me years to realise this, but you've got to get away! I call it beating a retreat.

It's only for a few days, I know, but that's enough! There simply isn't a machine, pro-gramme or drug that can lift your spirits like this. We all go through years of excuses, not having the time, the inclination, the 'I'm needed' syndrome, family needs me, hus-band needs me, work needs me and so it goes on. Yes, they need you but they need you happy, fresh, invigorated, and full of life. One thing I do know is that graveyards are full of indispensable people. You've probably heard the one about the dying words that no one ever said: 'I wish I had spent more time at the office'!

Now I go away on my own, just once every couple of years, and DH is happy for me to do it. He can see just how much it benefits me and my whole outlook on many a thing.

So make yourself do it – guys, too. Book a few days away, get the train somewhere, travel cheap, stay cheap. Be with yourself. It's amazing what you can sort out. You'll probably find yourself making a few life-changing decisions. There are a million and one loca-tions. It could be a hotel in San Francisco, a beach hut in Whitstable or a convent on the Isle of Sky. Just escape! My first lone break was to Making Waves Vegan Guesthouse in St Ives, Cornwall, which I've mentioned earlier (www.making-waves.co.uk). It was perfect. The proprietor, Simon, aims to leave 'as light a set of footprints behind on this earth' as possible. He's one of my Imperfectly Natural People, as you'll see.

The food there is entirely organic, much of it from his own garden or allotment, and it's the best veggie breakfast you'll ever taste. When I first arrived, hassled from the long train journey and the London smoke, I felt grumpy and critical of the slightly shabby entrance to the house and the less than luxurious bathroom. I was doing a 'DIY makeover' in my head. By the time I'd relaxed in a hot bath with candles and the essential oils provided, it was a case of 'Lawrence Llewellyn Bowen, eat your heart out!'

I went for a run on the beach every morning, then had breakfast on the tiny terrace in the wild garden overlooking the sparkling sea. Simon wants you to have as leisurely a breakfast as you like. There's no rush to get you out, and I found myself drinking a whole cafetière of his fair-traded coffee and an amazing melon smoothie late into the morning. He speaks passionately of his eco-friendly principles and, if you get him started, you'll find that he's very knowledgeable about permaculture.

After three days, I left a different person, relaxed, chilled out and seeing things in perspective. I came home and threw away all of my chemical cleaning products and ordered a huge stock of wholefoods and healthy stuff from my local supplier.

There are of course specific retreat programmes and places and, many years ago when I was a novice at this, I got myself a copy of a publication called *Retreat*, which lists UK venues. I took myself off to New Hall, a convent in Essex, for some soul searching and solitude. It was a life-changing experience. I spent three days in a beautiful old building in a very basic room using the communal kitchen. I ate with the community of nuns, who were an absolute scream.

During the day, I went for long walks, attended a couple of the services in their chapel just to hear them sing and sat around dreaming or writing down all my thoughts. A few months later I went back to the same venue and took a Myers-Briggs course. It's a kind of personality testing system but it's not at all limiting - in fact I found it freed me up to know who I was and where I wanted to be. Well, that was then, but, fifteen years and four children later, beating that retreat is still so important to me. Many of the organised retreats (remember, yours doesn't *have* to be organised) run courses but offer accommodation on a B&B or full-board basis.

Another great one is Monkton Wyld Court in Dorset. Their blurb describes it like this:

> A holistic education centre run since 1982 by a resident community, with help from visiting volunteers. The main building is a beautiful Victorian rectory, set in 11 acres of grounds, which can sleep up to 35 visitors in shared bedrooms. The group rooms and communal areas are heated by wood-burning stoves. In addition to the two main group rooms we have a beautiful sitting room with a grand piano. Other resources include a meditation hut, a healing room, a well-stocked library and facilities for arts and crafts.

Our diet is vegetarian and fully organic, and some of it is provided by our own organic vegetable garden. Our small farm provides us with milk and eggs and we have our own water supply and reedbed sewage system. We have a commitment to a sustainable lifestyle.

Monkton Wyld is set in beautiful, peaceful countryside close to the sea. We invite you to come and share our lovely home, take a break and maybe learn something new.

It's all true. I heard about this one from two sources: one a girlfriend who'd been, had a fantastic time, and met her future husband; and also from a frazzled mum of four who just took off to learn sacred drumming. If you want to have the best of both worlds, and concoct a mix of retreat and family holiday, this is a great place to try it out; but make sure your entourage know what to expect. Remember it's an escape. We're not talking Butlin's here!

I took off for two nights' bed and breakfast and I must be honest and say that I was a bit nervous. I was worried that I'd find a bunch of holier-than-thou, lentil-munching hippies who wanted to practise silent meditation even at the dinner table and who would be absolutely horrified by my imperfections. I needn't have worried. I had a grand room overlooking the grounds, ate wonderfully wholesome organic meals, lovingly prepared by whoever was on the cooking rota and spent a lot of time just pondering.

Don't get me wrong, this is not luxurious, but I knew that the Jurassic coastline of Lyme Regis was only three miles away in case I got desperate for a newspaper and cappuccino fix. At Monkton Wyld there's no TV, which was quite refreshing, no *en suite* bathrooms and definitely no room service or bar. But, for a simple break, I found it perfect and fantastically cheap. I'd highly recommend it for a group of people to go away together, either an organisation you're part of or just a bunch of families. I came away feeling more chilled out than I have in ages.

The courses on offer include all the stuff you'd expect from a bunch of Mother (and Father) Earth types, including yoga, meditation, life drawing, decorative stained glass, permaculture, creative textiles, 'the courage to sing' and many more. I didn't partake in any of that. Painting for fun in their fully stocked art hut, picking out a few one-finger tunes on their lovely old grand piano and just simply beating a retreat was enough for me. Check out their website: www.monktonwyldcourt.org.

I mentioned a beach hut in Whitstable and, while that doesn't sound relaxing, trust me, it is. If you're not familiar, Whitstable in Kent is a charming little town with a quaint harbour and a pebbly beach and one of the best fish restaurants in the southeast. The

Whitstable Oyster Company has a rustic bistro-style place right on the beach and, if you love your fish, it's hard to beat. When you've eaten you can stroll back along the beach to the sound of the clanging bells on the boats in the harbour to the Fisherman's Huts. These are lovely wooden fishermen's huts that have been refurbished to create the perfect romantic night away. (See www.oysterfishery.co.uk.)

I can't speak of breaks and holidays without banging on about Cornwall. It's a special place for me. There's something about the quality of the light that I find hard to explain. If I'm going to St Ives with the children and I want a break for myself too, it has to be the Garrack Hotel. It's a family-run hotel full of open fires and bookcases and a cordon bleu menu. They're very child-friendly, too, and there's a leisure club in the grounds with an ozone pool and a great little café where the children can have their meals if you don't think they're quite ready for the gourmet dishes on offer in the restaurant. It's not the cheapest but for a few days it is good value and you will feel relaxed and very well fed. (See www.garrack.com.)

> If women were convinced that a day off or an hour of solitude was a reasonable ambition, they would find a way of attaining it. As it is, they feel so unjustified in their demand that they rarely make the attempt.
>
> ANNE MORROW LINDBERGH

If it's a family break you're looking for, in my humble opinion, you won't find anything better in the UK than Bedruthan Steps Hotel a bit further up the coast. They have one of the best sea views from a hotel window ever; children are really well catered for in children's clubs; they serve great, healthy food; and there's a luxurious leisure club. (See www.bedruthan.com.)

If you want to jet away as a couple and it's luxury and romance you're after – and you've got the cash – (don't forget to factor in the carbon offsets!) check out my favourite hotel in the world, which is in Sausalito, at the northern terminus of the Golden Gate Bridge in San Francisco. It's the Casa Madrona Hotel and Spa.

This charming family-run hotel has been going since 1885 and overlooks the bay. It has totally individual rooms. Book into the Artists' Lodge and you'll find a balcony, a log fire and everything you need to light it for those cosy winter nights, a fully stocked minibar and, best of all, a full-size easel, canvases and paint. It's totally exhilarating, even if you've never painted before, just to sit and splash vibrant colours all over a canvas.

The breakfast is the best in the States. I just love the exotic fruits and continental breads, cheeses and cold meat. If you get a chance to eat in the restaurant, do so: it is one of the finest in the world. It's not cheap, but, if you want to spoil yourself for a couple of nights or celebrate an anniversary, it's perfect. (See www.casamadrona.com.)

If you want to try an actual retreat, there can be no better way to get in touch with your spirituality and revitalise yourself. Many of them offer short courses or are themed, but most also take guests just for a few days. I can't personally recommend these, since I haven't been there, but they appeal to me from their description. If you go, send me your review.

- **The Iona Community, Iona, Scotland**. A vibrant, ecumenical Christian community from different traditions in the Christian church. I have lots of Christian friends from all denominations who've been on residential courses and retreats there. The general view is that it is life-changing and wonderfully inspirational. (See www.iona.org.uk.)

- **Self-Realization Meditation Healing Centre, near Yeovil, Somerset**. This one offers Yoga and meditation with counsellors and healers available. (See www.selfrealizationcentres.org.)

- **Ard Mhuire Retreat House, County Donegal, Ireland**. Here the Capuchin Friars serve their home-grown food in the family kitchen on the Irish shores of Sleaphaven Bay. (See www.irishcapuchins.com.)

- **The Taraloka Buddhist Retreat Centre for Women, Whitchurch, Shropshire**. This centre provides inspiration for women. Look at www.taraloka.org.uk for more information.

- **Scargill House, Skipton, North Yorkshire**. This is a beautiful building in a gorgeous setting. They offer a rich programme that includes eco-spirituality retreats on planting trees, dry-stone walling and global deforestation. Their web address is www.scargillhouse.co.uk.

- **Middle Piccadilly, Holwell, Dorset**. Not so much a retreat centre as a natural healing centre or alternative health farm. Located in peaceful surroundings, it is a real escape from the rat race offering vegetarian food and a full range of natural complementary therapies. My editor tells me she's escaped there several times. After just a couple of days of treatments and wholesome food, she was so completely detoxed that her expensive scent smelled like chemicals! (See www.middlepiccadilly.com.)

You'll find loads of ideas at www.thegoodretreatguide.com.

Simon

Simon Money, 34, Making Waves Vegan Guesthouse proprietor. St Ives in Cornwall (www. making-waves.co.uk).

Bright and early
Up at 7.30. Large glass of hot water, sometimes with lemon. Quick walk to see the sea and get a paper. In season – no food until guests are fed and out for the day. Off season – yoga for ten minutes or up to an hour.

Typical brekkie
Homemade organic gluten-free muesli made as porridge to ease digestion. With chopped fruit and plain Sojasun soya yoghurt.

Lunch
Sometimes a vegan pasty if I'm busy. Or sandwich bursting with salad. Home made hummus 'healthed up' with hemp or flax oil and spirulina powder. Pack of crisps or some pistachio nuts for a bit of salty naughtiness.

Dinner
Millet, fried dry in a pan with a little oil (only use organic extra virgin for all cooking), then soaked in boiling water for 30 mins and boiled 30 mins. Served with stir fry veg, cut very thin for quick cooking, and peanut sauce mixed with sprouted mung beans. Mmm.

Drinks – water – bottled or tap?
Peppermint tea, beer or organic red wine. All drinking and cooking water from NSA tap filter on sink. Luxury after years making do with a jug filter!

Favourite superfoods I couldn't live without
Spirulina, tahini, broccoli, watercress, millet. I could go on!

Wild horses wouldn't get me to eat…
… any animal products which harm me, the animal and the planet. I've been vegan thirteen years and, honestly, it's no big deal!

Vitamins and minerals
Vitamin C after alcohol or if getting ill. Zinc (I'm not celibate!), B complex with B12. Multivit off and on.

When I'm under the weather
Large doses of echinacea – 150 drops a day for a few days only. Bracing sea walks with lots of clothes on!

Favourite treatments
Sports massage – very good deep-tissue massage for muscular problems. Self-treatment and prevention using yoga and knowledge of Alexander technique, fundamental in curing me of back problems from years of misuse of my body!

For exercise
See above. Also cycling, walking and, most importantly, being active and energetic through-out the day. Jogging into town and running up the stairs. Being hyperactive helps!

For relaxation
After a big cycle ride, soaking in a large roll-top bath lit by candles with dinner and a bottle of red wine waiting downstairs. My daily paper read with a small strong coffee is relaxing after guests are out the way!

Save my skin
Hemp oil. If you can't eat it, don't put it on your skin.

Sunscreen
Causes cancer. Limit time in sun and cover up before you go red.

Cleaning and laundry products
Ecover cream cleaner. Bio D toilet cleaner. Bicarb of soda. For washing, Ecover liquid.

Recycling and composting tips
Cut up old washing-up gloves to make elastic bands for whatever. No composting tips – as long as you do it, that's the most important. A pile in the corner of the garden is fine. Nature will do the rest.

Gardening naturally
Plant food-producing perennials – can feed you and the birds for little effort. The less you dig the soil the richer the organisms in it. See www.PFAF.org, an educational charity of which I am a trustee.

I'd also like to recommend...
... hanging, or standing, upside down.

To achieve balance in my life
Yoga, in all ways.

To revitalise my soul I go to...
Guess! Or a big cycle over the hills.

The one thing I couldn't live without
Sunglasses.

Guilty secrets and imperfections
Drinking too much as a reward for a hard day's work. Control freak who finds other people's lack of optimism frustrating. Must be very annoying.

If I had a magic wand, I would...
... leave for a faraway place for a few months to do yoga and eat simply.

" Life should not be a journey to the grave with the intention of arriving safely in an attractive, well preserved body, but rather to skid in sideways, chardonnay in one hand, strawberries in the other, body thoroughly used up, totally worn out, screaming 'woo...woo...what a ride!!!'

(IMPERFECT) AUTHOR UNKNOWN "

Keep in Touch

To contact Janey Lee Grace, email janey@imperfectlynaturalco.uk or check out www.imperfectlynatural.com for more tips, updates and info on forthcoming projects.

Natural Extras

More websites and other stuff you might want to try

(Addresses correct as book goes to press)

Food and Drink

Fairtrade goods
www.fairtrade.org.uk
www.traidcraft.co.uk

Shopping locally
www.regionalfoodand
drink.co.uk
www.farmersmarkets.net

A raw food diet
www.fresh-network.com

Vegetarian Society UK
www.vegsoc.org

National Pure Water
Association
www.npwa.freeserve.co.uk

Biodynamic Farming and
Gardening Association
www.biodynamics.com

Dietary advice for emotional
and mental health
www.foodandmood.org

Health

Massage training and
complementary health care for
companies and individuals
www.stressbusters.co.uk

Bags for men and women that
contour the body and reduce
back strain
www.presentandcollect.co.uk

Pillows for the relief of neck
pain
www.pillowcentre.co.uk

An authoritative critic of
conventional medicine
www.wddty.co.uk

Alternative views on health,
info and products
www.zeusinfoservice.com

Personal experiences of health
and illness
www.dipex.org

The title says it all –
www.embarrassing
problems.com

Alternative news magazine
and fascinating info on urine
therapy
www.nexusmagazine.com

Wellbeing

Workshops, talks, psychic
development and books /
tapes
www.innerpotential.org

Healing crystals, minerals and
natural gifts, tapes / books
www.scienceofnature.co.uk

Courses and workshops in
crystal energy healing
www.crystalandhealing.com

National spinal injury charity
offering sporting challenges
www.aspire.org.uk

Eco-friendly living

Friends of the earth
www.foe.co.uk

Conservation and
environmental issues
– Earthpulse
www.nationalgeographic.com

Global conservation and
ecology
www.ecology.com

Worldwide careers in ecology
and conservation
www.earthworks-jobs.com

Opportunities for volunteers

Worldwide opportunities on
organic farms
www.wwoof.org.uk

Field experiences for
volunteers in marine
conservation
www.blueventures.org

Changing the way electricity is
made
www.ecotricity.com

Green 'forum' including
articles on eco-friendly cars
www.theenvironmentsite.org

Rent a car for an hour or two
only when needed
www.smartmoves.co.uk

Links to all things green
www.greenchoices.org.uk

Doing your bit

Aluminium, packing and
recycling organisation
www.alupro.org.uk

Don't throw it away, give and
get for free
www.freecycle.org

Recycle your mobile phone
www.fonebak.org

Recycle your computer
www.computer-aid.org

Recycle your books
www.bookcrossing.com

Recycle your specs
www.vao.org.uk

Use public transport
www.liftshare.com

Decline plastic bags
www.recoup.org

Turn off lights
www.saveenergy.co.uk

Give blood
www.blood.co.uk

Save paper
www.paper.org.uk

Offer your services for nothing
www.timebank.org.uk

Leave a will
www.surefish.co.uk/ethical_
living/money/wills/wills.htm

Personal finance – ethical
investment co-operative
0845 458 3127

Plant a tree
www.woodland-trust.org.uk

Imperfectly Natural People

 Mariano
13

 Amanda
27

 Janice
42

 Rosi
55

 Tiggy
61

 Liz
69

 Carl
79

 Hatty
89

 Dani
112

 Ingrid
132

 Felicity
153

 Lynda
158

 June
172

 Sue
182

 Dinka
208

 Josie
220

 Simon
226

Directory

(Details correct as book goes to press)

Alexander technique

The Complete Guide to the Alexander Technique
www.alexandertechnique.com

Sally Tottle
www.bodysenseuk.com

Allergies

Allergymatters
www.allergymatters.com

Aromatherapy

International Federation of Aromatherapists
www.ifaroma.org

Natural Magic
www.naturalmagicuk.com
Supply scented organic candles

Bowen technique

European College of Bowen Studies
www.thebowentechnique.com

Fiona Meekes, Bowen therapist
Tel: 0208 876 3010

Breast care

The Liv Breast Self-Exam Kit
Can be purchased from:
www.goodforhealth.com
www.drugstore.com

Association of Breastfeeding Mothers
www.abm.me.uk

Breastfeeding Network
www.breastfeedingnetwork.org.uk

La Leche League
www.lalecheleague.org

Christianity

www.vurch.com
Daily inspiration and support from a liberally Christian point of view

www.moot.uk.net
For more 'alternative' Christian ideas and support

Cleaning

Soda crystals
www.soda-crystals.co.uk

The New Homemaker
www.thenewhomemaker.com

UK Parents
www.ukparents.co.uk
Click on 'Forum info' and 'Families on a budget'

Ecover UK Ltd
Tel: 08451 302230
www.ecover.com

E Cloths
www.e-cloth.com

Natural Clean
www.naturalclean.co.uk

Soap Nuts
www.inasoapnutshell.com

Clothing and fabrics

Gossypium
Tel: 0800 085 6549
www.gossypium.co.uk

Earth Collection
www.theearthcollection.com

FunkyGandhi
www.funkygandhi.com

Tatty Bumpkin
www.tattybumpkin.com

Greenfibres
www.greenfibres.com

Organic Towel Company
www.organictowel.co.uk

Ethics Trading
www.ethicstrading.com

Composting

Community Composting
Network
www.communitycompost.org

Can-O-Worms
www.wigglywigglers.co.uk

Cranio-sacral massage

The Cranio-Sacral Therapy
Association
Monomark House, 27 Old
Gloucester Street, London,
WC1N 3XX
Tel: 07000 784 735
www.craniosacral.co.uk

College of Cranio-Sacral
Therapy
9 St George Mews, Primrose
Hill, London NW1 8XE
Tel: 020 7483 0120

Dental health

Soladey
Toothpaste-free solar
toothbrush
Available from www.
hippyshopper.com

Munro-Hall Clinic
Dr Graeme Munro Hall's
holistic dental practice
Wick End Farm, Wick End,
Stagsden, Beds MK43 8TS
Tel: 07050 611333
www.hallvtox.dircon.co.uk

Holistic Dental Association
www.amalgam.org

Dietary supplements

DHA (docosahexaenoic acid)
www.dha-in-mind.com

Morepa
www.minami-nutrition.com
Also available from www.
healthyandessential.com/
shop/

Groovy Food Company
www.groovyfood.co.uk
Producer of Cool Oil, a blend
of organic seed oils rich in
Omega 3, 6 and 9

Supajus
www.supajus.co.uk
Orange juice drink enriched
with Omega 3 DHA

BioCare
www.biocare.co.uk

Vitamin Service
www.vitserve.com
Suppliers of vitamins and
supplements at discount prices

DIY

Society for the Protection of
Ancient Buildings (SPAB)
37 Spital Square, London
E1 6DY
Tel: 020 7377 1644
www.spab.org.uk

Ecos Organic Paints
www.ecospaints.com

Auro
www.auro.co.uk
Manufacturer of natural paints
and wood finishes

Green Building Store
Tel: 01484 854898
www.greenbuildingstore.co.uk
Suppliers of building products
which promote energy-
efficient, sustainable and
healthy homes

Eco Merchant
www.ecomerchant.co.uk
Supplier of sustainable and
environmentally friendly
building materials

Drink

The Organic Wine Co Ltd
PO Box 81, 1 Brands Hill
Avenue, High Wycombe,
Buckinghamshire HP13 5PZ
Tel: 01494 446557
Mail order organic wine
wholesalers

Vintage Roots Ltd
Farley Farms, Bridge Farm,
Reading Road, Arborfield,
Berkshire RG2 9HT
Tel: 0800 980 4992
www.vintageroots.co.uk
Mail order organic wine
wholesalers

Black Isle Brewery
Old Allangrange, Munlochy,
Ross-shire IV8 8NZ, Scotland
Tel: 01463 811871
www.blackislebrewery.com

Coffee Plant
180 Portobello Road, Notting
Hill, London W11 2EB
Tel: 020 7655 4574
www.coffee.uk.com
Mail order organic coffee
wholesalers and coffee shop

Celestial Seasonings
www.celestialseasonings.com
US manufacturer and marketer
of speciality teas

Clipper Teas
www.clipper-teas.com

Irma Fingal-Rock
www.pinotnoir.co.uk
Organic wine merchant

Electromagnetic radiation

EM Radiation Research Trust
www.radiationresearch.org

Sitefinder Mobile Phone Base
Station Database
www.sitefinder.radio.gov.uk

Environmental affairs

Ecologist
www.theecologist.org

Women's Environmental
Network
www.wen.org.uk

Environmental Working Group
www.ewg.org

Eyes

The Bates Method of Vision
Education
www.seeing.org

Pinhole Glasses
www.pinholes.com

Feminine care

NatraCare
www.natracare.com

Mooncup Ltd
Dolphin House, 40 Arundel
Place, Brighton BN2 1GD
Tel: 01273 355021
www.mooncup.co.uk

TreeHugger Mums
www.treehuggermums.co.uk

Magnopulse Health Products
Tel: 0800 977 5070
www.magnopulse.com

The Nice Nappy Company
www.nicenappy.co.uk
For washable menstrual pads
and cloth nappies

Fertility

The Billings Method
www.billings-centre.ab.ca

Fertility UK – The National
Fertility Awareness and Natural
Family Planning Service UK
www.fertilityuk.org

Fitness

Natural Swimming Pools
Available from:
Fairwater
www.fairwater.co.uk
Michael Littlewood
www.ecodesignscape.co.uk

Rebounders – PT Bouncer
Super Tramp Ltd
Tel: 01884 841305 or call
0800 197 1897 for stockists
www.supertramp.co.uk

Carl Munson
www.healthchampion.co.uk
Natural health practitioner,
health centre owner, writer
and researcher

The Chi Machine
www.chinow.com

Flower remedies

Dr Edward Bach Centre
Mount Vernon, Baker's Lane,
Brightwell-cum-Sotwell, Oxon
OX10 0PZ
Tel: 01491 834678
www.bachcentre.com
For further information on
Bach flower remedies

Kavenga Publishing
www.kavenga.com
For further information
on Australian bush flower
remedies

Crystal Herbs
Tel: 01379 642374
www.crystalherbs.com

Institute of Phytobiophysics
www.phytob.com

Gardening

Dutch Nursery Garden Centre
Great North Road, Brookmans
Park, Hatfield, Herts AL9 6ND
Tel: 01707 653372
www.dutchnursery.co.uk

Plants For A Future
www.PFAF.org
Permaculture, edible and
medicinal plants

Hair

Full range of products
available by mail order from
www.honestycosmetics.co.uk

Aubrey Organics
www.aubrey-organics.com

Jason
www.kinetic4health.co.uk

Herb UK
www.herbuk.com

Avea
www.avea.co.uk

Health products

Wholistic Research
Company Ltd
Tel: 01438 833100
www.wholisticresearch.com

Heating

EBC Ecofuels
Tel: 01953 455854
www.ebc-ecofuel.co.uk
Supply a range of recycled
woodfuels

Solar Twin Ltd
www.solartwin.com

Green Systems UK
www.greensystemsuk.com

Herbs

Bioforce (UK) Ltd
www.bioforce.co.uk
Offer a range of holistically
standardised fresh herb
tinctures and tablets

Hambleden Herbs
www.hambledenherbs.co.uk
Mail order supplier of herbal
products, including teas,
tinctures, infusions and
culinary herbs and spices

Halzephron Herb Farm
www.halzherb.com
Mail order supplier of a range
of medicinal herbs, foods and
spices

Granary Herbs
The Granary, Bearsted, Kent
ME14 4NN
Tel: 01622 737314
Supply tinctures and creams
made from fresh organic
home-grown herbs

G. Baldwin & Co
171/173 Walworth Road,
London SE17 1RW
Tel: 0207 703 5550
www.baldwins.co.uk
Sell a huge range of herbs
for teas, tinctures and flower
remedies

Home education

NatureKids
www.naturekids.co.uk

Education Otherwise
www.education-otherwise.org

Free Range Kids
www.freerangekids.co.uk

Homoeopathy

Ainsworths Pharmacy
36 New Cavendish Street,
London W1G 8UF
Tel: 020 7935 5330
www.ainsworths.com
Offer a range of homoeopathic
and Bach flower remedies

Helios Homoeopathic
Pharmacy
Tel: 01892 537254
www.helios.co.uk

The Society of Homeopaths
Tel: 0845 450 6611
www.homeopathy-soh.org

Mary Taylor
www.marytaylor.co.uk

Magnet therapy

Magna Jewellery Limited
Tel: 020 8958 9719 or
020 8421 8848
www.magna-health.com

Ecoflow
Tel: 01752 841144
www.ecoflow.plc.uk

World of Magnets Ltd
www.worldofmagnets.co.uk

Menopause

Dr Marilyn Glenville
www.marilynglenville.com

Hormone Replacement
Therapy Cake
www.anniebakes.com/
favorites.htm#hrt

Organic meat

Save The Bacon
Tel: 01604 696859
www.savethebacon.com
Organic farmer's market

Higher Hacknell Farm
Tel: 01769 560909
www.higherhacknell.co.uk
Mail order organic meat

Sheepdrove Organic Farm
Tel: 01488 71659
www.sheepdrove.com
Mail order organic meat

Organic Butchers
Tel: 0800 085 1340
www.organicbutchers.net

Purely Organic
Tel: 01985 841093
www.purelyorganic.co.uk

Mitch Tonks Fishworks
Restaurants and Fishmongers
www.fishworks.co.uk

Fish 4 Ever
Range of sustainably-fished
tinned fish. Available from
independent health shops and
farm shops and also http://
organico.homestead.com/
fish4ever-products.html

Organic vegetables

Riverford Organic
Vegetables Ltd
Buckfastleigh Farm, Devon
TQ11 0LD
Tel: 0845 600 2311
www.riverford.co.uk

Local Farmer's Markets
www.local-farmers-markets.
co.uk

Infinity Foods
www.infinityfoods.co.uk
Organic and natural foods
wholesaler

Organic Festivals
Refer to
www.soilassociation.org

The Organic Delivery Company
www.organicdelivery.co.uk

Perfume and cosmetics

Aubrey Organic Colognes
www.aubrey-organics.com

Organic Natural Enterprise
www.sheerorganics.com

Earth's Beauty
www.earthsbeauty.com

Jane Iredale - The Skincare
Makeup
www.janeiredale.com

See also
www.totallyorganics.co.uk
www.lemonburst.co.uk

Cosmetic, Toiletry and
Perfumery Association
www.ctpa.org.uk

Personal growth

Heal Your Life Courses and
Workshops
www.aplacefortheheart.co.uk

Pregnancy and birth

Dr Gowri Motha, The Gentle
Birth Method
www.gentlebirthmethod.com

Zita West
www.zitawest.com
Clinic and pregnancy shop

Active Birth Centre
25 Bickerton Road, London
N19 5JT
Tel: 020 7281 6760
www.activebirthcentre.com

Help! I'm Having A Baby
Book and DVD with practical
tips on pregnancy, birth and
looking after a new baby
Can be ordered from 01637
831001 or visit www.
babiesdirect.com

Baby Carriers
www.kari-me.co.uk
www.freerangekids.co.uk

Onelife World
www.onelifeworld.com

Reflexology

Association of Reflexologists
27 Old Gloucester Street,
London WC1N 3XX
Tel: 01823 351010
www.reflexology.org

Reiki

UK Reiki Alliance
www.ukreikialliance.co.uk

Retreats

Making Waves Vegan
Guesthouse
3 Richmond Place, St Ives,
Cornwall, TR26 1JN
Tel: 01736 793895
www.making-waves.co.uk

Monkton Wyld Court
Charmouth, Bridport, Dorset,
DT6 6DQ
Tel: 01297 560342
www.monktonwyldcourt.org

The Whitstable Oyster
Fishery Co
17-20 Sea Street, Whitstable,
Kent CT5 1AN
Tel: 01227 276856
www.oysterfishery.co.uk

The Garrack Hotel &
Restaurant
Burthallan Lane, St Ives,
Cornwall, TR26 3AA
Tel: 01736 796199
www.garrack.com

Bedruthan Steps Hotel
Mawgan Porth, Cornwall,
TR8 4BU
Tel: 01637 860555
www.bedruthan.com

Casa Madrona Hotel and Spa
801 Bridgeway, Sausalito, CA
94965
Tel: 001 415 332 0502
www.casamadrona.com

The Iona Community
Isle of Iona, Scotland
www.iona.org.uk

Self-Realization Meditation
Healing Centre
Tel: 01935 850266
www.selfrealizationcentres.org

Ard Mhuire Retreat House
Creeslough, County Donegal,
Ireland
Tel: 074 9138005 or 074
9138301
www.irishcapuchins.com

The Taraloka Buddhist Retreat
Centre for Women
Taraloka, Bettisfield,
Whitchurch, Shropshire
SY13 2LD
Tel: 01948 710646
www.taraloka.org.uk

Scargill House
Kettlewell, Skipton, North
Yorkshire BD23 5HU
Tel: 01756 760234
www.scargillhouse.co.uk

Middle Piccadilly Natural
Healing Centre
Holwell, Sherborne, Dorset
DT9 5LW
Tel: 01963 23468
www.middlepiccadilly.com

The Good Retreat Guide
www.thegoodretreatguide.com

Saving water

Hippo the Water Saver
www.hippo-the-watersaver.
co.uk

Environment Agency
www.environment-agency.
gov.uk

Seaweed

Artisan Bread
www.artisanbread.ltd.uk
Wholesale bakery supplying
Biodynamic bread and loaves
baked with Norwegian
Seaweed

Wales Direct
www.wales-direct.co.uk
Internet shop for all things
Welsh, including laver bread

Xynergy Health Products
Tel: 08456 58 58 58
www.xynergy.co.uk
Supplier of superfood
supplements, some of which
contain seaweed

Skin

Neal's Yard Remedies
www.nealsyardremedies.com

Coconut Oil UK
www.coconut-oil-uk.com

Elemis
www.elemis.com

Himalaya Salt
www.soothingsouls.net

Sensitive Skincare Company
www.sensitiveskincareco.com

Spiezia Organics
www.spieziaorganics.com

Living Nature
Tel: 01794 323222
www.livingnature.com

Green People
Tel: 01403 740350
www.greenpeople.co.uk

Urtekram
www.urtekram.dk (Danish)
Urtekram products are
also available from www.
goodnessdirect.co.uk

Dr Hauschka
www.drhauschka.co.uk

Sun-Togs
www.suntogs.co.uk

Weleda
www.weleda.co.uk

Crystal Deodorant
www.crystaldeodorant.co.uk

Essential Oils
www.essentiallyoils.com

Green Hands
www.greenhands.co.uk

Amazing Health
www.amazinghealth.co.uk

Totally Organics
www.totallyorganics.co.uk

Akamuti
www.akamuti.co.uk

Lavera
www.lavera.com

Naturally Tejas
www.naturallyTejas.com

Purely For You
www.purelyforyou.com

Avea
www.avea.co.uk

Space clearing

Dinka Cinnamon, Feng Shui
Consultant
www.fengshui4you.co.uk

Naomi Saunders
www.clearlyorganised.co.uk

Fly Lady
www.flylady.net

Organized Home
www.organizedhome.com

Free Cycle
www.freecycle.org

Sweet stuff

Gluten-Free Bakery
E-mail:
rebeccaprout@ntlworld.com
www.glutenfreebakery.co.uk

The Organic Sweet Shop
E-mail: theorganicsweetshop@
tiscali.co.uk
http://stores.ebay.co.uk/The-
Organic-Sweet-Shop

Active manuka honey
Nature's Nectar Ltd, 21 The
Briars, Ash, Surrey GU12 6NX
Tel: 01252 330850
www.manukahoney.co.uk

Green & Black's
www.greenandblacks.com

Tea tree oil

Those Amazing Tea Tree Oils
Tel: 0871 784 3007
www.teatreebook.com

Washing

Aquaball Laundry Ball
www.aquaball.com

Also available from www.
healthy-house.co.uk

Eco-Ball
www.ecozone.co.uk

Soapnuts
www.ethicstrading.com
www.soapods.com
www.inasoapnutshell.com

Glo Care
www.colourcatcher.co.uk

Water filters

Dryden Aqua
www.drydenaqua.co.uk

Thanks to the following companies who have given us the info to promote their work and loan us a few items to photograph:

Crystal Herbs

Beauty Without Cruelty

Natural Health

Coconut Island

Daniel Field Organic and Mineral Hairdressing

EBC Ecofuels

Ecoflow

Ecover UK Ltd

Gossypium

Green People

Ladycare Health Products

Living Nature

Nature's Nectar Ltd

Mooncup Ltd

Riverford Organic Vegetables Ltd

Super Tramp Ltd

The Healthy House

Wholistic Research Company Ltd

Index